# Object Relations
# Couple Therapy

## THE LIBRARY OF OBJECT RELATIONS

ॐ

### A Series of Books Edited By
### David E. Scharff and Jill Savege Scharff

Object relations theories of human interaction and development provide an expanding, increasingly useful body of theory for the understanding of individual development and pathology, for generating theories of human interaction, and for offering new avenues of treatment. They apply across the realms of human experience from the internal world of the individual to the human community, and from the clinical situation to everyday life. They inform clinical technique in every format from individual psychoanalysis and psychotherapy, through group therapy, to couple and family therapy.

The Library of Object Relations aims to introduce works that approach psychodynamic theory and therapy from an object relations point of view. It includes works from established and new writers who employ diverse aspects of British, American, and international object relations theory in helping individuals, families, couples, and groups. It features books that stress integration of psychoanalytic approaches with marital, family, and group therapy, as well as those centered on individual psychotherapy and psychoanalysis.

ॐ

# Object Relations Couple Therapy

David E. Scharff, M.D.

&

Jill Savege Scharff, M.D.

JASON ARONSON INC.
*Northvale, New Jersey*
*London*

**Library of Congress Cataloging-in-Publication Data**

Scharff, David E., 1941–
    Object relations couple therapy / by David E. Scharff & Jill Savege Scharff
        p.   cm.
    Includes bibliographical references and index.
    ISBN 1-56821-436-7 softcover
    1. Marital psychotherapy.   2. Object relations (Psychoanalysis)
I. Scharff, Jill Savege.   II. Title.
RC488.5.S364   1991
616.89'156 – dc20                                                                              90-19182

Printed in the United States of America on acid-free paper. For information and catalog
write to Jason Aronson Inc., 230 Livingston Street, Northvale, NJ 07647-1726, or visit our
website: www.aronson.com

For our children and our parental couples

# Contents

## Part II: EVALUATION AND THERAPY OF MARITAL PROBLEMS

## Part III: THE TREATMENT OF SEXUAL DISORDERS

## Part IV: SPECIAL TOPICS

## Part V: ENDINGS

# Preface

This book follows from our previous book, *Object Relations Family Therapy*, and functions as a clinical companion volume to David Scharff's earlier theoretical book, *The Sexual Relationship*. Like both of those, this book expresses a point of view that derives from British object relations theory integrated with the theories of small groups, infant development, and sex research. Here we develop a way of thinking about and working with the couple as a small group of two, held together as a tightly knit system by a commitment that is powerfully reinforced by the bond of mutual sexual pleasure. As a physically and emotionally intimate relationship, marriage is the inheritor of the earlier psychosomatic partnership of the infant-mother relationship. Repressed aspects of their personalties determine the unconscious fit between spouses and later seek expression in consciousness in the safety of the marital dyad. These aspects generate a marital personality that emerges in daily interaction, in sexuality, in management of children, and, of course, in relation to us as therapists.

Our way of working in couple therapy focuses equally on all these aspects. Object relations couple therapy is based on the value of non-directive listening to create psychological space for understanding, working with dream and fantasy material, and following affect to reach the unconscious conflict. Repetitive patterns of interaction are recognized and linked to the need for defense from intolerable anxiety, which can only later be named and worked on. There is no promise of a quick cure, though that sometimes happens. No paradoxical interventions are made. The method is one of interpretation of conflict, with the goal of bringing the unconscious to consciousness, where it can revitalize the couple's impoverished relationship.

Two special features differentiate our approach from other forms of psychodynamic couple therapy. The first of these is our emphasis on sexuality. Sexual difficulty obviously affects marriage in the initiation and maintenance phases, yet work on sexual dysfunctions and disjunctions due to unconscious conflict has not been sufficiently integrated into marital therapy but has been split off to be dealt with in behavioral approaches. In this book we recognize the importance of sex therapy and apply knowledge gained from that field to our work with couples. In addition, from his experience as a certified sex therapist, David Scharff has contributed material from sex therapy that illuminates the couple's object relations. Understanding of the sexual relationship is always part of the work of couple therapy, whether or not specific sex therapy is required. Our comments about marriage and sexuality derive from work with heterosexual couples because, although we have treated individual homosexuals in psychoanalysis and in couple therapy, gay and lesbian couples have not consulted us, presumably because as marital therapists married to each other we are "straight identified." Many of the issues we describe are applicable to the homosexual marriage, but the same-sex object choice introduces fundamental differences that we do not address.

The second characteristic of our approach is our focus on transference and countertransference. We join the couple at the deepest level of unconscious communication. When we allow the couple's unconscious to resonate with our own, we arrive at interpretation that comes from inside the shared experience. Since all this occurs inside the therapist, indeed unconsciously, it is not easy to describe. It might embarrass us, or it could upset patients who might be unfortunately surprised by this material. Another reservation about illustrating countertransference is that it tends to spell out an impossible ideal of instant and penetrating clarity that, in practice, is an impossibility. In fact, striving for that kind of constant in-touchness is a major distraction for therapists. But we have set ourselves the task of reviewing our countertransference anyway, because it is the only way we know of teaching how we work. We hope that any negative consequence is offset by the gain from sharing these moments of personal experience and therapeutic insight that enliven our practice and are the highlight of our work.

Readers often assume that because we have written together we also work as a co-therapy team. Occasionally we do work together on a diagnostic consultation for teaching purposes, but in general we prefer to work separately at different locations. Of course, there are financial and administrative reasons to eschew a co-therapy model, but the main reason is to preserve our clinical independence. Although married co-therapists are in a unique position to experience in their relationship the projective identification of the patients' internal couple in couple therapy, the time and effort they require to distinguish patient fantasy from preexisting unconscious marital conflict when processing their countertransference can detract from their work with patients—and also from the therapists' marital harmony. Theoretically, this could be most beneficial to both patient and therapist couples, but practically we have elected to forego the benefit of professional work-related marital introspection in favor of investing in the everyday work and pleasure of marriage.

We would like to thank Jo Parker and Lisa Ribiat for their help with word processing, deciphering of scribbles, and laborious entering of corrections to produce a final manuscript. Jason Aronson was, as ever, enthusiastic yet patient, and gave us wonderful editorial help from Muriel Jorgensen and Jane Andrassi and promotional expertise from Nancy Scholem. David Scharff thanks the administrative staff, especially Anna Innes, and the board of the Washington School of Psychiatry for support of his writing. We both are deeply grateful to the faculty of the Psychoanalytic Object Relations Couple and Family Therapy Training Program of the Washington School for developing ideas, sharing work, and planning programs together. We also thank those groups around the country from Miami to Los Angeles that invited us to teach our approach and drew our attention to the need for a book on the object relations approach to couples.

We are continually grateful to Pearl Green for keeping our home and hearth together and to our children for putting up with us during the writing process.

We would like to acknowledge the trust and cooperation of those couples that allowed audiotaping for our study of interaction and those that gave permission for videotaping for further learning and teaching. In our case examples in this book, individual identities have been disguised and data about each couple altered or merged with material from other couples to preserve anonymity, which we have tried to do without compromising the integrity of our account of the relationship of symptom, pathology, and unconscious object relations. The only aspect not disguised is that of countertransference. We hope that any patients reading this book will be able to tolerate our revelations in the spirit of scientific enquiry. Finally, we thank our patients for their confidence in our work and for contributing to our learning, teaching, and writing.

# Part I
# Object Relations

not be supported in future contact. There may be quite a discrepancy between the capacity for intimacy in brief encounters, or for charm in social settings, and the ability to sustain relationships of longer duration. The short-term intimacy of early courtship consists of a rapid interpenetration, a sudden recognition of similarities and complementarities, often emphasizing one shared aspect of internal objects, which does not, and cannot, take into account the total balance of internal economies. The engagement period allows for some checking out of the defensive structures of repression, but more thorough testing of fit usually awaits the longer term commitment after marriage.

The problem of intimacy shows up when a courting couple, enjoying a sense of closeness and a mutually rewarding sexual life, make a commitment to each other, only to find that this is the moment of withdrawal for one or both. The withdrawal we refer to is not the complete one of actual separation and breakup of the courting couple, but that of partial withdrawal into the self, a retreat from intimacy that is occasioned by the sudden finding of new and unwelcome features in the partner, characteristics that have burgeoned inexplicably since the day before. This is the moment of reckoning with the other person as a whole person, good and bad—for better *and* for worse—and in an immediate and reciprocal way, with the whole of oneself. Marital therapy and sex therapy recognize that self and other are inextricably intertwined. Furthermore, the marital relationship and the sexual functioning of the couple are closely connected. The treatment of the sexual dysfunction cannot get far without considering the marital relationship because sexual problems express and give access to difficulties in relating that stem from unconscious factors.

For many years psychoanalytic therapies struggled to treat sexual problems without the benefit of specific knowledge about sexual functioning and dysfunction. But now, from sexological research, we have information about the specifics of sexual function and dysfunction. At the same time, we have learned from psychoanalysis about the problems of relating in intimate situations, including that of the analyst–patient couple as a prototype. This knowledge is now more accessible than previously, because we have the analytic language of object relations theory, which links the individual's developmental struggle in the intrapsychic dimension to the interaction in relationships with significant others. A product of the last fifty years, object relations theory has been applied to the marriage relationship by Dicks (1967) and Zinner (1976), to the dynamics of families by Shapiro and Zinner (Shapiro 1979, Zinner and Shapiro 1972), Skynner (1976), Box et al. (1981), Slipp (1984) and most recently ourselves (Scharff and Scharff 1987). In addition to our work linking psychoanalytic object relations with family therapy, David Scharff has described the links between sexuality and general development in his book *The Sexual Relationship* (1982), where he documented the ways that the individual's sexual development expresses family concerns and currents while at the same time changing the family forever.

Object relations theory begins with the individual's need for relationships. From the beginning, what motivates the infant is its need for a relationship with its mother, and it is within the matrix of the attachment to her that the baby grows. This earliest attachment is a *psycho-somatic partnership* (Winnicott 1971), a relationship that is at once entirely somatic and entirely psychological. Through holding and handling the baby, through early attempts to understand the baby's innate rhythms and needs, the mother learns what is happening inside the baby, and as she does so, the baby drinks in the experience with the mother. Because it offers the only other crucial psychological experience of intense pleasure that is entirely somatic at the same time it is entirely psychological, the adult sexual relationship retains a resonance with the embedded history of the earliest relationships.

The major contributors to object relations theory explored the way in which this early experience with primary caretakers was absorbed by the infant and child, becoming the substance of the child's inner world. This theory, taken in its least rigid form, offers an even blend of emphases. The environment that is shaped by the caretakers and the child's contribution in modifying what is taken in are equally considered (Mitchell 1988).

In the early years of psychoanalysis, Freud introduced the theory that actual events and deprivations constituted the nucleus of difficulty for the individual: childhood seduction, masturbation and its prohibition, and coitus interruptus were seen as the causes of psychological trauma (Freud 1895, 1905a, Breuer and Freud 1895). But then when he made his extraordinary discovery that young children modify and distort the actual events that occur, Freud's theory moved into the area of unconscious intrapsychic conflict, and he eschewed his earlier seduction theory, interestingly one of only a few of his theories that he turned his back on. His clinical descriptions, which clearly credit the importance of actual experience in the child's history, suggest to us that he believed that the quality of a child's experience with the world determined, to a large extent, the quality of development. But his theoretical elaboration from this early point on stressed the unfolding of a set program of drives and structures that exhibited a predetermined form. Modifications by contact with experience were seen as having only a secondary role. We see individual development, from a Freudian point of view, as being like a missile with its program built into it, so that it moves by predesign, equipped even to accommodate for interferences in its path, but still moving and seeking a predetermined target. Chance encounters with the environment have a secondary quality compared to the predestined unfolding.

Family therapy theory has focused on the environmental aspect to which Freud allotted secondary status. As a field of theory, it has stressed the importance of the external world, the family system, and the structure of relationships in the immediate, original, and extended family, acknowledging in only a secondary way the importance of the contribution of the individual's capacity to initiate and modify experience. For this theory, external events have a solid reality and internal, psychological events an insubstantial, mythical quality. The behavior therapies stand midway, stressing action and observable events as what matters, being as far removed from the internal life of the individual as family therapy, and as far from family systems as is psychoanalysis.

Object relations theory covers both directions. It is a psychoanalytic theory of motivation, development, and relationships. It began as a theory of individual unconscious organization that, since it developed from the study of the analytic relationship rather than of the patient's pathology, could be applied readily to the study of marital, family, and group dynamics. It provides the tools to explore both the actions that occur in fundamental relationships throughout life and the unconscious determinants and results of those actions.

However, the object relations approach is more than a theory. It is a way of working, an approach to the patient, couple, or family that centers on understanding as the vehicle for relating. It is the way we take patients in, just as the mother must take in the baby in a form of wordless understanding in order to respond. Our therapeutic stance echoes the parenting process of sitting with, listening, reflecting, digesting, and responding based on empathy modified by further feedback, and conceptualizing the whole experience in verbal form. And when we do so, we credit equally the power of external events and people on the life of the individual, couple, or family, and the power of individual psychology to modify experience. The breadth of the theory enables us to work with the full complexity of the experience. For instance, in psychoanalysis or psychoanalytic psychotherapy, we pay the most attention to the individual's internal world as the focus of work with the patient. In the conjoint therapy setting, we start with external interactions, often asking what actually happened between the people, as a point of departure from which to ask what those events meant to the people involved. But within this way of working we can note that we are simply taking different vantage points from within a comprehensive theory, moving just as each of us does in life, back and forth between a view of the events in the "real" world around us, and the data from the "subjective" world inside us. This way of working offers us the opportunity to think about both equally.

## OBJECT RELATIONS THEORY

Let us now turn to object relations theory of the individual, most coherently described by Fairbairn (1952, 1954, 1963). While he did not specifically discuss intimacy, what he offered will nevertheless move us a long way toward understanding it. He began by proposing that what organizes the baby in the beginning is the need for a relationship with a primary caretaker, usually its mother (although a father or substitute can do the "mothering"). The baby takes in the *unsatisfying aspects* of its interactions and splits them off from experience, repressing them from consciousness because they are too painful to be borne in consciousness. Two major aspects of painful experience are thus put underground: the *need-exciting* (which he called "libidinal") relationship with the mother, and the *rejecting or frustrating* (which he called "anti-libidinal") relationship with the mother. The need-exciting relationship is one in which the baby feels the mother is seductive or anxiously smothering, and the baby is left longing for satisfaction, which is beyond reach. In the rejecting constellation, the baby feels the mother is rejecting, angry, or frustrating its needs. The baby therefore becomes angry and sad. Finally, there is an area of reasonably satisfying relating between the child and mother, which Fairbairn located in the realm of the "central ego" in relationship to its internal object, the "ideal object." A reasonable range of affects characterizes this area of relating. Fairbairn also described the way that the rejecting object system acted to exert a further "hostile repression" on the need-exciting object system. Clinically, we see this commonly when couples fight endlessly rather than acknowledge their painful mutual longing in failing relationships. Figure 1–1 summarizes Fairbairn's theoretical construction of endopsychic structure.

Other theoretical ideas from the British object relations theorists enable us to put Fairbairn's theory of the development of the individual to work in the interactive family context, an application that enables us to study unconscious communication as a feature of observable relationships. From the work of Melanie Klein, we draw on *projective and introjective identification* (Klein 1946, Segal 1964, Ogden 1982). This complicated concept requires a chapter to do it justice (see

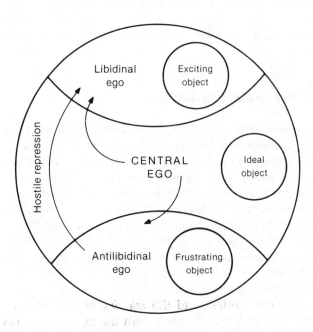

**Figure 1–1. Fairbairn's model of psychic organization, by D.E. Scharff, from** *The Sexual Relationship: An Object Relations View of Sex and the Family.* **Reprinted courtesy of Routledge and Kegan Paul. The central ego in relation to the ideal object is in conscious interaction with the caretaker. The central ego represses the split-off libidinal and antilibidinal aspects of its experience along with corresponding parts of the ego that remain unconscious. The libidinal system is further repressed by the antilibidinal system.**

chapter 3). For now, perhaps it will suffice to say that projective identification is the process through which a person projects a disclaimed part of the self into the other, and the other person unconsciously takes it in and feels like that projected part through introjective identification, and then behaves in such a way as to confirm it or, in more mature states, to modify it. In normal relationships, projective identification is the basis of empathy for the other's experience, but in states of anxiety it possesses and controls the other in uncomfortable ways that may or may not be tolerated. Figure 1–2 shows this interactive process.

Projective identification is similarly the basis for intimacy. Through projective identification, a couple tests the fit of their internal object constellations. While this can happen in brief encounters, a longer

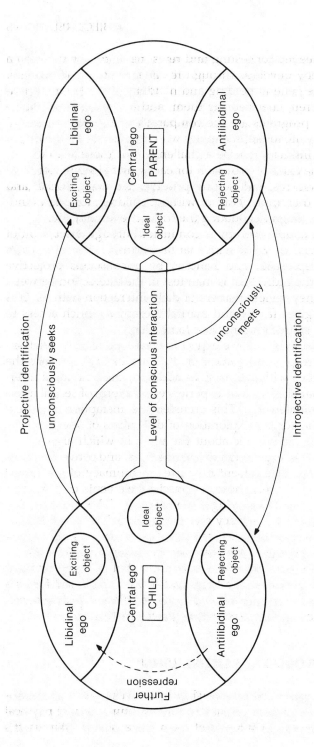

Figure 1–2. The action of projective and introjective identification. The mechanism here is the interaction of the child's projective and introjective identifications with the parent as the child meets frustration, unrequited yearning, or trauma. The diagram depicts the child longing to have his needs met and identifying with similar trends in the parent via projective identification. The child meeting with rejection identifies with the frustration of the parent's own antilibidinal system via introjective identification. In an internal reaction to the frustration, the libidinal system is further repressed by the renewed force of the child's antilibidinal system. Reprinted courtesy of Routledge and Kegan Paul.

time is usually needed for testing and retesting. Intimacy between a mother and a baby develops through feeding, changing of diapers, giving baths—the general holding and handling of the infant. Feeding, raising children, chauffeuring them, and arranging their educational and social programs are the comparable nonsexual sources of intimacy in family life for adult couples who are parents. Finding time alone for sexual intimacy can be a challenge. For those who do not have children, the tasks of provision for eating and sleeping comfortably, sharing resources, and setting priorities for work, social, and private time together apply. With or without children, long-term intimacy develops through negotiating the trivia of everyday life.

It follows that couple therapy is conducted through discussion of these central trivia. In work with marital partners, that which has been split off, repressed, and handled by unconscious projective identification in the individual is manifest in the interaction between the partners as they review matters of daily interaction with us. It is this review that gives family and marital therapy so much access to the intimacies of shared unconscious family life.

In work with individuals, we expect to create an intimate relationship between therapist and patient that allows us to experience the patients' difficulties with intimacy. In addition, the emotional intercourse of psychoanalysis can be experienced as a form of sexual intercourse in the transference. This transference metaphor is an extremely useful one for the exploration of difficulties of sexuality, but we can now be more specific about the ways in which analysis, or psychotherapy, gives expression to sexual issues, and conversely may serve to hide them. The patient may use the intimacy of the verbal situation to further repress those unconscious elements contained in physical sexuality, while enjoying the protection of the situation. For some patients, then, the privacy and protection of the psychotherapeutic situation makes the repressed elements of sex less initially accessible, until time matures the therapeutic relationship. Then the repressed seeks to return. Not just in therapy, but in every primary relationship each person seeks to be understood and cared for as a whole person, and so the denied and repressed elements of personality seek expression and understanding (Fairbairn 1952).

## THE PSYCHOSOMATIC PARTNERSHIP

In order to explore the relationship between physical and emotional intimacy, we have to go back to the beginning, where physical closeness and emotional interpenetration were united. Winnicott's

(1960a, 1971) description of "the psycho-somatic partnership" between the mother and infant centers us in this territory of intimacy and of sexuality. He describes the way the earliest mother–infant relationship organizes the psychological interior of the baby through the medium of physical exchange. The relationship is simultaneously entirely physical and entirely psychological. The baby's physical interaction with the mother also organizes her psychologically as a mother. In other words, the psychosomatic partnership is a mutually confirming process. Revealing aspects of the infant–mother relationship have been studied by Spitz (1945, 1965), Mahler and colleagues (1975), Brazelton and his colleagues (Brazelton 1982, Brazelton and Als 1979, Brazelton et al. 1974, Brazelton et al. 1979), Greenspan (1981), and many others. Most recently this body of research has been summarized by Stern (1985), who described the progressive growth of the infant's self beginning in the observable exchanges between mother and infant that form the psychosomatic partnership: gaze and vocal exchanges synchronized with mutually attuned body movements form rudimentary conversations. Through the early months, adjustments and refinements of intimate mutual cue-and-response sequences are made by mother and baby in a long-term relationship.

## The Sexual Relationship

So, too, with sex. It is just such a psychosomatic partnership, in which the physical interaction between sexual partners resonates with the depths of their individual psychology, and specifically with their internal object relationships. Masters and Johnson (1966, 1970) mapped the specifics of genital function and interaction, providing the description of normal and abnormal genital physiology. D. Scharff (1982) developed the idea of the erotic zone as a projection screen for conflict. He wrote:

> The genitalia and the woman's breasts are the physical parts of the body most often chosen by an adult couple or individual to be the physical locus of the conflicts both with internalized objects (for instance, the internalized parents) and with current primary figures. The penis and vagina, those rather small organs, become a battlefront for personal and interpersonal conflict. Issues of enormous complexity have to be psychologically factored (added, subtracted, or multiplied like vector forces) and then distilled in order to fit in these very small areas. Massive conflicts barely remembered or long surrendered to the unconscious are projected in condensed form on the body screen of the genitalia. These screens are too small to allow the showing of a whole picture, so the outcome is, by neces-

sity, simplified and condensed, seen only as through the wrong end of a telescope. Important details can no longer be differentiated, and one conflict is superimposed on another, one internalized relationship fused with others, much in the same way that the ego of the dreamer condenses and distorts events in the process of creating a brief dream which may nevertheless express worlds of meaning and feeling.

Although the resulting mixture of feelings is about many people, about old relationships and current ones, it still must be expressed along the final common pathway of physicality in a relatively simplified and direct way. For instance, there either is or is not sexual activity and responsiveness in a given situation. There are complications of varying degrees of openness, withholding, sexual failure, or aggression, but the sexual encounter either feels good or it does not. [pp. 6–7]

If we approach the sexual relationship as a psychosomatic partnership, we can map the way these specific physical interactions between bodies—between genitalia, breasts, mouths, hands—express and speak to profound emotions and relationships. The adult sexual relationship is in part a replay of early relationships, which lends it a poignancy that few other relationships approach. In this setting, sexual excitement taps into the need-exciting object constellation, while sexual rejection and frustration resonate with rejecting object systems. The internal object relations that represent these tend to recreate these experiences in interaction with the external object, and a sexually heightened bodily experience of them magnifies their unconscious role for each of the participants. It is in these ways that adult sexuality is the inheritor of the earlier mother–infant psychosomatic partnership.

Sexual expression is a link both to the new love object and to the internal objects. Sex symbolizes the following (D. Scharff 1982):

1.  The longing to hold onto the image of the giving, loving parent as a living presence, and to care for him or her while being cared for.

2.  The struggle to overcome and tolerate the image of the withholding parent who does not seem to care, but who, if forgiven, paradoxically provides the opportunity to come together.

3.  The attempt to synthesize these two rehabilitated images into a whole, internal sense of a loving couple based on the parents' relationship. [pp. 9–10]

Successful sexual performance constitutes both an actual and a symbolic reparation, a reinfusion of loving from the body to the multiple sources of physical and emotional needs. In contrast, failed sex restimulates the feeling of deprivation and need without relief. Reasonable goals for sexuality are that it be a useful, tension-reducing, good-enough part of a marriage or relationship, and that it be capable of expressing and containing the average amount of frustration and conflict, giving the couple at some times exactly what is needed and wished for. We call this "good-enough sex."

Good-enough sex cannot happen when there is too much physical or psychological difficulty in one or both partners. The general term "sexual dysfunction" has been applied to pathological sexual interaction of physical, educational, and psychological origins. To differentiate the aspect of impaired sexual interaction that stems from internal object relations, we use the term "sexual disjunction," coined by D. Scharff (1982). In sexual disjunction, the problem of object relating may be of recent or of profound origin, usually in combination. Even sexual dysfunctions due to inexperience or physical deficit affect the emotional tone of the current relationship and stir internal object unrest. Thus every dysfunction includes a disjunction, but not all disjunctions constitute dysfunctions that require specific sex therapy. As couple therapists we want to be able to work with the full range of sexual disjunction and dysfunction, referring those cases at the dysfunction end of the continuum for specific sex therapy when necessary, or shifting into that behavioral format ourselves if we are trained to do so.

## WAYS OF WORKING

Thus object relations theory gives us a way of working with and talking about sexual and marital issues. It is quite consistent with individual psychoanalysis or psychoanalytic psychotherapy, couple therapy or the behavioral framework called for in sex therapy. It does not preclude the giving of advice or even the prescriptions of the sex therapy format. It does differ markedly, however, from approaches that assume that what happens inside the individual is essentially unknowable and irrelevant to the therapeutic process. It centers on valuing what happens inside individuals, even in the conjoint therapy situation when we organize therapeutic interventions upon understanding the interaction of the couple.

Our aim is to join patients at the level of their unconscious experience and then to relate to them through interpretive work based on our understanding of it. Everything else is adjunctive to that, even in the more behavioral methods of sex therapy or in counseling parents of young children or adolescents. Since understanding unconscious communication is at the core, we must then have a method of achieving that understanding in depth. Transference and countertransference provide vital information about unconscious organization and communication and their use is central to this way of working.

## TRANSFERENCE AND COUNTERTRANSFERENCE

Freud (1895, 1905a) originally described transference as the patient's transposing impulses appropriate to earlier situations onto the analyst. The concept was originally limited to the analytic situation and was closely allied to the concept of resistance, the force that operated against the therapist's efforts to make what was unconscious conscious. It is inherent in the structure of the mind that those things that are repressed are resistant to derepression.

When a person finds part of a relationship too painful to be consciously borne in mind, it is split off and put underground. This inevitably involves burying the three aspects that constitute a relationship: a trace of the object, a part of the self or ego, and the affect that characterizes the interactions between ego and object inside the self. What is repressed is too painful to be consciously tolerated, so a central part of the self acts to keep these painful elements buried away from awareness. With force equal to that of the repression, the central ego resists derepression in order to avoid anxiety.

Guntrip (1969) has noted that there is also an interpersonal aspect to resistance. The patient is reluctant to reveal parts of himself or herself to the therapist, because of shame and imagined interpersonal consequences determined by early experience. Resistance now refers to the difficulty in revealing parts of oneself to another, and transference becomes the vehicle for the inevitable revelation of these unconscious elements despite the reluctance.

Why do these split-off and repressed objects and parts of the self emerge as transference? The answer, according to Fairbairn (1952), lies in each person's need for a relationship. Just as each person seeks a relationship, each part of the personality seeks to be acknowledged in any primary relationship. So in the relationship with parents, spouse or lover, children, and therapist, the average person will seek to be understood completely, and the denied parts of the self will tend to rise to the surface, as if seeking acknowledgment, each in its turn. These elements of personality act almost as if each were a separate person, seeking recognition just as the whole person seeks recognition, powered by the overarching motivation each of us has to become integrated and accepted and loved as a whole person.

Transference in this view is a general phenomenon of relationships, no longer defined as unique to the therapeutic relationship. Rather it exists in all relationships. Even in brief or casual ones, aspects of transference reflect the way a person tends to view others. Thus, qualities of suspiciousness, grandiosity, optimism, or fear with which a person approaches new relationships represent a set of personality traits that are up front and that color central ego functioning. In the more enduring and intense relationships, the unconscious elements of internal object relationships are transferred in greater depth. It is here that transference moves from mere projection of elements of the self and internal object onto the other, to the interpenetration of unconscious elements through projective identification.

A therapist will begin by being able to spot the projections that a patient brings, but not the projective identifications that must emerge over time. They become knowable because the therapist absorbs them, in a way that must be unconscious because insisting on being conscious of them at every moment means having to be outside the situation, and therefore remaining forever a stranger to them. Therapists who are willing to be open to being taken over will eventually sense in themselves various states of mind that are foreign to their own personalities and therefore have arisen in unique response to each individual patient or couple. The clues to this discovery of a projective identification lie in the countertransference, the therapist's response to the patient. Here the therapist has an uneasy feeling that reaches consciousness as a set of uncomfortable affective responses that are discordant and that can be seen to represent responses to that particular patient. As the therapist struggles to understand these, and then to connect them to the experience with the patient, the meaning of the patient's communication takes shape.

To reach this understanding, the therapist may use a fantasy that has been elicited or a dominant feeling that has erupted without fantasy elaboration. Sometimes the words to a song may echo through the therapist's mind, or the memory of an event from childhood or an association to current experience may present itself. All of these constitute the first responses, which then need to be linked to the experience with the patient before sense can be made of the situation. This does not mean that the therapist should simply share the countertransference response. That is a frequent error of inexperienced or self-gratifying therapists. Awareness of the therapist's own experience is the starting point.

Then the work of making sense of the response has to be done before a communication is made to the patient. We shall present many examples of this throughout the book. It is the hardest part of the work to learn and takes the most training. Even when it is part of the therapist's armamentarium, countertransference-based interpretation constitutes a minority of the spoken responses to the patient. When it is used, though, it tends to come at a moment of major understanding of the situation, and often creates a turning point in the therapy.

The countertransference is the primary guide to navigation in the therapeutic path. If the therapy proceeds apparently effortlessly, we can assume good unconscious alignment between patient and therapist. But there are times when things do not feel right: progress is stopped, hopelessness and futility abound, or anger dominates the situation. Equally, when a rosy glow pervades the atmosphere, unrealistically idealizing patient and therapist, something is askew. In all of these situations, the contertransference becomes crucial. There is scarcely a treatment in which these matters do not emerge at a crucially difficult point. The capacity to analyze these affectively charged moments through the use of countertransference is one of the major hallmarks of analytic object relations psychotherapy.

## AN EXAMPLE FROM THE BEGINNING OF THERAPY

Rebecca and Quentin Rawsthorne had been married ten years at the time they were referred to me [D.E.S.]. He was a 40-year-old lawyer, she a 32-year-old musician. They reminded me of naïve, religiously Orthodox couples with unconsummated marriages, but my fantasy was not borne out. They did have intercourse, but I was unable to imagine it. I learned from them that penetration was frightening to Rebecca. Virginal when she met Quentin, Rebecca had vaginismus in some and vaginal tightness in the rest of her sexual encounters with him. She usually failed to lubricate and experienced the whole episode with anxiety and a sense of imposition. Quentin had had many partners before he met Rebecca, but never any relationship that, looking back, he would consider caring or sustained. They met when Rebecca was recently graduated from college and sexually naïve. Upset because his father was dying, Quentin latched onto her. In the beginning she felt pulled toward sex and physical closeness with Quentin but her arousal was not relieved by orgasm. From the moment of marriage, she became less and less interested in sexuality, felt that Quentin ignored her needs for closeness, and was generally consumed with anxiety. Quentin said that in the many years before he met Rebecca he had enjoyed sex, but that it had never occurred to him that women had any needs. He was clear, in a matter-of-fact way, that he had simply used women as vessels into which to discharge himself. Although he could see that there might be other ways to think about it he wanted me to know that in fact he could not really believe there was any other way of having sex.

*I felt from the beginning how anxious both were, like two porcupines constantly bristling toward each other. Their attitudes toward me differed. Quentin was loving and idealizing of me. He had majored in psychology in college, and although avoiding therapy until now, he was an aficionado of sex therapy. He thought I was too marvelous, which worried me. What other thoughts was he keeping at bay? Rebecca was wary of me. She was worried that she would be ganged up on by the two men in the room, both interested in psychologizing on her. So my reaction to the beginning constellation was to feel that Rebecca could not trust me, and I could not trust Quentin. Furthermore, I felt inclined to agree with her suspicion about his agenda: I thought he seemed to want me to fix her up for him, preferably without his having to change. I found that I wanted to distance myself from them, to get away from a "gooeyness" about them that reminded me of the slime the ghosts left on the heroes when they swept by them in the comedy movie* Ghost-busters. *My feeling of infantile disgust and "get away from me" seemed to be a response to their clinging quality, and my association to ghosts made me wonder about the quality of the internal ghosts that might haunt our work.*

After an evaluation, we agreed they would begin sex therapy, acknowledging that it would offer a vehicle for exploring the difficulties in their relationship. I gave them the first assignment, a nongenital pleasuring exercise in which they were to alternate giving each other massages while nude. They reported back that neither had liked the exercises. Rebecca said, "I felt really nervous, not because of the massage, but because of being nude with Quentin. And I didn't like seeing his body—his body hair and genitals were weird." The fifteen-minute turns seemed to drag out forever for both of them and the fact that Quentin had not come home from the office until 10 P.M. meant she had the excuse of feeling sleepy. Furthermore, she thought being playful about massage or sex seemed disrespectful and bad.

Quentin did not feel interested in the exercises either. He said, "I had trouble looking at *her* genitals, too."

She said, "Now I really don't want to do it!"

He went on to say that looking at her made him think about his mother and the demands she made on him. He felt a sense of "anxiety all over about what I should do for my mother." The exercises had taken place before and after a weekend when his mother had visited them. When Rebecca had massaged him, his thoughts had wandered so that he was not aware of feeling anything about the massage itself. He had trouble keeping his mind in the room where the exercise was occurring.

*Here in the first sex therapy session I was confronted with enormous resistance to physical and emotional intimacy. It was almost as though my therapeutic invest-*

*ment in their sexual life met with strong objection from both of them. Their resist-ance was voiced by Rebecca as disgust and by Quentin as preoccupation with his mother. Both these negative reactions were associated with their mothers, while I seemed to be cast as the father who was supposed to draw them out of their en-trapped distaste and fear of sex. So far, I didn't mind the job. Couples frequently find the first assignment hard in just this way, but there was something about the way each of them rejected the other and turned to me to validate their distaste for sexual closeness and their disapproval of each other that bothered me. It struck at my identity as a sex therapist, always vulnerable to contempt from analytic col-leagues, but usually not from the patients who seek my help.*

I told them to do the exercise again before the next session, and I con-fronted Quentin about his working late hours. I thought he did so on their shared behalf, in order that they could easily avoid not only sex but also intimacy. I said they could never confront their shared reluctance at such late hours. He seemed reluctant to change his ways, full of protest that the law firm required these hours. I left it for him to think about.

When they returned three days later, they had not done any exercises. Rebecca said, "Quentin's mad at me, so I'm lonely. I feel good about my body but when I feel mad at him, then I have problems being touched. I *have* enjoyed sex at times, but not when I feel like this."

Quentin said, "I don't think I'm mad at her. I started changing office hours the day we met. I told my managing partner that I wouldn't work so late."

Rebecca said, "We didn't do the exercises. Quentin wanted to sand-wich me in between the office and going for a run."

Quentin corrected her, "It was *instead* of going for a run."

"I didn't hear you say that," she answered. "And changing your whole work schedule just like that, without any discussion!" she scoffed. "It's just as rigid a way of doing things as refusing to change because I asked you. Look, Dr. Scharff, I'm anxious because you are making me do the exercises, and because Quentin is so highly strung. And when you tell him to do something, he jumps. He wouldn't do that for me. He never has. Then he wants me to praise him at dinner for doing what *you* wanted."

"I want you to validate me," he said. "Given that you remind me all the time that I'm a rigid person, I want you to acknowledge it when I've done something to help."

"I'm not going to say 'Good boy, Quentin.' It's just as rigid to change behavior immediately without mulling things over, with no change in the way you feel."

*I felt pretty battered with her spoiling of what I felt to be his efforts to comply. I found myself liking it that he had done what I asked him to do, and was upset by her belittling his attempt at change. I realized I was feeling angry at Rebecca for spoiling my efforts at treatment and that I was for the moment pretty thoroughly identified with Quentin. But as I thought about my taking his side, I realized that she was speaking for both of them. They were feeling coerced by me into doing things they could not feel ready for. Both of them were frightened of me, as though, in offering treatment, I were making them risk the intimacy that threatened each of them with being taken over by the other. They each wanted to be intimate without being touched or risking emotional penetration.*

I said that in their worry, Rebecca began to spoil Quentin's efforts, and then he lashed out at her for not appreciating him. But they were both more comfortable with the angry exchanges than with the risk of the closeness the exercises would impose on them.

Rebecca cried, "I feel hurt that you tell me I'm spoiling things. That's what my mother would say to me. He's not so easy to be with, you know. And you and he want me to accept his changed behavior without his feeling any different."

He said, "I'm scared of losing control to Rebecca and to you. So I scream at her."

"But the anger is also at me," I said.

"I guess it is," he said. "When I get mad at Rebecca, it's like shooting fish in a barrel."

"But the barrel you're shooting into is this therapy. And you're in there, too, swimming with the fish you're shooting at!" I said, "You're both afraid you'll be shot by me or each other in the dangerous situation I've put you in."

*Now I could say to them that they were both frightened of me, because they felt I would coerce them both without understanding their plight, forcing Quentin to change quickly without any gain in understanding, and forcing Rebecca to submit. They each felt trapped like fish in a barrel. That feeling was at the bottom of their sexual and emotional impasse, and they had already established it jointly with me in their shared transference. As I said this, they both acknowledged the shared anxiety, and both seemed to relax, feeling understood. And as I was able to say this, I no longer felt angry at Rebecca for resisting my "prescription" or at Quentin for his over-compliant behavior and his refusal to feel.*

This example presents an ordinary beginning phase of sex therapy. What we want to illustrate is the way the therapist's understanding of the couple's fear of intimacy, brought to the treatment as a shared transference, occurred from inside his own experience with the couple. At times he felt unfairly on the side of one or the other of them, at other times he felt burdened with them as a couple. His exploration of how their individual and shared anxieties contributed to their transference wariness enabled him to analyze his own reaction—not yet in terms of the origins of their internal objects, which were the prototypes for what they projected onto him, but in terms of what his feeling annoyed, burdened, and resisted conveyed about their shared difficulty, which bound them together in ways such that neither could reach out to help the other.

With the resolution of this beginning resistance through the vehicle of the transference and countertransference, their treatment was secured and the couple could move toward exploring the internal object relationships expressed in their difficulties with physicality and intimacy. An account of the outcome of their ensuing treatment appears in Chapters 9 and 14.

Chapter **2**

# A THERAPEUTIC APPROACH TO
# MARRIAGE AND SEXUALITY

Sexuality in the marriage relationship reflects the physical aspects of the early mother–infant relationship that fade from the relationship as the child masters bodily needs autonomously and that only fully reappear in the interdependence of adult sexuality. The series of diagrams in Figure 2–1 will help us explore this relationship.

In the beginning, the fetus dwells completely inside the mother, physically and psychologically, penetrating her inner space with deep communication to conscious and unconscious parts of her organization while she holds inside her the future psychological organization of the fetus.

Birth establishes the psychosomatic partnership (Winnicott 1971). At birth, the intrauterine physical symbiosis gives way to a physical partnership, with the moment of birth being an intense shared physical experience. In almost all cases, the mother has already been per-

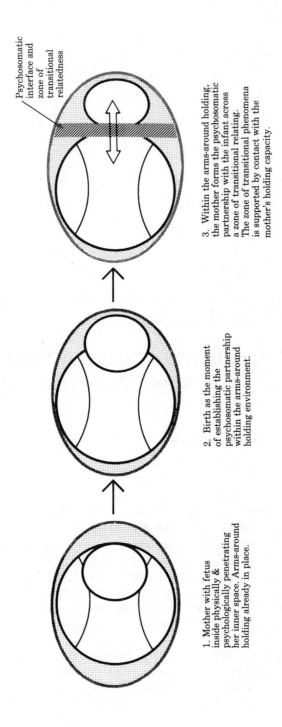

Figure 2–1. The movement from the pre-birth somatic partnership to the establishment of the psychosomatic partnership at birth. The transitional zone, across which the psychosomatic partnership occurs, is mediated and supported by its intimate contact with the arms-around holding of the mother.

forming the role of providing arms-around environmental holding, not only with her body, but with her mindful planning for the baby's arrival. In two-parent families, the father has usually had a substantial role in holding the mother beforehand, and in providing an outer envelope of holding for the mother–infant relationship from before the time of the infant's arrival.

In the early months, the psychosomatic partnership is dominated by physical exchange. Admittedly, the baby is often drowsy or asleep, but when awake, much of the time is engaged in receiving direct care such as feeding, holding, changing diapers, positioning, rocking, and bathing. There are other components of the partnership less clearly based on physical urgency, such as gaze interaction and vocalization, but even these early forms of relatedness are easier to characterize by their physical biologically determined characteristics rather than the emotionally obvious meaning we assign to them.

Figure 2–2 continues to show the path of development in the mother–infant relationship. In this early period, the mother contributes to the organization of the infant across the physical interface and exchanges gaze and vocal conversations through which she imparts the stuff of the infant's precipitating psychic organization. This happens across the physical interface, but even at the beginning there is a nonphysical aspect of this zone, namely the area of transitional phenomena (Winnicott 1951, 1971). In this area, the infant is discovering new things, including newfound aspects of the mother that she has put there for the baby to find. Yet the parents experience them as the baby's own inventions, as part of their child. The baby is discovering its self and the influence of the self on the world, a process described in detail by Stern (1985).

The physical aspect of the mother–infant partnership rapidly lessens over the months and years. We may note that while there is still a good deal of physical interaction between mothers and toddlers, it is progressively less than at first. Even by 6 or 8 months, infants spend a much larger part of their alert time looking at the wider world, exploring beyond their mothers. In this period, the psychosomatic partnership becomes weighted increasingly toward psychological collaboration and interchange. The infant's interior continues to be organized by these interactions. The area of transitional relatedness becomes larger, more under the infant's control, and less concretely connected to the mother. We should note, however, that in its origins, the transitional area was connected to the mother's provision of holding: so there remains, throughout life, an important connection between the transitional area of relatedness, the quality of holding, and the child or adult's need for holding. When there is se-

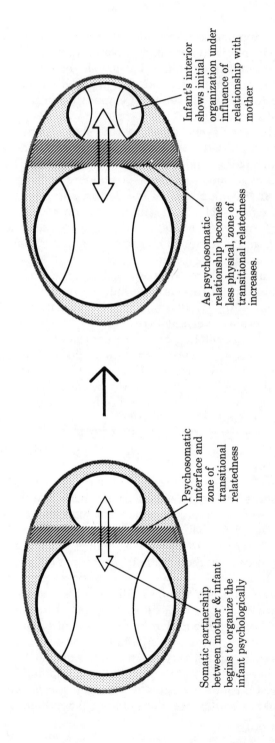

Infant's interior shows initial organization under influence of relationship with mother

As psychosomatic relationship becomes less physical, zone of transitional relatedness increases.

Psychosomatic interface and zone of transitional relatedness

Somatic partnership between mother & infant begins to organize the infant psychologically

Figure 2-2. The earliest psychosomatic partnership between mother and infant. This begins the organization of the infant's psyche and of the mother-as-mother. As the physical component of the relationship wanes, the area of transitional relatedness and transitional phenomena takes prominence, inheriting the core issues of the psychosomatic partnership. It is still closely connected to the functions of arms-around holding.

cure, safe, and reliable holding, satisfying relationships mediated across the transitional area build secure internal objects. Conversely, experience with excessive bad object relations in a situation of flawed holding will increase the need for holding in the current relationship.

## SEX AND THE PSYCHOSOMATIC PARTNERSHIP

The psychosomatic partnership gives birth to all relatedness including the adult sexual relationship. Nevertheless, the adult sexual relationship is the only other pleasurable psychosomatic partnership in maturity, offering a union of physical and psychological aspects of intimacy, as had the mother–infant relationship. It therefore has an ancient inheritance reinforced by physical gratification, which accounts for its intense poignancy.

Adolescent sexuality, though certainly qualifying as psychosomatic and pleasurable is, however, a period of learning appropriately preceding full adult commitment. Adolescence should be a time of practice, a way station on the road to longer-term adult relationships, an experimental phase without the raised stakes of a committed relationship.

Physical sexuality is important in relation to emotional commitment. When it goes well, the sexual bond renews the forces inherent in the psychosomatic partnership, resonating with the loving and nurturing aspects of the partners' internal object worlds. But when sex does not go well, there is a magnification of split-off and repressed object constellations, of both the unrequited longing for the exciting object and the unsoothed anger and frustration at the rejecting object. An adequate sexual adjustment supports the growth of love in courtship and later it strengthens the bonds of marriage, repairing the wear and tear of everyday life and supporting the couple through times of strain. But a frustrating or threatening sexual relationship attacks the sense of trust and safety, erodes other currents of love and caring, and fails to offer support to the central bond of marriage.

Sex, a fundamental part of the bonding process, deepens commitment both in the formative and mature years of the relationship. Because of this, sex also increases the possibilities for rejection, disappointment, and anger when it fails or is withheld from the relationship. The quality of sexual life is intimately related to the quality of mutual holding within a marriage. While a good sexual relationship rests on a secure mutual holding relationship, it also performs a reciprocal function of supporting the holding between marital partners. Within this secure contextual holding occurs centered holding in which there is a deep unconscious communication of internal object relatedness through the interpenetration of mutual projective identification.

During the phase of courtship or early in romance, sexual life takes its color from the couple's emphasis on the exciting aspects of relating. If the romance is to proceed, the excited object qualities must be magnified to overshadow the rejecting ones, so that areas of central ego functioning become infused with excitement. This is a normal aspect of formation of a new primary bond. Sexuality is a universally required feature of bond formation toward marriage. This does not mean that the couple must have a physical relationship, but that emotional sexualization is there with or without consummation. The resulting skewing of psychological life tends to repress those aspects of the rejecting object constellation that are normally present, either burying them beneath a blanket of exciting object activity and idealization, or, under their influence, projecting them outside the couple into the wider world. Thus Romeo and Juliet hold all the excited idealization, the antagonistic world peopled by their own projected but denied dangerous impulses.

With the moment of marriage or of equivalent commitment, the rejecting object issues for each of the partners can no longer be ignored. As soon as the relationship is confirmed as a permanent primary relationship, which often but not always occurs at the moment of marriage, then all personality aspects of each of the partners press for recognition and acceptance.

When it is the case that one or both partners have rather fragile excited object sets, the rejecting object and ego can now swamp the excitement and sexualization of bonding. It is for this reason that we frequently see a marked decrease of interest in sex at the moment of marriage or of commitment. A man or woman who is threatened, consciously or unconsciously, by sex because it is associated with frightening object relatedness may well muster a sexual response with pleasure and excitement under the conditions of courtship and bond making, only to have those feelings disappear once the bond seems secured.

All points of development in the marital life cycle may stress the couple: the birth of a first or subsequent children, shifts in career, new challenges of different phases such as the oedipal phase or adolescence, new phases of adult development such as midlife crises or aging. All these life transitions carry the twin possibilities of growth and regeneration or of threat and retreat. And any of these threatening aspects may undermine the couple's sexual relationship.

Sex not only expresses the loving side of the couple's relationship, injecting energy and excitement into the creative pairing, it also expresses difficulties that derive from the couple's shared rejecting object system. A good-enough sexual life supports the overall relatedness of a couple, providing solace and holding for domestic strain, and offers a pleasurable regeneration of the couple's loving bond. Absence of sex has the opposite effect, aggravating the wear and tear, spreading frustration and a sense of rejection, and undermining the maintenance of the bond. For this reason, difficulty in a couple's sexuality can be expected to take a toll in its own right. Sexual dysfunction is a secondary difficulty for a couple whose sexual life is mainly eroded because of causes in their general relationship, but it is a primary difficulty when there is situational performance anxiety, lack of knowledge about sexual functioning, or physical impairment. Well-trained psychodynamic therapists may not look out sufficiently for these latter cases that are uncomplicated by relational pathology, while therapists trained in sexual disorders but not in psychodynamic psychotherapy may underestimate the primary role of object related issues in the genesis of many sexual disorders. Examples of both causes are included throughout this book. Nevertheless, in our view, a poor sexual relationship is most often a product of object relations difficulty, and then unsatisfying sex takes a further toll of its own.

## THERAPY FOR SEXUAL DISORDERS WITHIN MARRIAGE

Therapy to help couples with their marriages is a much older clinical field than direct therapy for their sexual difficulties. At first the attempts to help marriages were, from the psychodynamic point of view, based heavily in the understanding of the individual, beginning with Flugel's (1921) attempt to apply psychoanalysis to marriage. Other contributions, such as the edited volume of Paolino and McCready (1978) continued to take individual psychoanalytic theories and techniques and to stretch them to apply to couples.

The pioneering work of Dicks (1967) and his colleagues (Pincus 1960, Bannister and Pincus 1965) at the Institute of Marital Studies of the Tavistock Institute of Human Relations first explored object relations theory as the language of an analytic approach to marital therapy. Still at this date there were no references to direct work with the couple's interaction, nor to explicit understanding of the role of sexuality in the couples' marriages.

This is not surprising. Masters and Johnson's first volume, *Human*

*Sexual Response,* was published in 1966. Work on direct therapy of sexual disorders was still found only in patches, without any organizing theory or approach. When it did burst on the scene in 1970 with the publication of *Human Sexual Inadequacy,* Masters and Johnson used educational and behavioral theory and formatting for their work. They eschewed psychodynamic theory and interpretation, having known little about it, and specifically taught that interpretation of underlying causes was irrelevant. Yet they identified many causes of sexual dysfunction in the anxieties of the couples' interaction that they thought of as being close to consciousness.

For instance, they described *spectatoring,* in which a man stands outside himself looking on at his erectile difficulty, anxious lest his erection fail, thus precipitating its failure because of this anxiety. The concept of spectatoring is an important contribution to understanding the way anxiety about the situation contributes, as an independent factor with a life of its own, to sexual failure. Masters and Johnson's detailed descriptions of sexual physiology and of the sexual response cycle gave us a capacity to understand the surface and therefore the interaction of surface and depth that was entirely lacking before. No longer were we limited to the speculations of the sort Freud made from deep analysis that mature female sexuality was characterized by the vaginal orgasm. We could now see the mechanism of orgasm as a physiological mechanism, which is sometimes immune to, and sometimes affected by, internal object life. In our practices, we find that experience of orgasm is no arbiter of emotional maturity. Clinical experience tends to confirm Kaplan's (1974) assertion that most women cannot obtain orgasm from penile stimulation alone. Fisher (1972) found that only 20% of the women in his study of orgasm were reliably able to achieve orgasm in intercourse without manual assistance. Of the 3,000 women surveyed by the *Hite Report* (1976), 30% experienced orgasm from penile stimulation alone during intercourse and the remaining 70% required additional manual stimulation of the clitoris.

Helen Singer Kaplan's *New Sex Therapy* (1974) led the way to integrating the analytic and behavioral ways of seeing couples, giving the first case examples of conjoint marital work that ran the full range. Her cases explored the origins of the individual's relationships, but they also relied on an intimate understanding of the physiology of sexual functioning. She understood, in a general way, the reincarnation of each partner's interaction with old primary figures in the current relationship, and she learned and taught about the ways these showed up in sexual impasse.

Kaplan's early work did not stress the in-depth exploration of the earlier and more pervasive causes of sexual difficulty, those rooted in character and in long-standing, dysfunctional, emotional patterns, but, after further experience with cases that did not respond promptly, she did move toward this area in her description of the disorders of sexual desire. Masters and Johnson (1966) had described a four-phase model of sexual response: Arousal, Plateau, Orgasm, and Resolution. To these, Kaplan (1977, 1979) added a preliminary Desire Phase, and described the most common sexual difficulty, Hypoactive Sexual Desire. She noted that disorders rooted in this phase were the most difficult to treat, and were the most likely to require long-term, psychodynamically oriented psychotherapy of one of the partners. Nevertheless, she said, some of these could be treated with brief sex therapy.

Decreased desire is one of the disorders that exists most frequently at the interface between sexual and marital difficulty. Decreased desire may originate in either of the individuals, just as often in the husband as in the wife. In the course of development, sexual interest and its diminishment represent a way of compartmentalizing and containing the relationship to the rejecting object. In these cases, a person may have had a lifelong inhibition of sexual interest, or may have managed a good show of interest in adolescence or courtship only to have the decrease in desire set in soon after commitment to a relationship or actual marriage. These long-standing and deeply embedded difficulties often require intensive psychotherapy or psychoanalysis, but there are cases, just as Kaplan originally suggested, that appear to be in these categories but that nevertheless yield to couple therapy. An example is given as the final illustration in this book, the case of Dr. and Mrs. T, for whom brief sex therapy accomplished a great deal despite the initial presentation of profoundly depressed sexual desire in both husband and wife. Even when the disorders of low desire do not respond to brief sex therapy, the process of trying and proving it to be inadequate is nevertheless useful: it crystallizes the understanding of areas of difficulty for the individual with hypoactive desire and ways in which the partner has usually unconsciously supported those areas.

At the other end of the continuum are those couples for whom sexual interest has declined because of conflict between them, repeated fighting, or strain that comes from identifiable sources in their lives—for instance, an exhausting job or a new baby. In these situational examples, the quality of the marriage and the sexual situation may improve when the overall situation eases, but it may also be that the strain sets up conflict and resentment that take on a life of their own and continue to invade the marriage and the sex. Or sexual reluctance may remain as a residue of the strain, with the couple unable to return to their previous adjustment.

When the decline in sexual desire is the leading edge of a more profound resentment and conflict, we do not expect to see its easy resolution with time. For these couples, for whom sex once worked well, there is usually little need of specific sex therapy. The difficulties in interest in sex, or in sexual interaction, usually yield to an investigation of the general conflict, both in the day-to-day interaction between the couple and in the causes rooted in their individual development, unconscious object relations, and mutual projective identifications. That is to say, object relations marital therapy will usually be sufficient without specific recourse to the behavioral framework of specific sex therapy.

However, many—perhaps most—couples present with a mixed picture. Marital distress rests on a mixture of object relations developmental difficulty in both partners, the strain of developmental life crises, and marital conflict. The sexual difficulties do stem from original internal object issues, but these have been reinforced by marital strain. For many couples, the relative contribution from each source cannot be precisely determined, and we remain in a muddle. We are forced to make an educated guess as we design the intervention that most seems to address the underlying causes, and then see how far we can get, switching to other ways of working if we hit an impasse. The switch may be from marital therapy to sex therapy, from sex therapy back to marital, or to individual work with one or both partners. Sometimes, the most helpful switch will be from couple's work to family therapy in order to explore the way in which issues from the whole family impinge on the couple. Conversely, in family therapy, we can study the way the couple's issues have an impact on their children, which in turn yields a better understanding of the couple. Chapter 11 gives an extensive example of this situation. Graller (1981) found that psychoanalytically oriented marital therapy was at times useful as an adjunct to psychoanalysis, and Sander (1989) has described the use of couple therapy as preparation for individual work, paving the way and demonstrating the usefulness of individual exploration. But the work can move in any direction—as easily from individual to couple as from couple to individual, and can include a specific phase of sex therapy, which may be necessary to the overall approach though not necessarily sufficient in itself.

An extensive example will illustrate many of the relationships between these factors.

Chloe Johnson presented for individual consultation with me [J.S.S.] to discuss her difficulty with her sexual interest and responsiveness to her husband, who she felt was an ideal husband. He had rescued her from a difficult family situation, which, we eventually learned, included a sexually threatening and sometimes psychotic stepfather and a provocative and promiscuous mother. Sam was easy for her to idealize: he was a major intellectual figure on campus, and he offered to take care of her. They married while she was still in college, where she continued her studies and then graduated. Sam had no difficulty getting an excellent first job working for an architectural firm, but Chloe had more difficulty getting satisfactory work in graphics. Sam was upset when she became pregnant soon after the marriage, but he did not mind a great deal, as Chloe agreed to put their son in day care. The second pregnancy threw him even more, and this time Chloe had more difficulty giving up the urge to stay home with the children.

Now resentment began to build but in unnoticed ways. Chloe felt the strain of working, feeling she was not progressing as well in her career as Sam, who was streaking ahead with major projects seeming to fall in his lap. And she felt the tug to the children, feeling she was ignoring them in a way that echoed the pattern between her and her mother. When she was small, her mother had gone on to have two more children in rapid succession. Chloe was born when her mother was 17 and unmarried, and had been given to her maternal grandmother to raise until her mother married two years later. She had been close to her grandmother, a brittle and often bitter woman. Chloe had been the one the grandmother idealized and loved rather easily. It was an uneasy relationship, nevertheless, because Chloe soon became aware of the grandmother's rage at everyone else around her. Throughout Chloe's childhood, her mother and grandmother had used her as an object of conflict, sometimes fighting to have her live with them, denigrating each other to Chloe, and sometimes ceding her to the other when life was overwhelming.

It was this early atmosphere of resentment that Chloe now feared would return. In her attempt to keep Sam idealized, she unconsciously split the fear and resentment into her sexual response and it began to wither. Not that it had ever been a completely mature and integrated function. In their adolescent courtship, Chloe had loved the physical closeness and enjoyed the holding, while having no trouble with intercourse and penetration. However, she was not orgasmic, and maintained a certain hands-off attitude about her own body. The underlying causes of this emerged only gradually in subsequent individual therapy, but she knew from the beginning that her stepfather had frequently acted sexually threateningly and on one occasion had come into the family's photographic darkroom with his erect penis extended toward her when no one else was present. She was nauseated, and ran from the room to vomit. She then left the household for a year to live with her grandmother.

None of this was known in detail when I suggested a couple assessment interview. There I could see the strain in the couple's marriage. Sam felt it came from Chloe's withdrawal from sex, which left him feeling deprived, while she felt rejected by his insistence on a regular sex life she felt to be increasingly burdensome.

From Sam's side, the withdrawal Chloe was making felt like a cruel assault. He had, in many overt ways, led a charmed life. The only son of doting parents, he had been idealized and given whatever he asked for. He saw his parents' marriage as good, but he saw it somewhat distantly, as through the sunglasses of someone on whom the sun never stopped shining. He had enjoyed the idealization Chloe had shone on him during their courtship, and he missed it now that the children's needs pulled on her. Her waning sexual interest hurt him even more obviously, because he could ignore her suppressed resentment in other areas by turning to his satisfying work life. But the sexual difficulty left him feeling rejected in an immediate way. In the wake of this, he would rage and sulk, increasing Chloe's resentment, wariness, and especially her sexual withdrawal.

In the initial evaluation, I could understand the interaction between Sam's sense of rejection that threatened his self-esteem, which he had not previously understood to be shaky, and Chloe's threatened withdrawal. Her history of a provocative, intrusive, and often unavailable mother made sense of the wariness that had emerged with Sam, especially as she felt increasingly pulled by her own children and her guilt that she might be ignoring them in the way she had felt ignored by her mother. It already made sense to understand, as Fairbairn (1954) described, that the sexual difficulty embodied the internal bad object. The bad object was embedded in Chloe's genital difficulty, while the idealized and exciting objects were embodied in Sam. Between the couple, Chloe became the rejecting person, as the sex and its strain embodied issues that could not be negotiated between them. With her persistent unconscious interest in idealizing Sam, Chloe blamed herself and initially presented for therapy alone, but when Sam came along also, as he was invited to do, he joined in blaming her.

I elected to recommend sex therapy as the place to begin, because both partners were most aware of the sexual difficulty. To not have done so would have violated Sam's sense of urgency, although both of them would have accepted a suggestion that put Chloe's individual difficulty first and recommended individual work for her. I referred the couple for sex therapy with David Scharff.

The sex therapy was successful up to a point. It succeeded in teaching the couple to provide more safety to their relationship, and to decrease the urgent invasion that had happened on every occasion as Sam pressed forward while Chloe retreated. During the initial period of nongenital pleasuring, Sam's urgent insistence could be related to his hidden anxiety about rejection, produced by his mother's anxiously hovering overattention and idealization of him. Chloe learned to help him understand her sense of threat, and could, in appreciation and relief for his slower, less insistent approach, warm to him and breathe more freely. In this manner, as she became less the reluctant mother to him, he became less the mother who would leave if she did not comply, and less the threatening stepfather.

This work continued with the next phases of the sex therapy. Sam learned how to create new tenderness, and Chloe learned to bind her anxiety about penetration. Chloe feared Sam's penis would invade and assault her, but she also feared for the damage she would do to him. As she said, "It isn't *just* that I'm afraid he will hurt me, though I am afraid of that. Sometimes I have a fleeting image of his penis tearing me apart. But I am also starting to feel that I could hurt him, that this isn't safe for him either. It's almost like I'm protecting him by staying away from him. Sometimes I even think I retreat to the children to protect Sam from me."

The sex therapy taught them a way of relating that gave them a shared sense of increased safety, but it could not go so far as to give Chloe an easy and relaxed acceptance of sex. Repeatedly during the phases of the sex therapy in which the penis is contained quietly in the vagina and then thrusts gently with slowly increasing movement, she was on the verge of anxiety, even when Sam's newfound patience was everything she asked for. The sex therapy ended with intercourse now a possibility, but it continued to require an exceeding tolerance by Chloe for her anxiety and her fear of invasion. Chloe's previous shying away from sex altogether had stemmed from the issues that now were understood specifically to relate to penetration and her fear of invasion. These ultimately stemmed from the experience with her mother and stepfather, which led up to her lifelong lack of safety. This constellation, she now felt, was no longer Sam's fault, and she requested a shift to individual therapy to work with these issues. Sam was able to be supportive and patient about her anxiety in a new way, and they were able to enjoy their partially restricted sexual life while she worked on her inhibitions in intensive psychotherapy.

The example of Chloe and Sam describes a sexual problem that stems primarily from difficulties in the early life of one of the partners, though both can be seen to have issues that contributed to the shared areas of trouble. In this case, a difficulty that began in reaction to trauma in one spouse was exacerbated by the internal object influence of the other. In the beginning, the sexual disorder can be seen to be congruent with the general underlying strain between Chloe, who feared mistreatment, abuse, and abandonment from her primary objects, and Sam, whose experience with an overanxious and idealizing mother left him vulnerable for rejection and anxious when not being indulged. However, there was then a secondary effect on their marriage when the lack of sex itself left them feeling additionally rejected, hurt, and anxious.

# THE ASSESSMENT OF SEXUAL FUNCTIONING WITHIN MARRIAGE

The quality of sexual functioning within a relationship should always be inquired about as part of our standard marital assessment, just as the question of affairs should always be broached. Some couples present their sexual relationship as the leading edge of their problem with the notion that sex is all that is troubling them. Other couples, in a more insightful vein, immediately let us know that their sexual difficulty embodies general aspects of their relationship that they have not been able to manage. For them, sexual disjunction is a way of characterizing widespread difficulty. Finally, some couples come for marital difficulty of a general sort and do not identify the role of sexual difficulty in its origin or maintenance.

## A Framework for Assessment

We can view sexual difficulties as stemming from difficulties at one of four places in the marital relationship. While many cases are of mixed origin, it is nevertheless useful to locate the areas of most significance.

### INDIVIDUAL INTRAPSYCHIC CONFLICT

First, the difficulties can stem from problems of intrapsychic origin in one or both of the individuals. In object relations terms, the marriage relationship is beset by conflictual internal object relations of one or both individuals.

### PROBLEMATIC MUTUALITY OF PROJECTIVE IDENTIFICATIONS

In the middle ground are the relational difficulties due to interpersonal conflict that follow from problematic mutuality of projective identification. This is an area that is not quite the difficulty of the individual spouse, in that either one might have a better sexual and marital adjustment with other people or in other circumstances. Yet the conflict between them draws on or magnifies the object relations difficulties in their internal worlds.

DEVELOPMENTAL STRESS

Another area of the middle ground is the sexual difficulty that follows from life stress, imposed by development, life circumstances, or illness. [We are not thinking of the organic sort of sexual difficulty that is a direct and inevitable consequence of an illness.] While these situations are independently stressful, they also often resonate with the internal object relations of the couple so as to interfere with sexual functioning. Then the sexual difficulty takes an additional secondary toll on the marriage.

INDIVIDUAL PHYSICAL LIMITATION

At the other end of the continuum are the learning difficulties and physically handicapping conditions that create problems with physical sexuality, causally independent of object relations issues. These problems with the physical aspects of the sexual relationship have, however, a direct effect on the emotional bond by forming a deficit or assault on it. In these cases, secondary effects accrue, as resentment, frustration, loss, and disappointment take their toll in producing conflictual areas.

A few examples will illustrate some differences in etiology that determine the choice of therapy.

## INTRAPSYCHIC DIFFICULTY IN ONE SPOUSE

Tamara and Tom Sands came to see me [J.S.S.] for assessment because Tamara had lost her interest in sex in this marriage, which was her second and his first. Sex had been a regular and well-functioning part of their premarital life, even when, in the early phases, she was unsure she could fully trust Tom. When he finally won her trust by sticking with her through an unusually difficult visit with her parents, she felt enormously relieved and decided she was ready to marry him. But she also promptly lost interest in intercourse and even became somewhat aversive. However, she managed to cover over this reaction, and he was still unaware of this when they actually married six months later. She then quickly became pregnant, nursed her son, and became pregnant again during the year of nursing. During these times, she complained that these altered bodily conditions caused her sexual disinterest. Since she also nursed her second son, she continued to have "legitimate excuses" for a low level of interest in sex until they had been married for almost four years. Then, for almost the first time since marriage, she was neither pregnant nor nursing.

Within a few months of her being unencumbered by the physical demands of nursing, Tom said he now insisted that they do something about her low level of desire and her aversion to sex. She quietly agreed.

When the couple was seen, Tamara revealed that a similar pattern had developed in her previous marriage. There, too, she had been interested in sex until the moment when she had made an emotional commitment to her first husband. Then, too, even without the excuses of pregnancy and nursing, she had been uninterested in sex for the duration of the marriage, which was fractured finally when her husband had an affair with her best friend.

Because there was no sexual dysfunction of physical origin and because as a couple they agreed that their marital relationship was gratifying, and since Tom, who had no demonstrable pathology, was supportive of Tamara while not supportive of the continuation of the sexual difficulty, it made sense to recommend individual treatment for her low sexual desire. Since she had had difficulty leading to the earlier loss of her first marriage, Tamara no longer denied her problem and asked for the most thorough treatment to help her avoid further loss. She therefore readily agreed to a recommendation for psychoanalysis where material eventually emerged that made sense of her sexual inhibition. Tom had taken on the transferential role in which she experienced him as her forbidding and intrusive mother, a religious woman who gave repressive messages about sex. Tamara had assumed that her mother was "sexually frigid," but she later had a dream that led to her curiosity about her parents as a sexual pair and to the recovery of a memory in which she had discovered the thermometer kept at her mother's bedside, a finding that had meant to her that her mother was using the thermal method of contraception and that, therefore, her parents had a sexual life.

Now she could see that her mother stood not just for the repression of sex, but for the tantalizing quality of the sexual pairing with father. Her envy of the parental pair, whom she unconsciously sexualized and hated, was at the same time an expression of her longing to be in a relationship like theirs or with them or in the place of one of them. She had been most exposed to the ravages of her repressed anger and envy at the time she made a commitment to a marriage of her own. She began to realize that she also repressed sexual feelings because of her envy of her husband, not only because he had the penis of her desire, while she did not, and because he had desire and she did not, but because she invested in him as though he embodied the composite couple she had longed to be a part of but ought not to be sexually involved with. When Tamara was able to bring these insights to her marriage from her individual analytic work, Tom did not make things more difficult. The work, to a considerable degree, led to an improved sexual relationship.

## INTRAPSYCHIC DIFFICULTIES IN BOTH PARTNERS

Velia and Lars Simpson sought help because of their sexual difficulty. Simply put, they had come because Velia hated sex and because Lars suffered from premature ejaculation after one to three minutes of intercourse.

The treatment with this couple is given in detail in Chapter 10, which discusses the treatment of sexual disorders and shows how the children internalized the parents' object relations, especially with regard to sexuality, and again in Chapter 11, which illustrates their family treatment. Data obtained only in the initial evaluation is used below to sketch the factors from each spouse's internal object world that led to their combined difficulty.

Velia was psychologically minded and able to reveal to me [D.E.S.] during a brief assessment that she had grown up in a house of fear and conflict. Her father, a heavy drinker, had been angry and verbally abusive to the children, and occasionally physically abusive to her mother. She was resentful that her mother had suffered this passively and had additionally failed to protect the children. In her loneliness, Velia had turned to her brothers for affection. There had been some sex play with them as young boys, some fondling and inspection of her body, and playing doctor. On one occasion she had handled one brother's penis and on other occasions, another brother had touched her breasts. As a mid-adolescent, she missed the sex and romance she had heard and fantasized about. Would she ever find them?

Lars was her first serious boyfriend. She and he had urgently cuddled and experienced arousal in their six-week courtship. But sex on their wedding night had been a disappointment when he could not enter her. After brief gynecological support and an operation, they could manage sex, but Lars now experienced premature ejaculation. Velia, who had never masturbated, was not orgasmic. She found arousal without satisfaction frustrating, but she seemed to retreat from the experience even before the frustration mounted. She quickly grew to avoid sex, although she could manage it on occasions by gritting her teeth.

Lars hated to hurt Velia and wanted to suppress his sexual desire with saltpeter. He seemed to have suppressed other male characteristics and appeared to be quite passive, was not psychologically minded, and could remember little of his childhood. He thought his parents had a good marriage, until one day when he was 16 or 17, he learned that his father had been picked up in a men's room for soliciting homosexual sex. His father had spent time in jail, and his parents were immediately divorced. Although Lars maintained contact with him, he said that his father, who lived with a man in a long-term relationship, was so defensive about his homosexuality that little closeness existed between them. He had stayed in close touch with his mother, but he could say little about her.

Lars's psychological opacity and the density of repression made it impossible to ascertain what issues in his inner world led to his premature ejaculation and to his intense interest in protecting Velia from harm, which he felt his penis would bring. But we could extrapolate from the suspicion that there were repressed, unknown issues in his early life that he had absorbed in terms of the threat of sex, which must have been embodied in his father's homosexuality and his mother's perhaps unknowing tolerance of it. Certainly the condensed memory of father's arrest for homosexuality portrayed the penis as destructive to the family. But for now, my comments were simply that there was more to know about his unconscious idea that sex threatened harm and that in some way this was complementary to Velia's fear of sex.

Velia's situation was easier to follow. Her father had been a threatening figure, and her mother lived a defenseless life, failing to protect both herself and her children. Longing for love had taken a sexualized route for Velia, which she repressed out of painful desire and guilt. This combination led to a fear of sex that was greater than her longing, and had led to a foreclosure of her desire. She had never experienced an orgasm, either with Lars or through masturbation.

One other piece of information supported the speculation that her capacity for desire lay buried not far below the surface. Once, when she had been quite depressed after the birth of her second child, she had received psychotherapy and had experienced a period of intense sexual desire, though she was still unable to achieve its resolution in orgasm. The psychotherapy lasted only for nine months, and was ended because of Lars's job transfer. When it ended, the desire faded. Nevertheless, that period of her life, which echoed her adolescent longing for arousal and sexual passion, gave support to the presence of a repressed but urgent longing.

This case represents the situation to the left of the continuum: a sexual dysfunction is the result, in all likelihood, of the internal object constellation of each of the partners, and is maintained in and between them through mutual projective identification. Velia put both the protecting and arousing parts of her internal world into Lars, while he sacrificed his wish for sex to protect a victimized part of himself that he had projected into her. In this case, treatment began with individual psychotherapy for Velia, although the recommendation was also for couples and family work. We will describe work on their mutual projective identifications in couple and family therapy in Chapters 10 and 11.

## SEXUAL DIFFICULTY DURING MARITAL CONFLICT

Sexual difficulty during marital conflict is known to marital therapists without specific experience in treating sexual disorders. It is quite common for the sexual relationship to wither as the strain in a marriage grows. On occasion, however, one of the spouses will ask for help with sex rather than with the marriage. At such times, it is not likely that any specific approach to sex will be of much help until the general difficulty between the partners is clarified, and to some extent cleared up. Since the quality of the sexual relationship often follows that of the general marital relationship, sex frequently deteriorates if the marriage is in serious decline. A brief example will suffice to illustrate this general situation.

> Barbara and Royce Allen came to see me [J.S.S.] because Barbara could not tolerate the way Royce seemed to turn away from her sexually. However, they were not in the office for five minutes when Royce began a litany of his grievances about Barbara. She was constantly critical, screamed frequently, and failed to take care of the children consistently. It was true that he had lost interest in having sex with Barbara, and he could not explain it except to say that he was so often angry with her that sex did not appear to make sense.
>
> From her side, Barbara was also furious with Royce for being preoccupied with his work and for the way she felt he turned the children against her. But she relied on sex to maintain a fragile sense of security in an increasingly anxious marriage. She imagined that a successful sexual encounter with Royce would relieve her feeling that he did not love her and that the marriage was in danger. Her intense longing for sex assumed a demanding quality that arose from her desperation, but it had the effect of driving Royce further away, as he felt it threatened to engulf him when he was already angry. This situation could, in turn, be traced to more profound causes of discord between Barbara and Royce, but the sexual difficulty did not in itself stem from intrinsic difficulty in either of their individual internal object worlds, but from the issues between them that eroded their general relationship.

## WHEN ILLNESS THREATENS

There are many life crises that can threaten the marital relationship. The effect of some of these may exist outside the couple's awareness. Spouses may manage to compensate for strain, but fail to make the connection that strain in their situation is related to an ensuing sexual difficulty. Such difficulty may arise in a couple who have previously done well. If it is not understood, it runs the risk of becoming chronic because of the toll of the accruing secondary anxiety.

> Pete and Rachel Rothstein had a late-life marriage, the first for her and the second for him. Their sexual adjustment had been satisfying for both until a year and a half before they sought help. Then Pete had a mild coronary, and became extremely anxious. Soon after his recovery both of

them thought about the dangers of exertion and especially the risk of sexual activity. It was during this period that Pete first experienced episodes of erectile difficulty. However, the erectile difficulty took on a life of its own, for even after Pete recovered from the worst ravages of coronary anxiety, he continued to fear that he would be impotent.

For Rachel, the initial erectile failure had not constituted much of a difficulty. She had thought it stemmed from Pete's fear for his health, and despite her own worries about his survival, she had been prepared, even eager, to coax him through the early anxieties. But she could not understand why, when he seemed more confident about his capacity to survive, he continued to have trouble with his erections. She now began to feel not only frustrated, but worried as well that there was something wrong in their relationship that she had not understood.

Here, the therapist's capacity to trace the origin of the difficulty to the original death anxiety to do with the coronary and then to name the subsequent performance anxiety that had supervened allowed the couple to recover their previous level of sexual relatedness. In this case brief therapy was enough.

## WHEN PHYSICAL DISABILITY IS THE CAUSE

There are times when physical disability is the cause of a sexual dysfunction: the couple suspects that from the beginning, and comes in to ask for help with the physical cause. This is more frequently true in men over 40 with erectile difficulty (Kaplan 1983, Levine 1988). More than half of these men, and a larger percentage with increasing age, suffer from organic impairment of the erectile mechanism. When the partners are clear and accepting about this, there is often no secondary invasion of their overall relationship. But if their relationship was compromised to begin with, or if the organic cause is not recognized, it is common to see a secondary invasion of their relationship and of their shared sense of well-being.

An additional complication occurs when an organic cause supervenes in couples who previously had difficulty of psychological origin, either in their overall relationship or only in their sexual relationship. This was so in the case described below.

Blair and Jo Ellen Foley were in their mid-fifties, and had been married for thirty-five years. They told me [D.E.S.] that they had, for the most part, an extremely happy marriage, and were each other's only lovers. They had been teenage sweethearts, and had first had intercourse when they were juniors in high school. On that first occasion, Blair had difficulty in achieving an erection, and then had premature ejaculation. Since then, he had had considerable help in his late twenties from psychoanalysis. He could describe the guilt that had characterized his early sexual adjustment, making him feel, in retrospect, that it was no surprise that he had trouble. Nevertheless, he had never overcome his sense of sexual inadequacy, and he had experienced severe difficulty with erections all his life. Despite the fact that the couple had five children, they were rarely able to have successful sex. Blair would not usually be able to have a firm erection, and if he achieved penetration, he had an orgasm within thirty seconds.

Not surprisingly, Jo Ellen had never experienced much satisfaction in sex. She remembered the passionate, anticipatory arousal of adolescence, but she had long ago learned not to expect much. She had stopped looking forward to sex, and found the experience of asking for sex therapy a painful prospect.

"Doctor, why should I go through this just to be dissatisfied yet again?" she asked. "Blair keeps hoping there will be a solution for his trouble. This isn't the first time he's tried. He tried psychoanalysis, and we have tried sex therapy before. We're told you may have some things to offer that are different, but I don't know if I can stand to get my hopes up again and have them disappointed."

Blair had a firm conviction that his difficulty was psychological. After all, he had had it all his life, and he knew that he had been enormously anxious as an adolescent. In fact, he thought it correlated with his difficulty living up to his image of his father and his standards, and he cited his failure in his career as evidence. There, too, he felt he had been impotent. He did think he had real organic difficulty—but with his memory, not with his penis!

I judged Blair's erectile difficulty as likely to be organic, but I was not impressed with an organic quality to his memory loss. But it seemed my guess about his erectile problem was wrong. After a Nocturnal Penile Tumescence Test, done by a reputable laboratory, indicated that he had the capacity for adequate erections, we agreed to proceed with psychological sex therapy. It was striking to me that Blair was willing to have the NPT for his erectile difficulty, but he was unwilling to put his memory to the test.

The sex therapy went generally well. In sessions Blair and Jo Ellen learned a new level of expression of tenderness for each other, and Jo Ellen learned a new capacity for arousal and shared orgasm. They brought in dreams. They worked with the issues that caused the underlying strain between them, including considerable difficulty around occupational dissatisfaction. But when sex therapy got to the point of "containment" of the penis in the vagina, and of helping Blair investigate and cope with his anxiety concerning erections, things did not work. Although I felt he did everything I asked of him, although he brought insight and some of the most passionate motivation of any patient I have had, his erection continually failed.

With this experience, I became convinced that he had more of an organic component than he or the NPT could credit. We considered referral for newly available vascular insufficiency evaluation and possible surgical intervention and for injection therapy with papaverine. The urologist also thought that Blair's history was indicative of psychological causation, but since psychological therapy had not worked, he prescribed papaverine injections. The papaverine worked like a charm to stimulate erection. In the majority of patients with likely psychological causation but who resist sex therapy and opt for injections from the beginning, papaverine does not change the situation much because it falls into rapid disuse (Levine and Agle 1978). But the injections were warmly received by this couple, who were then able to have the first reliable sex of their long marriage. Jo Ellen took longer to warm to the importance of sex for herself, but she immediately felt that the relief Blair experienced was a considerable source of pleasure for her.

Blair was, from the first, ecstatic. "You don't know what it's like to have wanted something desperately for so long and finally be able to have it!" he said. "It has changed my life, and it's made me feel better about everything else as well. We still have a wonderful marriage, and I still love Jo Ellen very much, but now I feel complete. I wish I had had this long ago, but at least I'm thrilled to have it now!"

The relationship of sex to marriage or a long-term loving relationship is often complex. In every case it is important to understand with as much specificity as possible the relationship between them. This kind of understanding makes it possible to undertake therapy with the most useful combination of approaches and with the potential for furthering the investigation and therapy as things unfold.

# Chapter 3
## OBJECT RELATIONS THEORY AND PROJECTIVE IDENTIFICATION IN MARRIAGE

Object relations theory is an individual psychology that views the personality as a system of parts in interaction with significant others in the environment. It is an amalgam of the theories of a number of independent British thinkers: Fairbairn, Guntrip, Balint, and Winnicott. Although their work is generally recognized as influenced by Klein, they form a group that in Britain is quite separate from the group of theorists that gathered around her. In the United States, where we are less concerned with such boundaries, we tend to group Klein with the object relations theorists. Of them all, only Fairbairn systematically developed a clear concept of the personality sufficient to challenge Freud's instinct and structural theories. Thus we rely most heavily on the work of Fairbairn (1944, 1952, 1954, 1963) with some filling in from Winnicott (1958, 1960b, 1968, 1971). Klein's concept of projective identification (1946) provides the necessary bridging concept to extend the individual psychology of object relations theory to the interpersonal situation. We also refer to Dicks' (1967) use of object relations theory in marital therapy, to Bion's (1961) application of the theory to small groups, and to Zinner and Shapiro's extension of that to marital interaction and family dynamics (Zinner 1976; Zinner and Shapiro 1972).

## A BACKGROUND OF OBJECT RELATIONS THEORY

### Fairbairn: An Individual Psychology Based on Object Relations

Fairbairn (1952, 1963) saw infants as "object-seeking," compelled to reach for a relationship with their mothers so that their fundamental needs for attachment and nurturance could be met. During the long years of absolute, and later relative dependency, human infants develop relationships with their parents and their older siblings. Infant personality is built from the infant's perception of the actual family experience. Feelings of need or frustration color the infant's appreciation of actual events. This mixture of experience, affect, perception, and misconception not only affects the experience and the child's memory of events but, much more important, it determines the child's psychic structure. This structure is seen as one consisting of a system of conscious and unconscious object relationships that crystallize out of the infant's experience of real relationships. In summary, as Bollas (1987) put it, "ego structure is the trace of a relationship" (p. 50).

The endopsychic situation is reinforced or modified in the light of future experience, maturing cognitive abilities, and changes in the quality of the primary relationships at various developmental phases. Not only is the individual child moving through the classic stages of psychosexual development described by Freud (1905b) but the family is moving on through the life cycle too, perhaps dealing with death or illness of significant members in the previous generation, a geographic move, a change in life-style or economic circumstances, or the birth of another child.

The individual personality, composed of a system of parts, some conscious and some unconscious, is in dynamic relation to the family system and its parts and to the individual members and their personality parts. Beyond the fixed number of whole person relationships, an infinite number of ever-changing part-to-part relationships is extended as a culture medium for the growth of the child. The resulting personality is complex, reflecting multiple identifications and counteridentifications with parts of others, organized in conscious and unconscious areas of the personality. The conscious parts remain in an open system, flexible and changeable, and able to interact freely with others. The unconscious parts are split off into a closed system, rigid and unchanging under the force of repression, and not available for interaction with others or for learning and change at the conscious level (Sutherland 1963). One of Fairbairn's major contributions was to point out that all these systems and their conscious and unconscious parts are in constant dynamic interaction with each other internally. Needs, frustrations, longings, love, and hate are reexperienced inside the self. These affects characterize the exciting and rejecting object relationships that were internalized and that continue to interact dynamically within the overall personality. These inner relationships are being actively repressed and are equally actively seeking to return to consciousness.

## Bion: Containment, Group Assumptions, and Valency

From studies of group communication, thought process, and mother–infant dynamics, Bion (1962, 1967, 1970) postulated that the mother in a special state of thought called "reverie" is able to bear her infant's anxiety and frustration so that her child feels contained. By identifying with the mother as the container, the child develops a secure self capable of thinking through. This kind of identification is an example of *introjective identification,* introduced by Klein (1946) and defined by Segal (1964) as "the result when the object is introjected into the ego which then identifies with some or all of its characteristics" (p. 105). Bion's concept of *container-contained* describes a situation where the infant's projective process can occur without damage to the mother and introjective identification is benign and growth-promoting. This is to be distinguished from Winnicott's (1960a) description of the *holding environment,* which refers to an empathic *psychosomatic* partnership between mother and baby permitting the management of physiological and psychological experiences rather than to a cognitive function of the mother that creates psychological space in the realm of *thought* as Bion intended. Containment is also distinct from Winnicott's (1971) description of the transitional space between mother and infant, the area in which the infant uses an object that represents the mother but is under the infant's control.

Winnicott's description of the holding environment and transitional space refers to the interpersonal process, which expresses much of what the mother has modified and which the infant has then to re-work, whereas containment refers to the mother's capacity for introjective and projective identification in fantasy.

As couple and family therapists, we use both terms—container and holding environment—for the provision by the family or the couple of the normal context that facilitates spontaneous mutative, mutual projective identification among family members.

From his study of small group process, Bion (1961) noted that members tended to unite in subgroup formations that expressed and met unconscious needs not satisfied by the leader. The subgroups formed on the basis of members' shared unconscious assumptions about how to find gratification of wishes for dependency, aggression expressed as fight or flight, and pairing to produce a savior for the group in distress. How did individuals self-select to respond to one of these themes? Bion suggested the concept of *valency*: "the capacity for instantaneous, involuntary combination of one individual with another for sharing and acting on a basic assumption." "It is instantaneous, inevitable, and instinctive" (p. 153). Most evident in the formation of the couple that falls in love, valency operates between marriage partners and family members and determines future personality development. We return later to consider how valency helps us to understand projective identification.

## Dicks: The Introduction of Projective Identification to Marital Studies

Another British theorist, Dicks (1967) grasped the value of Fairbairn's individual psychology for understanding the marital relationship. Dicks studied sets of spouses. He conceptualized each individual personality, in Fairbairn's terms, as consisting of conscious and unconscious object relationship systems. Based on his study of parallel individual psychotherapy of spouses, each partner seeing a separate but collaborating therapist, Dicks noted in the spouses a degree of fit between these systems and their parts at both conscious and unconscious levels. He suggested that marital choice, apparently based on conscious factors, was also determined by a congruence between unconscious object relations. He called the need for this fit "unconscious complementarity." Perceptions of the spouse occur "*as if* the other was part of oneself. The partner is then treated according to how this aspect of oneself was valued: spoilt and cherished, or denigrated and persecuted" (p. 69). As the marriage progressed, this unconscious fit persisted along with a blurring of boundaries between self and other, to the point where the couple developed a "marital joint personality." "This joint personality or integrate enabled each half to rediscover lost aspects of their primary object relations, which they had split off or repressed, and which they were, in their involvement with the spouse, re-experiencing by projective identification" (p. 69).

To account for his findings, Dicks invoked Klein's (1946) concept of projective identification. The dynamic relation between parts of the personality described by Fairbairn could now be conceptualized as occurring between the systems involving parts of two personalities uniquely joined in marriage. Projective identification gave Dicks the explanatory link he needed to apply Fairbairn's object relations theory of individual endopsychic structure to marital interaction. But what exactly is projective identification?

## SOURCES OF CONFUSION ABOUT PROJECTIVE IDENTIFICATION

Although Dicks referred to projective identification frequently and gave many theoretical descriptions and clinical examples of its occurrence, he did not formally define the concept himself. Like Klein, he tended to demonstrate it in action—in his case, in application to marriage—and to assume that his readers knew about the basic concept already. Those of us with a working familiarity with the term tend to think that we have got the hang of it and talk about it together, not realizing that some of us think of projective identification as an intrapsychic or *one-body phenomenon* and others as an interpersonal or *two-body phenomenon* (Meissner 1987). On the one hand this points to the remarkable flexibility and applicability of the concept; on the other, it demonstrates a lack of conceptual clarity.

We postulate that this confusion is to some extent an inevitable consequence of the ambiguity of the process of projective identification. It has been contributed to by unacknowledged differences in meaning of the term identification in the writings of various authors, following one and ignoring the other aspect of the dual meaning introduced by Segal (1964), because of the difficulty of holding complexity and ambiguity in mind. There have been differences in view as to where in the identificatory process the identification itself is located, either in self or other, in ego or object, in internal object or in external object. On the subject of projective identification, our opinions are influenced toward the intrapsychic or interpersonal dimensions by our personal experience of the relationship between self and other in the early months of life, in other words, by our resolution of the phase Klein called the paranoid-schizoid position, in which projective identification emerges as the major defense. Finally, the lack of conceptual clarity originates with Klein's discursive writing style.

## KLEIN'S CONCEPT OF PROJECTIVE IDENTIFICATION

In her paper on schizoid mechanisms Klein (1946) introduced the concept of projective identification through an illustration of its occurrence in the paranoid-schizoid position during the first months of life. Without formally defining it, Klein mentions projective identification as the name she gives to the mechanism for dealing in fantasy with object relations when the infant is struggling with hatred due to anxiety during the earliest relation to the mother and her breast. Thus in hatred, the anxious infant seeks to rid itself of destructive parts of the self by spitting out or vomiting them out or excreting them in fantasy in its urine or explosive feces and projecting them in a hostile stream into the object residing in the mother's body. Then the infant experiences this part of itself as if it were the mother attacking the infant. The infant identifies with this persecutory maternal object, which further fuels the paranoid-schizoid position.

Klein then qualifies her discussion of projective identification by reminding us that the good parts of the self may also be projected. By identifying with the projected good parts of itself the infant personality can experience good object relations; this is important for integration of the ego. She goes on to say that projective identification occurs in love as well as hate under the influence of the life instinct as well as the death instinct. Splitting, projection, projective identification and introjection are part and parcel of projective and introjective processes characteristic of object relations in the paranoid-schizoid position normally achieved during the early months of life.

Segal (1964), who has given the clearest exposition of Klein, wrote that *projective identification* "is the result of the projection of parts of the self into an object. It may result in the object being perceived as having acquired the characteristics of the projected part of the self, but it can also result in the self becoming identified with the object of its projection" (p. 105). Thus Segal gives a dual meaning to the term. It could mean that the object was misperceived as if it was like the self and/or that the self became like the misperceived object. Segal extends this one-body view to a two-body view when she describes the effect of the projections on the other person: "the external object . . .

becomes possessed by, controlled and identified with the projected parts" (p. 14). The link between the two views is provided by the concept of introjective identification, which refers to "the result when the object is introjected into the ego which then identifies with some or all of its characteristics" (p. 105). According to Segal these processes occur only under the influence of anxiety in the paranoid-schizoid position, whereas in normal development, projections return undisturbed and are reintegrated into the self. Modern expositors of Klein, like Steiner, Williams, and Segal agreed in discussions at the present time that in projective identification the external object is affected by the projections into it. In projective identification a state of mind of the self is evoked in someone else (Williams 1981).

## OTHER CONTRIBUTIONS: MALIN AND GROTSTEIN, MEISSNER, KERNBERG, OGDEN, SANDLER

A review of the literature on projective identification (Scharff [in progress], Jaffe 1968) reveals that many authors tend to use the term projection as synonymous with projective identification, while others expend much energy arguing about the differences between them. For instance, Malin and Grotstein (1966) said that the term projection alone should be reserved for the projection of displaced instinctual drives, whereas projection of parts of the self cannot exist alone but is always accompanied by projective identification when the object receives the projected, disclaimed parts of the self "and then this new alloy—external object plus newly arrived projected part—is reintrojected to complete the cycle" (p. 26). Meissner (1980) deplores the confusion and gives the following distinguishing points:

> In *projection*, "what is projected is experienced as belonging to, coming from, or as an attribute or quality of the object."
> In *projective identification* "what is projected is simultaneously identified with and is experienced as part of the self." [p. 55]

Meissner then declares that since it involves loss of ego boundaries and taking the object as part of the self, projective identification is inherently a psychotic mechanism, thus contradicting Klein's view of projective identification as a normal developmental process that can only become pathological if the degree of anxiety due to the death instinct is too great to bear. Unlike Freud (1894), who viewed projection as an abnormal mechanism found in paranoia, Meissner sees projection as a normal mechanism, while Kernberg (1987) finds it a normal or neurotic one. Agreeing with Meissner's view of projective identification as always abnormal, Kernberg describes it as a primitive but not inevitably psychotic defensive operation, which, however, is most evident in psychosis and borderline conditions. Kernberg (1987) defines projective identification as follows:

> Clinical experience has led me to define projective identification as a primitive defense mechanism consisting of (a) projecting intolerable aspects of intrapsychic experience onto an object, (b) maintaining empathy with what is projected, (c) attempting to control the object as a continuation of the defensive efforts against the intolerable intrapsychic experience, and (d) unconsciously inducing in the object what is projected in the actual interaction with the object. [p. 94]

Meissner (1980) also addresses himself to a "certain vogue" in using the concept in family dynamics. He agrees that complex projective-introjective processes occur but not projective identification. He agrees with Zinner and Shapiro (1972) that indeed when "the subject perceives the object *as if* the object contained elements of the subject's personality," then truly the term projective identification applies. But he states that that is not often the case except in psychotic interaction. Yet Meissner gives no clinical or research evidence to disprove Zinner and Shapiro's conclusion that it does occur in nonpsychotic interaction. Zinner and Shapiro's argument is, however, based on their documented clinical research.

More recently, Ogden (1982) brought some order to the chaos, attempting a definition of projective identification as he experienced it in clinical situations. He, too, makes a distinction between projection and projective identification:

> In *projection*, ". . . the aspect of the self that is in fantasy expelled is disavowed and attributed to the recipient."
> In *projective identification*, "the projector subjectively experiences a feeling of oneness with the recipient with regard to the expelled feeling, idea, or self-representation." [p. 34]

Here Ogden elaborates upon identification as a feeling of oneness. He also specifies what is projected: not just a part of the self, it may also be a feeling or an idea. Later in his text, he concludes that he views projective identification as "a group of fantasies and accompanying object relations" (p. 36) in the intrapsychic dimension. These operate in interpersonal interaction in three phases outlined by Ogden (1982) and derived from Malin and Grotstein (1966) (see Table 3–1).

This model of projection, coercion, and reclaiming brings out the interactive sequence. From the intrapsychic perspective of the projector (the one who is doing the projecting), Ogden goes further to ask

Table 3–1.  Ogden's Phases of Projective Identification

1. Expelling part of the self into someone else, where it takes hold
2. Pressuring the other person to experience it
3. Getting it back from the other person

why the projector goes through all these stages.  What are the intrapsychic and interpersonal benefits of projective identification? He finds that there are four purposes of projective identification, summarized in Table 3–2:

Consider Ogden's (1982) opening statement on projective identification: "The concept integrates statements about unconscious fantasy, interpersonal pressure, and the response of a separate personality system to a set of engendered feelings. Projective identification is in part a statement about an interpersonal interaction (the pressure of one person on another to comply with a projective fantasy) and in part a statement about individual mental activity (projective fantasies, introjective fantasies, psychological processing). Most fundamentally, however, it is a statement about the dynamic interplay of the two, the intrapsychic and the interpersonal" (p. 3). Primarily an individual therapist, Ogden does not refer to Dicks on marital studies. Yet interestingly enough, based on his study of the patient–therapist relationship and its evocation of the primitive processes of infancy, he comes up with the foregoing concept of projective identification that is in the mold of Dicks and certainly just as applicable to understanding marital dynamics.

In later writing, Ogden (1986) has been concerned with explaining the change in the quality of the infant's experience after a projection has been metabolized by the mother and returned to the infant in a more useful or manageable form. Ogden suggests that "in the process of creating the type of emotional linkage that is involved in projective identification" there occurs an actual alteration in the infant, be-

Table 3–2.  Ogden's Four Functions of Projective Identification.

1. Defense–to distance oneself from the unwanted part, or to keep it alive in someone else
2. Communication–to make oneself understood by pressing the recipient to experience a set of feelings like one's own
3. Object-relatedness–to interact with a recipient separate enough to receive the projection yet undifferentiated enough to allow some misperception to occur and to foster the sense of oneness
4. Pathway for psychological change–to be transformed by reintrojecting the projection after its modification by the recipient, as occurs in the mother–infant relationship, marriage, or the patient–therapist relationship.

cause the "simultaneous oneness and twoness (unity and separateness of mother and infant)" involved in projective identification "creates a potential for a form of experience more generative than the sum of the individual psychological states contributing to it" (p. 36). In his view, both infant and mother, patient and therapist, projector and projectee contribute actively to the process and the infant/patient/projector is changed by it. By including the therapist's elaboration of what has been projected, Ogden explores the two-body projective identificatory system. Although we welcome his expansion, others do not; for instance, Kernberg (1987) deplores such "unwarranted" broadening of the concept (p. 93). Ogden goes beyond Klein to emphasize the interpersonal aspects of projective identification and the importance of the environment that were only implied in her work, but like Klein, he emphasizes the infant's experience. Drawing on Bion (1962), he deliberates upon the effect on the contained infant, (or the "mother–infant" as he prefers to call the infant in the mother–infant dyad), and the containing function of the mother rather than upon the formation of altered psychic structure in the mother. Thus he points us back to the intrapsychic dimension of the interpersonal process of projective identification.

There is a correspondence between the phases of the interactive sequence in the process of projective identification described by Ogden and stages of theory building identified by Sandler (1987). He noted that the concept had gone through three stages, in which it was viewed as (1) an intrapsychic process in which the real object is not affected by the fantasy; (2) an interpersonal process in which the object is affected by the fantasy (as occurs in countertransference); (3) an interpersonal process in which the object affects the fantasy when the projected parts are modified by the thought or reverie (Bion 1967) of the containing mother. (Sandler remains unconvinced of the validity of this third stage concept).

## CONTRIBUTIONS FROM FAMILY RESEARCH: ZINNER AND SHAPIRO

Zinner and Shapiro (1972) applied their understanding of the intrapsychic process of projective identification to interpersonal situations in family life. Zinner (1976), having read Dicks (1967), brought the concept to bear in marital therapy in the United States. He emphasized that projective identification is an *unconscious* process with defensive and restorative functions. His emphasis on the unconscious is helpful; other writers describe projective identification in such tangible terms that it may seem conscious and sometimes even willful. Zinner writes:

> "Projective identification is an activity of the ego that modifies perception of the object and, in a reciprocal fashion, alters the image of the self." He adds, "Again through projective identification, the individual may locate the object not inside the self, but as if it were inside the other partner in a relationship." [Zinner 1976 in J. S. Scharff 1989, p. 156]

For Zinner, projective identification is an unconscious intrapsychic process through which conflict can be contained inside the self or projected out into a relationship. He noted, as Dicks had, that this happens in marriage and that the process not only alters how the self perceives the object but actually evokes a collusive response in the object. This fits with Ogden's idea of interpersonal pressuring of the object. But Zinner, like Dicks, goes further to point out that both spouses are involved in processes of projective identification. In modern terms we might say both are simultaneously projectors and projectees. Thus, Zinner describes a marriage as "a mutually gratifying collusive system" (Zinner 1976 in J. S. Scharff 1989, p. 156). Here is projective identification as a mutual process. The goal of marital therapy in Zinner's view is to help each spouse reinternalize these projected conflicts.

Zinner also has a useful concept of projective identification as a process that is both healthy and unhealthy. Depending on the extent of the use of projective identification, the nature of a marriage relationship may fall anywhere on a continuum from normally empathic to frankly delusional:

> The location of a particular relationship along this continuum is determined by the quality and developmental level of internalized nuclear object relations, by the capacity of the spouses to experience each other as separate, differentiated individuals, and by the intensity of the need for defense. To the extent that a spouse uses projective modes less as a way of externalizing conflict and more as an instrument for approximating shared experience, the marital relationship approaches the healthy end of the continuum. [Zinner in J. S. Scharff, p. 159]

Projective identification as a concept can now be seen to have the power to offer a conceptual bridge between individual and interpersonal psychology. We have seen that marital choice is "motivated by a desire to find an object who will complement and reinforce unconscious fantasies" (Dicks 1967). Thus adult development continues to be strongly affected by projective identification. Family studies by

Zinner and Shapiro (1972) go further to show its influence on individual development. They write: "Projective identification leads to authentic and lasting structural change in the *recipient* of the projections. A prime example of this phenomenon is the effect of family interaction on the developing personality of the child" (Zinner and Shapiro 1972 in J. S. Scharff 1989, p. 110).

In contrast to what he wrote then on projective identification in family interaction, Zinner says in discussion that he now regards projective identification as entirely an intrapsychic process occurring between parts of self and internal objects inside the projector. For Zinner, it is a one-body phenomenon. Similar intrapsychic processes occur in significant others, but Zinner says that the idea of projecting into another person or vice versa is too mystical for him to accept. Although in his writing he had emphasized the interpersonal context, in his teaching now Zinner focuses on the intrapsychic dimension, on what happens in the individual. So if projective identification is entirely an intrapsychic process, how does Zinner account for the process of mutual projective identification, which he has described and to which he still subscribes? How does he explain the effect on the object? For Zinner, the missing link is interpersonal behavior. Zinner states that the wife's intrapsychic operation of projective identification, which affects her perception of the spouse, leads to changes in her behavior toward him. Her husband then responds with his own intrapsychic processes of projective identification and corresponding relevant behaviors. Zinner does not regard this statement as a shift in his view but rather as a clarification of precisely where projective identification occurs.

Integrating the contributions from family therapy research with our clinical experience as family therapists, we conclude that multiple individual processes governed by shared unconscious assumptions about family life eventually lead to the identification of parts of the family inside individuals. At the same time, the intrapsychic situation is projected onto the intrafamily group unconscious. An individual is selected as host for, or object for projection of, the unwanted or disavowed parts of the central self of the family. In health, the host role rotates among family members, but when projective identification focuses and fixes on one member, a pathological situation has arisen. An index patient now holds disavowed parts for the other family members, and stands for a family group problem in metabolizing the unwanted aspects of the family unconscious.

## CONTRIBUTIONS FROM SEX THERAPY

In projective identification in the marital dyad, the projection induces a state of mind in the external object. We have tended to think of this happening through the stirring of behavior, thought, or feeling relevant to the received projection. But in the sexual situation, as in infancy, the medium for projection tends to be the body. The projector projects not into the psyche, but into the soma of the projectee, and vice versa in mutual projective identification. Sometimes, in order to protect the other, the projector projects into his or her own body parts directly or indirectly after introjective identification with the returned projection, in either case the object of projection now being located inside the self. Any body part of self or other can become identified with the disclaimed projection, but the erotic zones are particularly likely targets. Conflicts are projected in condensed form on the body screen of the genitalia (D. Scharff 1982). Penis, vagina, and the woman's breasts become the physical locus of the repressed rejecting and exciting object systems. Repressed objects then return directly through contributing to or interfering with physical love in the married state.

## FURTHER CONTRIBUTING CONCEPTS

### Valency

In his study of small groups, Bion (1961) had noted the engagement of personalities around unconscious group themes. To account for it, he suggested the concept of valency: the instinctive capacity for instantaneous involuntary combination of one individual personality with another. Bion simply said that valency was "a spontaneous unconscious function of the gregarious quality in the personality of man" (p. 136). But this does not take us far enough into understanding how it happens. So we turn to the work of Racker.

### Concordant and Complementary Identification

Racker (1968) described countertransference as the therapist's reaction to the patient's projections organized as projective identifications occurring unconsciously in the therapist. These identifications might be of two types:

In *concordant identification*, the therapist identifies with a projected part of the patient's *self*.

In *complementary identification*, the therapist identifies with a projected part of the patient's *object*.

We have applied these ideas to the family therapist's experience of identifying with family group projections (Scharff and Scharff 1987). We can also take Racker's formulation out of its therapeutic context and apply it to the marital relationship where it helps us to fill out Bion's concept of valency and Dicks' concept of unconscious complementarity. To put it simply, a wife's self (or part thereof) may be seen as her husband's object or as a part of his self, exclusively, alternately, or simultaneously. The result is an exponential progression involving mutual projection of and identification with parts of self and object in a growing cybernetic system of unconscious object relationships in the couple and the family.

## Extractive Introjection

We also find helpful Bollas's (1987) concept of *extractive introjection*: "an intersubjective process . . . in which one person invades another person's mind and appropriates certain elements of mental life" leaving the victim "denuded of parts of the self" (p. 163). The mental theft may be of ideas, feelings, mental structure such as superego, and parts of the self. For instance; when a wife fails an exam for reasons that seem unfair and finds her husband more upset than she is, she is robbed of her right to outrage. In extreme cases, extraction may be "followed by vaporization of the psychic structure" (p. 164). In other cases, Bollas continues, "as a person takes from another person's psyche, he leaves a gap, or a vacuum, in its place. There he deposits despair or emptiness in exchange for what he has stolen." Thus, "each extractive introjection is accompanied by some corresponding projective identification" (p. 164).

Now we can say that projective identification occurs along with introjective identification and in more violent examples it is associated with extractive introjection. These interlocking processes are the basis for valency. We find that spouses connect through valencies for concordant or complementary identification that determine the "unconscious complementariness" of fit described by Dicks (1967, p. 69). A match in valencies leads to the instantaneous combination of two personalities falling in love. The balance of the projective and introjective processes is determined by the nature of the object relations of each personality and the degree of fit between the parts of self and internal objects of the spouse and the partner. In sickness and in health, valency is determined by inner object relationships seeking expression, repetition or healing in current life relationships (Scharff and Scharff 1987).

## FURTHER DISCUSSION AND DEVELOPMENT

Now we will present our own view of projection and projective identification based on this literature, on our experience as analysts, as couple and family therapists, and on previous elaboration of the concept (J. Scharff [in progress]).

In projection a part of the self—either a part of the ego or of its internal objects, or a feeling or an idea originally connected to the self or objects now split off from them—is expelled from the intrapsychic domain and displaced to an external object during an unconscious mental process. The person doing the projecting (the projector) has no awareness of the projection onto the other person (the projectee), and so has a feeling of separateness from the external object that possesses the expelled part of the self. The object is believed to be invested with qualities that it does not have. The only identification occurring is that of recognizing a quality in that object. The projection does not necessarily fit. This process may be a delusion as in paranoia, a misperception as in neurosis, or a normal momentary expulsion followed by reintrojection.

In projective identification, a number of steps follow. The first step is always a projection. Whether it remains a projection or becomes a projective identification depends on whether the second step of affecting the object occurs. If the only object affected is the internal object, then the process remains an intrapsychic one. When the external object of the projection contributes to the process, either passively or actively, then projective identification has entered the interpersonal dimension. Then the object may simultaneously project parts of itself into the subject in a process of mutual projective identification. If all the steps are completed, the process of projective identification goes beyond its description as a one-body or two-body phenomenon to a multipart-and-object phenomenon, a description that does justice to the recruitment into the process of any number of parts of self and objects of one, two or more personalities in unconscious communication during interaction in family life.

## THE STEPS OF PROJECTIVE IDENTIFICATION

The following steps characterize projective identification in marriage (J. Scharff [in progress]):

1. *Projection.* The projector spouse expels a part of the self and identifies the external object in the projectee spouse as if it were imbued with qualities that do not pertain to it in fact but that pertain to the self. (This is the original projection. Identification occurs only in the sense of naming or recognizing a quality.)

2. *Object induction.* The projector spouse so convincingly identifies the part of the self in the external object that the feeling state corresponding to that part of the self is evoked in the projectee spouse.

3. *Introjective identification by the object.* At this point the projectee spouse has identified with the projection of the projector spouse through the process of introjective identification at the unconscious level.

4. *Transformation by the object.* Since the projectee spouse has his or her own personality, the projected part of the projector spouse's self with which the projectee identifies is not the same as that part was when still inside the intrapsychic arena of the projector. The part has been transformed by its temporary lodging in the psyche of the spouse, its goodness or badness being confirmed, exaggerated, or diminished.

5. *Valency of the object to receive a projection.* When the projectee spouse has a valency for a certain projection, then the projectee will tend to accept that projection and identify with that part of the other spouse's self. This valent part is not passively inducted but actively seeks parts of another to identify with to the point of stealing part of another person's mind through a process called "extractive introjection" (Bollas 1987, p. 5).

6. *Complementary and concordant identification by the object.* The part of the self projected may, however, be a part of the ego (part of the self representation) or a part of the object. Thus the projectee spouse may be induced to embody the ego in relation to the object that is located in the projector spouse or to embody the object in relation

to the projector's ego. This is determined not only by which part of the self is actually projected but also by the projectee's valency to respond in identification with the projector's projected part of self or to respond as the nonprojected part of the self that is in relation to the projected part. In other words, the introjective identification of the projectee spouse may be, in Racker's (1968) terms, concordant or complementary to projector spouse's self or object.

7. *Introjective identification by the self.* The self identifies with or assimilates itself to the reinternalized confirmed or modified part of the self. Then psychic structure is "cemented" or slightly altered. Cementing can be a healthy process if accurately received projections are accurately returned by the external object but it can be unhealthy by not permitting change. Alteration in the range, flexibility, or acceptability of responses can promote growth if the modification is slight and is based on the projectee spouse's unconscious capacity to appreciate the otherness of the marital partner and to harbor and return the projected part of the projector spouse without fundamental distortion.

8. *Mutual projective identification.* The projector that projects into the projectee is at the same time receiving projections from the projectee. Projector/projectee marital pairs unconsciously match up based on valencies for identifying with each other's projections. Thus, projective identification is a mutual process: husband and wife connect according to unconscious complementarity of object relations. Similarly, couple and therapist relate through the transference and countertransference.

## CONCLUSION

We hope to have minimized confusion and miscommunication on this topic without robbing the concept of its versatility or creating further complications. Underlying the confusion is the elusiveness of the process of projective identification. We have to remember that this is an unconscious process, a form of primitive, primary communication originating in the early months of life before we had words or thinking as we now know it. Thus the problem is to find words for experience that lives on not as ideas or memories but as psychic structure. That very structure is what we bring to bear on the cognitive task of understanding projective identification, the process through which the structure formed is continually being modified.

We propose that projective identification be agreed upon as an umbrella term subsuming processes of varying degrees of completeness along a continuum involving the intrapsychic and interpersonal dimensions. This gives us a theoretical basis for describing unconscious conflict occurring in individual spouses and portrayed in the interaction of their marriage.

Chapter 4

# MODELS OF THERAPY

In this chapter we will attempt to give a theoretical model of couple therapy based on the types of transference and countertransference specific to marital work. These types differ from the transference-countertransference dimension in individual psychotherapy and in family therapy. The respective differences generate a continuum on which these various treatment models can be located.

## THE ORIGINS OF FAMILY AND MARITAL TRANSFERENCE

In the therapeutic process are two kinds of transference relationships. Although these two kinds of transference relating go on at the same time, they can be differentiated according to their origin in two distinct aspects of the mother–infant relationship. We call these two aspects the contextual and focused relationships respectively. These two aspects give rise to a contextual and a focused transference respectively (Scharff and Scharff 1987).

## THE ORIGIN OF THE CONTEXTUAL TRANSFERENCE

The first aspect of mother–infant relating is seen when the mother holds the infant in her arms and secures the environment for herself and her baby. Here she provides for the baby's needs and creates a safe environment with her husband's support. She makes sure her child is clean and positioned comfortably, is fed and content, and gives appropriate attention to sleep, play, and the necessary functions of living. In providing all these things, she is offering what we epigrammatically call "the arms-around" relationship; she is providing the *context* for their relationship. Then the baby's interest in the relationship and responsiveness to the mother gives her a feeling of being held, in turn. But the majority of the responsibility for providing this holding goes to the mother. We have called this her capacity for *contextual holding*.

## THE ORIGIN OF THE FOCUSED TRANSFERENCE

The second aspect of the early relationship is seen when mother and infant look into each other's eyes, converse with vocal and gaze exchanges, and respond to each other with the subtle changes in body position that convey their mutual responsiveness. This is the *focused* relationship that centers on and penetrates to the core of both infant and mother, affirming identity and building psychic structure. The focused relationship depends on the physical and psychological tone of the relationship and on the interpenetration of personal qualities. Stressing the subjective quality of the relationship for both mother and infant, we refer to this graphically as the "eye-to-eye" and the "I-to-I" relationship. The focused relationship is fostered by an intimate kind of holding, which we call *centered holding*, through which the mother is psychologically able to reach into the infant's inner world, see it, and grasp its meaning. In the *holding, arms-around* situation, the infant finds *itself* while held in the mother's arms. In the focused *I-to-I* situation, it finds the *other*.

## CONTEXTUAL AND FOCUSED TRANSFERENCE IN INDIVIDUAL THERAPY

An individual patient's transference to the therapist stems from each of these two aspects of relating. First, the patient has expectations based on prior experience of other people's capacities to provide arms-around holding in relationships. The previous experiences began with the parents and were then extended to the widening world of primary objects in the family and in loving relationships, to social settings as with teachers of the young child, to adolescent peers, and later to partners in sexual and marital relationships. These expectations and fears of failure in holding contribute to *the contextual transference* when the patient comes for therapy.

The patient also brings expectations and fantasies based on the experience of centered relating, which are recorded as the discrete structures of the patient's internal world. Here the presence of exciting and rejecting objects and part objects, and of the parts of the self in relationship to them and all the feelings evoked therein, provides the stuff of a more discrete transference, which we call the *focused transference*. It consists of the projection of these internal object relations into the therapist through projective identification, as we have discussed earlier.

In individual psychotherapy the contextual transference is prominent in the early phases of work. It must be attended to in order to facilitate the later development of work on the focused transference. Not understanding this difference in early and later transference has led to an inexact understanding of the role of transference in individual psychotherapy and in the ways it differs from psychoanalysis on the one hand, and from marital and family therapy on the other. Most important, this confusion has narrowed the application of transference in marital and family psychotherapy, at times to the extreme where it is held that transference is not relevant to conjoint therapy at all.

In psychoanalytic work, where transference is the central focus, transference refers to the patient's feelings about and way of dealing with the analyst as a representative of the patient's internal objects. This happens in a most organized and forceful way during the transference neurosis in which patients, although fully able to test reality, nevertheless treat their analysts as though taken over by their internal objects. A fully organized transference neurosis does not crystallize for at least a year or two of four- or five-times-a-week psychoanalysis, even if the work is going well.

## The Contextual Transference and the Alliance

Aspects of relatedness are found earlier than the transference neurosis. Greenson (1965) described the working alliance and Zetzel (1958) the therapeutic alliance. These were held to be nontransference aspects of the relationship, parts of the "real relationship," which were not subject to the usual considerations of transference. Zetzel in particular suggested that the elements that supported the patient's capacity for a therapeutic relationship originated in the early, preverbal aspects of interaction with the mother. Other writers became interested in aspects of the transference that surfaced early, sometimes as early as the beginning of analysis. Gill and Muslin (1976) describe aspects of negative transference that surface at the beginning and must be interpreted quickly to secure a working relationship between patient and analyst.

In our view, the capacity for a therapeutic or working alliance is based on contextual transference, and this is based on the experience of contextual holding by previous primary figures, just as the focused transference is based on centered holding. Specifically, contextual transference derives from the infantile experience of what Winnicott (1963) called the "environment mother," who provides the arms-around holding, and focused transference derives from the aspect of mothering that Winnicott called the "object mother." Like Winnicott, we do not confine our reference to the actual mother, but to an amalgam of caretakers that includes both mother and father and a few other primary care figures. Siblings and important regular substitute caregivers certainly contribute to the experience of early holding.

Early in any therapy, including individual psychotherapy, psychoanalysis, and the conjoint therapies, the emerging transference is to the therapy as a contextual holding environment. That early transference draws not on the discrete object and self images we may see later, but on more global internalizations of the experience of being held or not being held.

## Early Focused Transference Phenomena

These early transference problems are different from those that emerge after the psychoanalysis or individual psychotherapy has been well established and gone on for a year or more. Then we begin to see the transferences that are based in discrete self and object structures played out through the projective identifications of the transference. When there is an early demonstration of such focused transference phenomena, in individual therapy or analysis, the therapist is treated as a distorted, misperceived figure in a premature way. This occurred in a number of Freud's early cases, most notably that of Dora, the case in which Freud (1905a) first described transference as more than a hindrance. We commonly find such early distortions in patients with hysterical or borderline pathology.

The substitution of a premature focused transference for a contextual one is shown in early eroticized transferences in which the patient attempts to identify the therapist as a sexual object to make up for the feared deficit in the holding relationship. For instance, after a few months one analytic patient began an hour by saying, "Aren't you going to be interested in having sex with me? Everyone else has been, and I can't believe you'll turn me down!" In this case, the comment did not constitute much of a seduction. It actually heralded a dawning recognition by the patient that her early sexualized appeal to people, which was designed to make up for a deficit in emotional holding by getting them to hold her physically, was not going to work this time. It served notice that the early sexualization of the contextual transference was already failing. In this situation, the patient was tentatively moving into a situation of slightly broadened trust, of being able to stay in a holding relationship that did not become sexualized. The comment was understood by the analyst as a small sign of growing confidence in the contextual transference.

## CONTEXTUAL AND FOCUSED TRANSFERENCE IN COUPLE AND FAMILY THERAPY

Both contextual and focused transference involve the patient's early experience with the parents, who supplied the holding environment. Both types of transference are there virtually from the beginning and have preverbal origins in the prehistory of areas of psychological structure to be elaborated upon during subsequent verbal epochs. Both occur in couple and family therapy as well as in individual psychoanalytic psychotherapy. Nevertheless, the two aspects of relating are experienced quite differently in our experience in various therapeutic modalities.

Individual spouses or family members bring their focused transferences—that is, their projective identifications—to the conjoint settings. These transferences have already been operating in their relations to each other. But the couple or family also bring a shared transference to the therapist. This shared transference is built around their shared hopes and fears about the therapist's capacity to provide therapeutic holding by shoring up their deficient ability to provide holding for themselves. This shared transference stems from the couple's or family's sense of having a deficit in their own capacity to provide holding for themselves—something we can assume since they have come to see us for help.

The transference that represents a couple's pooled difficulty with the holding situation constitutes *the couple's shared contextual transference.* This deficit in the couple's or family group's ability to provide holding for its members interests us most, because if the family can be helped to do a better job of holding, it will then, almost by definition, be able to provide for its individuals' needs for development and for centered relating. Therefore, in object relations couple and family therapy, therapists can most easily and usefully organize their understanding of a family around the information gained from the family's shared contextual transference. This level of understanding involves at least a rudimentary understanding of the sharing of unconscious processes in small groups. This is a more complex business in the larger groups of the family than it is for the couple.

## COUNTERTRANSFERENCE IN INDIVIDUAL, COUPLE, AND FAMILY THERAPY

Countertransference in family and couple therapy, as in individual therapy, refers to the affective experience of the therapist in joining with the family or couple. Their individual and pooled transferences get inside the therapist and reverberate, creating both fruitful and problematic responses in the therapist. The resonance may be simply with previously unexplored areas of the therapist's life, or more problematically with areas of discomfort or even pathology.

Countertransference, in our view, refers to the totality of the affective responses that occur whenever the couple or family creates an impact that penetrates beyond the therapist's conscious and relatively reasonable capacity to understand, beyond the central self. When this happens, the family or couple's object relations system reaches an area of the therapist's unconscious. There it resonates with the therapist's own repressed internal object relations. Training and personal therapy prepare the therapist's psyche as a fertile ground in which these internal experiences can take hold, in which the growth of meaning amidst uncertainties can be cultivated, and out of which is garnered a harvest of intimate understanding of the family from the ripened countertransference. In this way, therapists allow themselves to be the substrate for newly emerging understanding, which they then feed back to the couple or family in interpretations.

Two forms of countertransference correspond to the two forms of transference. The *contextual countertransference* is stirred by the couple's or family's expectations and projections concerning the therapist's capacity to provide contextual holding, and has to be calibrated against the therapist's internal issues about being a provider of holding, a parent to the growth of the couple or family. The focused transferences of individual family members stir various versions of *focused countertransference* in therapists, depending on the therapist's object relations set.

If focused transference and countertransference become dominant during the conduct of family therapy, we regard this as a skewing of the experience occurring when the family is attempting to substitute individual experience for their shared experience—using one member as a spokesperson for the group's shared contextual transference because the group cannot believe the therapist can hold the whole group in mind. This is analogous to the premature substitution of the focused transference by hysterical or borderline individual patients whom we described before.

For instance, if we find ourselves bullied by an angry adolescent boy in family therapy, it is likely that we have just experienced what the family group feels when bullied by him. The family is speaking through the behavior of this adolescent and through the ways they handle it. The family's attitude to the behavior shapes its meaning as an expression of the family's contextual transference. Imagine that the parents, without indicating their support or disagreement, leave the therapist to deal with the anger. That leaves the impression that the angry boy may be speaking for their anger about being there, too. It then seems that all three of them have a resentful and mistrustful shared contextual transference, the full wrath of which is turned on the therapist at the nodal point of the young male.

Now imagine another version: that the parents express frustration about the son's rebellion against therapy and regret that they could not help him. The family group attitude is one of dismay that caring holding is not enough and so the therapist does not feel isolated by a completely mistrusting group. Instead, a therapist will be likely to feel there are allies for the task. Here the countertransference is likely to be more easily empathic for the parents who feel frustrated and for the boy who is angry with them.

In summary, our countertransference to the focused transference of the single spokesperson is supported, modified, or even contradicted by our countertransference to the contextual transference message from the whole group.

## TRANSFERENCE, COUNTERTRANSFERENCE, AND THE TASKS OF THERAPY

The tasks of therapy in each of the situations of individual, family, and couple therapy differ based on the transference-countertransference dimension relevant to the treatment modality.

### In Individual Therapy

In work with an individual patient, therapist and patient share the task of examining the patient's inner world and its effect on current relationships as described by the patient or revealed in the relationship to the therapist. To do this work, they rely, in the beginning, on the patient's experience of the holding environment of the therapy. The therapist has the major responsibility for its provision, but the patient contributes as well, just as the baby also contributes to the overall holding for which the mother has major responsibility. The patient's contextual transference to the therapeutic environment and the therapist's corresponding countertransference tend to dominate this phase of individual therapy. It is only later, in intensive, long-standing psychotherapy or psychoanalysis that the transference becomes the focused transference where discrete inner objects and parts of the self are put into the therapist, metabolized there through containment and interpretation and then reintegrated in modified form (see Fig. 4–1). This formulation of the therapist's task as one of modifying the patient's projective identifications that are received by the therapist is consistent with Bion's (1962) concept of the mother as a container receiving the raw projections to be contained, withstood and transformed through her reverie, and then fed back in detoxified form. It also recalls Loewald's (1960) emphasis on the mother's responsibility for holding in mind the potential maturation of her child and by her vision, contributing to the maturational thrust of development.

### In Family Therapy

The situation in family therapy is summarized in Figure 4–2. The individual family members each have individual centered relationships to each other, characterized by discrete mutual projective identifications. This occurs in the area of the *centered holding*, the kind that exists when people who are each other's primary objects reach deeply

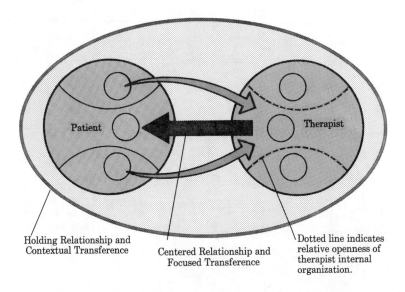

Holding Relationship and
Contextual Transference

Centered Relationship and
Focused Transference

Dotted line indicates
relative openness of
therapist internal
organization.

**Figure 4–1. Individual Therapy. Within the envelope of the holding rela-
tionship, patient and therapist examine the patient's inner object relations
and their effect on relationships. In the focused transference, these are projected into the therapist, where they are modified in interaction with the
therapist's less rigid splitting and repression of internal object relations,
and then fed back to the patient in modified form. The relationship itself is
the agent of change.**

into each other over time and hold each other at the center.

All of this is sustained, however, by the pooled *contextual holding*
contributed to by each individual but constituting something greater
than the sum of the holding relationships in the family. The myriad
dyadic projective identifications deriving from individual areas of
centered holding cannot all be followed thoroughly in family sessions. Instead, we focus on their interlocking in the area of contextual
holding, on the resultant of those forces, which forms an object relations set of the family as a whole, evidenced in how they relate to us.
This set gives rise to shared conscious and unconscious family assumptions (Shapiro 1979) which we can detect in the repeating patterns of family–therapist interaction. Once the shared family assumptions are understood, it may become possible to understand the part
played by each individual component relationship, but that is not the
primary task in family therapy.

In family therapy we do not dissect the contextual transference to

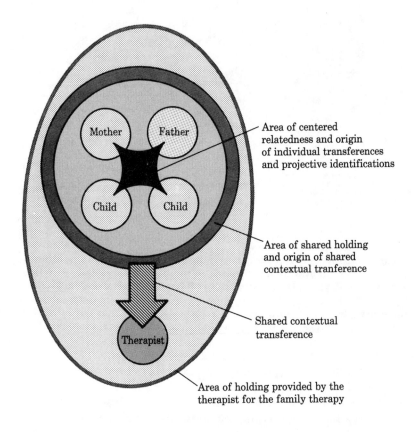

Figure 4–2. Family Therapy. In family therapy the therapist is outside the family circle. The members of the family have centered holding relation-ships to each other. Around this area is the envelope of their contextual holding to which each member contributes a share. It is from this area that the shared contextual transference comes. In providing a space for therapy, the therapist offers an area of psychological holding to the family. They react to the therapist's provision of this space with their shared contextual transference.

discover individual contributions. We conceptualize the contextual transference shown in the family's attitude toward the therapist as an expression of the family's deficits in holding that bring them to the therapist. Therapists' countertransferences represent their reception of the contextual transference that gets inside them to resonate with their own internal structures formed during experience with their own families of origin. We all have many overlapping models of families inside: good and bad families, aggressive and loving, strong and weak, ideal and denigrated that comprise our internal family. These alternate models co-exist within us and a specific one is activated when we engage with a family. Countertransference as a specific response to each unique family group is the most reliable guide to the therapy of unconscious family interaction.

## In Couple Therapy

The situation in couple therapy is an intermediate one. Working with only two people, the therapist can, to a large extent, keep track of the development of individual and discrete transferences. Nevertheless, a focus on the couple as a two-person group is essential and represents a level of organization that is qualitatively different from the view of them as two individuals.

Elements of the couple therapy situations are shown in Figure 4–3. This is conceptually more complex than that of either individual or family therapy, largely because of its employment of both contextual and focused transference equally, often in rapid oscillation.

The couple is a group of two, the smallest of groups. Breaching the dyad is not an easy task, for the two-person group is designed to have a tight holding pattern that supports intimate relationships. We might say this is because the area of shared environmental holding, analogous to that supplied to the baby by the mother, is here supplied by both husband and wife to each other as objects of devotion. In addition their commitment is reinforced by the powerful pleasure of the sexual bond. Because of that, the area of centered relating is much closer to the shared holding of the environment. The couple's environmental holding is easily susceptible to invasion from their mutual projective identifications.

Transference to the therapist originates from these two areas of centered relating and contextual holding. While this also applies in family therapy, it happens in a more fluid and rapid way in couples, and the work of couple therapy is often to understand the ways in which projective identifications assault or erode the sense of safe

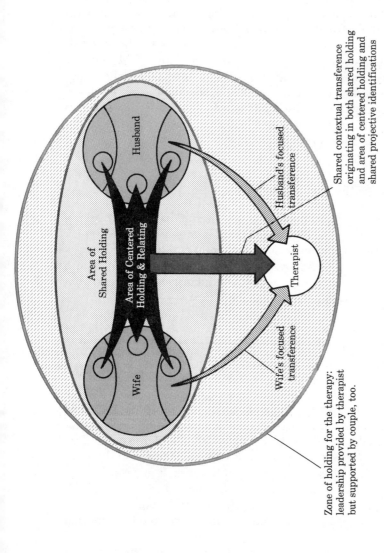

Figure 4–3. Couple Therapy. The couple has an intensified system as a group of two, with focused projective identifications or transferences in the area of centered holding. There is also an area of shared contextual holding to which they both contribute. The main and guiding source of transference in couple therapy derives from the area of contextual holding. In addition, there is shared transference that stems from the shared projective identifications of internal objects in the area of centered holding. Each spouse can, and often does, also develop individual focused transference to the therapist.

Labels within figure:

Area of Shared Holding

Area of Centered Holding & Relating

Husband

Wife

Husband's focused transference

Wife's focused transference

Therapist

Shared contextual transference originating in both shared holding and area of centered holding and shared projective identifications

Zone of holding for the therapy: leadership provided by therapist but supported by couple, too.

holding that the couple expects from the therapist and that marital partners want and need from each other.

Finally, each of the partners may develop individual transferences to the therapist. It is not infrequent to hear that one partner has developed erotic feelings for the therapist, or that another has become infuriated for transferential reasons. These manifestations can best be understood as the substitution of an individual transference for the transference from the shared areas of holding, skewed unconsciously to protect the integrity of the couple for complex reasons. Late in marital therapy, it may be possible to work directly with focused transference within an atmosphere of overall acceptance by the couple. This requires a good holding situation colored by a positive shared contextual transference.

Countertransference in couple therapy is best understood as a response to the couple as a pair, just as countertransference in family therapy is best understood as a reaction to the family as a group. Because there are only two other individuals in the room, therapists will more frequently find themselves cuing off one or the other partner. But this is a defense against the discomfort of being excluded from the couple system. The fundamental resonance between the couple and the therapist's internal world should not be to discrete inner objects, but to therapists' *internal couples*. Figure 4–4 summarizes the situation between the couple and the inner object relations of the therapist.

Experience with the couple resonates with the therapist's life experience of couples, especially those couples who have been or are primary in earlier and current life, including parents, prior relationships with partners in adolescence and adulthood, former marriages, previous therapeutic relationships, and current relationships with spouses or loved persons.

We each have many versions of couples inside us, just as we have many versions of families inside. These versions express angry couples, loving couples, and idealized and feared couples. At different points in the transference, different aspects of the internal couple constellation and the corresponding affects will be sensed by therapists in the countertransference. The most immediate clue to the kind of relationship being stirred up inside is the set of emotions that come into play. This clue leads to the couple's contextual transference to the therapist and its resonance with their shared projective identifications or transferences to each other.

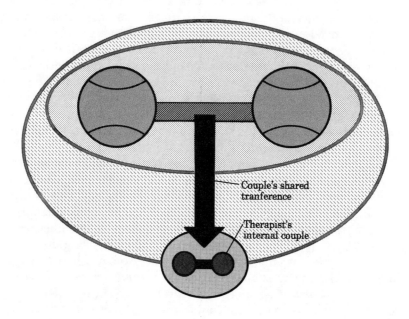

Figure 4–4. Countertransference in Couple Theory. Countertransference is experienced in response to each spouse individually resonating with individual internal objects of the therapist and most especially in response to the couple resonating with a specific constellation of the therapist's internal couple.

THE REJECTING COUPLE COUNTERTRANSFERENCE

A frequent occurrence in couple therapy is the situation in which the couple intensifies their shared holding like a brick wall that excludes the therapist. This is their attempt to maintain their relationship as a closed system, something analogous to what happens when an individual patient tries to maintain the inner world as a closed system and to press the therapist into supporting that desperate defense (Fairbairn 1958). In such situations, the therapist feels the frustration of not getting on with the work of therapy. The therapist who feels fundamentally excluded like a child from the bedroom experiences the couple as an exciting and rejecting object at each psychosexual level. This tends to increase longing and frustration on the part of the therapist, while leaving anger and loneliness in its wake. This situation is expressed in Figure 4–5.

Sometimes the exclusion is achieved not by an open negativity, but by emotionless and opaque presentation. For instance, a couple spoke of the way their relationship was formed around a shared feeling that other people were shallow and worthless. They spent their time enjoying the shared attitude that other people were not worth bothering with. The therapist felt excluded from the emotional life of this couple, though they were not overtly rejecting of her. She found them exceedingly boring and opaque, leaving her feeling deadened. They keep the relationship going this way because a livelier way of relating is too threatening in its evocation of desire. The therapist feels the repressed drive for vitality and relatedness and suffers from its rejection.

Other spouses actively seek our help but are unconsciously worried that we will come between them. While this often expresses the fear that the bond between them is fragile, the unconscious pact to exclude others has been practiced and cemented. Sooner or later, their shared but repressed longing has to emerge in order for work to proceed.

## THE EXCITING COUPLE COUNTERTRANSFERENCE

Another situation, shown in Figure 4–6, forms the complementary opposite of the shared rejecting contextual transference but is less frequently recognized or discussed.

In the exciting couple transference intense desire is experienced in the countertransference. It may be felt in an eroticized form, but there is a more subtle form that is perhaps more important. Here the therapist may be filled with a rather intense liking for a couple, each of whom feels strangely excluded from the other but is attractive to others. One therapist, in such a situation, found himself caught up in urging the marital partners on to an intensified relationship despite their intense fears of it. After some time, the therapist realized that in the contextual countertransference he had absorbed the projection of heightened longing that was making him a frighteningly excited figure for the couple. When he could interpret the couple's shared but denied fear of exciting objects, they began to work on the way they got others to represent the longing they feared to bring into their relationship.

What we wish to clarify here is that the focus of work in couple

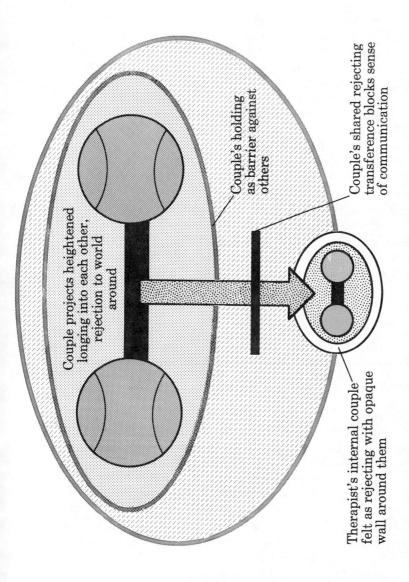

Couple projects heightened
longing into each other,
rejection to world
around

Couple's holding
as barrier against
others

Couple's shared rejecting
transference blocks sense
of communication

Therapist's internal couple
felt as rejecting with opaque
wall around them

Figure 4–5. The Rejecting Couple Countertransference. A couple may bond tightly together with heightened exciting objects projected into each other in order to jointly repress the rejecting object constellation. The rejecting object is jointly put outside the relationship. The couple then turns its shared holding into a massive wall against the outside world. Therapists feel excluded by such couples. Their own internal couples then feel rejected, heightening therapists' longing for a responsive object.

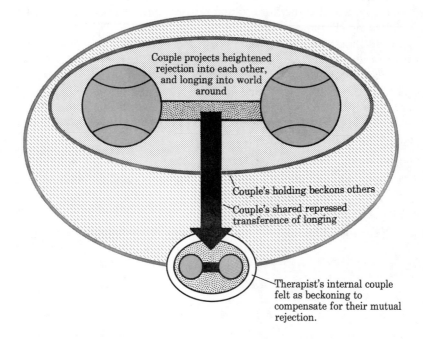

Figure 4–6. The Exciting Couple Countertransference. This is the situation of the heightened exciting contextual transference, felt by the therapist as a craving for a beckoning object. It comes from the couple's keeping of the rejecting objects repressed by the projection of longing outside their relationship in their shared transference.

therapy is not primarily on the focused internal object constellation of each member of the couple. It is on their shared holding capacity and its deficits. These deficits come both from the shared contextual holding and the centered holding the couple provides each other. It follows that the countertransference is organized by the therapist's relationship to his or her own internal couple in its various forms.

Work with the countertransference often begins with an experience of heightened affect, usually with some discomfort, and proceeds sometimes through a fantasy or thought, and sometimes without conscious organization to a dawning awareness of an internal relationship. However, in practice, much, and perhaps most, of the work goes on without such specific awareness. It happens with an affective nudge first in one direction, then in another, bringing the therapist into the couple's discomfort so that together they can work their way

out of it. Many examples of the use of countertransference to eluci-
date focused and contextual transference in couple therapy are given
in following chapters.

These models of the transference and countertransference situation in individual, family, and couple therapy are intended to help
therapists locate the task in each of the settings. The three kinds of
work are compatible with one another. More than one of them, and
occasionally all three, can be carried on concurrently. But when that is
done, it is important to know the focus of the task in each modality of
treatment.

Part II

# Evaluation and Therapy of Marital Problems

# Chapter 5
# THE ASSESSMENT PROCESS

In this chapter we define and illustrate the method of object relations couple therapy applied to assessment. Basically, technique remains the same as in therapy, with particular attention to setting the frame for treatment, and without any attempt at working through. Although our intention is to arrive at understanding, our main goal is to facilitate entry into therapy when it is needed. In other words, we do not worry about finding out everything or making magical interpretations. We just want to secure the therapeutic space and give the couple a fair sample on which to base a decision about therapy.

**Setting the frame.** We set a frame within which to establish a reliable space for work. Any reactions to the frame are explored in terms of contextual transference, both to secure the frame against unconscious forces tending to distort it, and to discover the nature of the flaws in the couple's holding capacity. The frame may be established at the beginning or may emerge according to need as the consultation proceeds. Usually about five sessions are needed before we are ready with a formulation and recommendation. This allows for one or two couple sessions, one or more individual sessions for each spouse as indicated, and a couple session where formulations and recommendations about treatment are given.

To maintain professional boundaries we address patients by their surnames and each of us introduces ourself as Dr. Scharff. In the intimate setting of intensive couple therapy sessions where spouses refer to each other by their forenames we do the same, reverting to formal forms of address outside sessions, for instance, during phone calls to change times. In writing this book, we have chosen to present using forenames or surnames for variety.

**Creating psychological space.** We create a psychological space, which the couple enters. We do this by our expectation of dealing with the couple relationship, not the individuals that comprise it, and by the way we listen, allow feelings to be expressed, experience those feelings in relation to ourselves, and interpret our experience. The couple identifies with our containing function and so develops the capacity to create space for understanding.

**Listening to the unconscious.** We listen in a relaxed way that is both attentive and yet not closely focused. We listen not to the individuals alone but to the communication from the couple as a system in relation to us. We listen not only to the conscious communication but also the unconscious communication. We do this by following the themes emerging from the verbal associations, by noting the meaning of silences, by integrating our observation of nonverbal language with words and silence, and by working with fantasy and dream material. We also attend to the unconscious communication expressed in the physical aspects of sexual functioning.

**Following the affect.** We are interested in affective moments because these provide access to the unconscious areas from which the feeling has emerged. These moments bring us a living history of the relationships in the families of origin. We find this more immediate and useful than a formally obtained social history or a genogram.

**Negative capability.** We apply negative capability, a refinement and extension of listening. The name is borrowed from Keats, who used the term to describe the poetic quality of Shakespeare. He defined negative capability as the capacity to be in "uncertainty and doubt without any irritable reaching after fact and reason" (Murray 1955). We try to be free of the need to get information and to make sense of things. As we listen, we let our senses be impinged on, we hold the experience inside, and then we allow meaning to emerge from within.

**Transference and countertransference.** Creating the space, listening, negative capability, and following the affect come together at a nodal point in the countertransference where we receive the transference from the couple and the individual parties. At times the countertransference remains unconscious in a way that is in tune with the transference and supportive to the work. At other times it obtrudes as a feeling of discomfort, a fantasy or a dream and then we can take hold of it and get to work. Through tolerating and then analyzing our countertransference we can experience inside ourselves the couple's transference based on unconscious object relations.

**Interpretation of defense.** Speaking from our own experience, we interpret the couple's pattern of defenses. We may already have recognized a recurring pattern of interactions that serve a defensive purpose and the couple may recognize it, too. But in our experience, our intervention is most effective when it is based in a countertransference experience. Only when we can point out the pattern and the way in which we have been involved in it can we work out what they and we have been defending ourselves against.

**Confronting basic anxiety.** Lastly, we work with the basic anxieties that have seemed too intolerable to bear in consciousness. When they are named, faced, and adapted to, the couple can proceed to the next developmental phase of the couple's life cycle. During assessment, we are content to identify some aspect of the basic anxiety revealed in the defensive patterns that we have pointed out, without any attempt at thorough exploration.

The following example illustrates the process of an assessment of a couple with difficulties in developing a sexual relationship, a mature marriage, and a shared ambition about life-style. The early use of fantasy in the countertransference is illustrated. Listening reveals the unconscious significance of the house in which the partners live. We resolve the dilemma of a shameful secret and we use this and other fantasies and dreams to gain access to the unconscious. The example was chosen mainly because it illustrates the way that the sexual and marital aspects of the relationship interdigitate and require an integrated approach in assessment and therapy.

Thelma and Yves Hamilton had been married for six years after living together for eight years in London. They came to see me [J.S.S.] for help with their sexual difficulties. Thelma, a tall, athletic woman wearing loosely fitted long dark clothes that were in odd contrast to her pale blonde hair had grown up in a Jewish section of London. She sat next to Yves on the couch. He was slightly shorter than she, with dark hair and beard, his deep tan set off to advantage by his short-sleeved shirt and shorts. I had a passing fantasy of him dressed as a woman in a show and could not reconcile that with his actual appearance. Nevertheless, I did not dismiss the fantasy, and regarded it as information of unclear significance as yet.

When I asked "What is the problem?" they replied in unison, "We don't have sex." They had not slept together for five years and had not discussed this until recently.

"We're like two great roommates," said Yves. "Or a brother and sister playing at being married," he added.

"Right!" said Thelma. "For us, living together is like playing house— but in our tiny flat. Yet I'm afraid to demand more. I love Yves, I depend on him. There are things I wouldn't want to lose. I've had more caring from him than I've ever had in my whole life. A more grown-up relationship would mean changes."

"But we don't need a house for the two of us. It's not something I want," said Yves, adding for my benefit, "She wants light and a garden."

*I was interested in this discussion of their living space. At the conscious level, they were dealing with a difference in aspirations. At the unconscious level, there were many meanings that I could only guess at. I waited for further elaboration.*

Thelma continued, "We do have a garden, but I had to carve it out of a jungle. I want a house I would feel good in, light and tidy. I hate any disorderliness and our flat is so small it's chaotic. The kitchen is my favorite room and I don't even want to be there."

"Thelma," Yves remonstrated quite kindly, "having a house wouldn't make things better. It would just be more space to take care of. I don't mind your mess. I only mind your freaking out about it."

*Now I got the idea that Thelma wanted a house to get away from herself and her pathology. The house represented for her a more mature ego. She longed for this, despite her fears, but Yves retreated from it because of his fears. Just as I was about to ask about the link between the house and their personal issues, Yves made the connection spontaneously.*

"I see our relationship as a function of our personalities. Both of us have a terrible lack of self-confidence and self-respect that reflects itself in our careers, sex lives, and everything else. At least Thelma is doing the public-interest law she loves, though getting paid is always dicey. I tried studying religion but I got bored with that and did some building and then started selling houses. I hate my job. Commercial real estate is dog-eat-dog, so I stick with domestic sales and rentals, where I just loaf along. I don't wanna own a house that puts you out in the world where you gotta do things."

*It seemed to me that the house had a phallic significance for Yves, an idea that his next association tended to confirm. He went on to talk of feeling better after a good day at work yesterday.*

"So I was feeling happier with myself. I got home and there was Thelma working out on her cross country ski machine in her bikini."

Thelma interrupted to explain, "I get hot and so I change into a bikini—actually I always do my exercises that way."

Yves continued, "And I got turned on! Previously I couldn't let myself," Yves concluded.

*Now the house seemed to be a space in which to have a grown-up relationship: Sexuality could be claimed and could flower in the light-filled space. I wondered if there was also an issue about their sexuality bearing fruit but I did not ask about their views on children yet. They were still talking about their sexuality.*

"What got you so excited?" asked Thelma. "You've seen me like that a hundred times."

"You just looked so sweet," he laughed.

"Sweet! That's just what I thought about you!" exclaimed Thelma. Then to me, "I'm glad he wanted to have sex with me. It was sad that we couldn't, though, because the spermicide was two years out of date. Still, I was happy to be doing it. I didn't get aroused though, until Yves was stimulating my clitoris. I feel so bad that's always so—as if I'm mechanical. I remember thinking French kissing would excite me but it didn't. . . ."

"It didn't turn me on either," said Yves as if to comfort her.

"I know," she replied ruefully. "What turns me on when he caresses my clitoris is a sexual fantasy I hate. I feel so ashamed of it."

"Does Yves know of it?" I asked.

"No, I'd feel too awful. I've worked on it in therapy for years and it never changes. I've had it since I was three. I try to stop it but if I do I feel no arousal at all."

*I was taken aback by this. Here was a central masturbation fantasy, an intensely personal and private area of mental life, that had not yielded to individual intervention. I did not want to invade Thelma's privacy or intrude upon her individual therapy. Yet it was obviously interfering with her sexual pleasure and with the couple's sexual experience. What was I to do? I said that I thought that Thelma had avoided sex in order to avoid this fantasy. I suggested that she consider letting the fantasy run its course during sex. Then in couple therapy they would have a place to work on the sexual experience. I have to admit I was still thinking that I could leave the details of the sexual fantasy to her and her individual therapist. Yet I knew this policy had not worked so far. A secret that cannot be shared tends to grow over time and to remain a major unconscious force expressive of split-off object relations. In the countertransference I was identifying with her shame. I was also feeling controlled into not asking too much. Like Yves, I was not ready to deal with this and even now I feel reluctant to write it down.*

He said, "I feel half angry and half taken aback. I'd forgotten about this fantasy. But I know there is something disturbing her, because we can't sleep in the same bed. And she has to have her own room. She needs to sleep surrounded by a nest of pillows and she tosses and turns all night. So back to the sex—why am I half angry? I resent the pattern that kissing her clitoris—which I like to do—is a necessary condition for orgasm. But then it's nice that the tension disappears and she's free to have intercourse."

Thelma added, "I resent it too. I hate to feel so passive when I don't feel I'm a passive person. But intercourse is painful if I don't have an orgasm first. Yves has pleasure in intercourse although he often does not come at all."

"I do come," he corrected her. "I don't always ejaculate."

*Penetration was frightening to Thelma, perhaps because of the fantasy, and for his own reasons Yves, too, was experiencing some anxiety in intercourse. By the end of this first interview, I could see that an extended consultation was needed, one that would assess their need for behavioral sex therapy as well as couple therapy. I explained the format of the extended consultation: two meetings for the couple, one meeting with each individually, and one more couple's meeting in which I would give my formulation and recommendation. I also gave them each a questionnaire about sexual behavior and attitudes (Lo Piccolo and Steger [1974]). The questions bring out what each member wishes for and dislikes in sex as well as what he or she thinks the other wishes and dislikes. I asked them not to collaborate on filling out the questionnaires but to return them separately. I said I would present my results from collating their responses in the meeting when I gave my recommendations.*

*Before the next session, I worked on my countertransference to the fantasy. I remembered the couple had declined my request that I videotape the first session for my study of interaction. Thelma had said, "No, it would feel as though there was someone else here." The fantasy must be about someone else, I thought, someone who behaved in the way I felt I must not, someone who got in somewhere forbidden. It also occurred to me that the fantasy was operating like an affair in a marriage, where a spouse's investment in a third party drains the marriage of both sexual energy and conflict.*

In the second session, Yves reported a wonderful dream. "It was about a former girl friend in Paris who had left her husband to return to me. I was walking around, carrying her, and it was just wonderful to have this. I had had to put down my glasses but I found them again. The depth of feeling of that reunion was really just wonderful." He thought that it symbolized how he felt so much more accessible to experiencing his sexual feelings for Thelma.

*As I write I am interested in his turn of phrase, namely that he felt accessible to the feelings rather than that they were accessible to him. It speaks of his per-*

*sonhood being less than his feelings. He, however, was just grateful to get back the feelings and thus feel more of a person.*

He cried with pleasure and relief, "I haven't told you this yet, but I heard a silly love song over the Musak about some guy's appreciation for a girl and how he longed for her sexually. It just went click and aha! I knew what he meant." Then laughing through his tears, he said, "What a relief, Thelma. Someone to have sex with and enjoy wanting it in your heart. I hadn't felt the wanting you in a long time."

Thelma, too, had felt her sexual longing to be dormant, tied up in the fantasy. But that week she, too, had had flashes of sexual feeling. She went on to discuss their recent lovemaking. "We made love," she told me, "and he thought I was pretty and sexy, which I've never felt, and I never felt he felt it before. I feel touched. Yves is very agile and I usually feel clumsy and not connected to my body. I could get aroused by kissing but then I always thought he felt revulsed by kissing. I guess we both had our walls up then. Here he was enjoying being kissed! I thought he wouldn't like that."

"We share the same turf," agreed Yves. "I've avoided sex like crazy. What an about-face!"

"When Yves entered, it was painful," said Thelma. "And I said so, for the first time. He found a way to stay inside that wasn't painful and I felt so relieved." Then to Yves, she said, "But even though you had kissed my clitoris and I had two orgasms, I still was not relaxed."

I said that intensity of feeling was not scary but that penetration was.

Thelma said that as a child she had been sexually molested by a friend's retarded relative who put his hands down her underpants. More influential in her sexual inhibitions, however, were her memories of the relationship with her mother, which was sexualized, though technically no abuse had occurred, according to Thelma. In contrast to her English parents' non-demonstrative style of child-rearing, Thelma's mother kissed her passionately on the lips and seemed to see no separation between herself and her daughter. Her parents were viciously disappointed in each other and expressed no affection at all. Thelma slept with both parents until she was thirteen and since her father tossed in his sleep, she was always afraid of being crushed. She explained that was why she could not sleep in the bed with Yves, though she wished she could.

*It occurred to me that she longed equally to stay in her bed with her parents, their bodies unconsciously represented by the pillows. But the thought evaporated and instead I tied her longing to be held safely in their bed by Yves to his wonderful dream of holding his recovered girlfriend. I was ignoring a source of resistance, caught up in the excitement of the longing.*

*This couple was rather exciting. They were very complimentary about me. Having heard my last book praised by Yves' pastoral counselor friend, they really wanted to work with me, and wondered what I would write about them. And they had a remarkable response to just one session. Having been in therapy, the woman was used to talking about intimate matters and the man had unusual emotional expressiveness. I felt that I was supposed to relate to them as a joint, exciting object and thus to gratify them and feed off them. As such, I would perhaps be enacting the fantasy that was being inhibitory to their sexuality. I was still puzzling over the fantasy. Perhaps it involved Thelma's sexualized relationship to her mother, a substitution for the loving parental sexual couple. I realized that I could not help them by guessing and hoping the work would get done elsewhere. That enabled me to resolve my problem of tact and confidentiality and to decide that the couple and I had to have access to the fantasy to continue the therapeutic task. I did not have to insist, however, I think because now I was ready to work and to face the return of the repressed when the secret was let go. (See Fig. 4–6, p. 77.)*

In the third couple session, Thelma began by telling of her dream about the consultation.

> "Yves and I had come to see you but you were busy with a little boy doing a puzzle as in an I.Q. test. Then there was a third person in our session, a man who was part of us. You said, 'Don't worry, you'll get your full forty-five minutes.' Then I told you that I hadn't answered all the questions on the questionnaire because I was too upset by them." She associated to the dream: "The third person was related to my sexual fantasy. My name is Sheila in my sexual fantasy. . . ."

*I worried that Thelma was about to launch into an individual session that would compete with her individual therapy and detract from this shared couple session.*

Just then she said, "Actually, I worry I'll talk too much."

Yves immediately sprang to life. "I sat here on the couch today next to Thelma so I'd be close to her 'cause I felt depressed last week sitting over there and listening to her talk so much. I sat next to her so you'd be looking at me too when Thelma is the more interesting client."

*I took his comment as a useful confrontation of Thelma and of me. I had felt, as he did, that she could use all the time for herself. She was holding for the couple many qualities—assertiveness, frustration, verbal competence, and therapy know-how. She seemed to be out front, larger than the couple, needy and swollen like a genital organ that has been stimulated but not relieved. I assumed that this was a substitution for Yves, who was afraid of being out front. So I welcomed his asserting himself.*

I said, "This dream introduces your fears and reluctance about starting therapy with me. Will I be more interested in a little boy or a little girl; will I focus on tests rather than on fantasy? I note that it also introduces your sexual fantasy as a third person. I wonder if this means you are ready to talk about that and if so is Yves ready to give the space for that, or will it feel to him like Thelma is taking up the time?"

"Both," said Yves.

"I felt upset that Yves was so depressed and withdrawn and didn't feel like trying to have sex again," said Thelma.

Yves explained that he was mainly depressed about his career going nowhere and about his difficulty learning from people at work. "Oh, selling houses to suburbanites, classes in statistics," he groaned. "I'm doing it but I'm not in it."

"Then where are you?" I asked.

"Nowhere. I could read Herman Hesse all summer, listen to music, fuck it! If I'm put on the spot in class, I clutch. I can learn things but only if I teach myself by listening." As he talked, Thelma sat very still. She held his hand and tried to encourage him to remember his talents. I thought perhaps that she was giving Yves a long turn of talking to me. I said that Yves' response to my question could mean that he wasn't ready to give Thelma the space, or perhaps his talk of a self-defeating part that would not take in was actually quite connected to the nature of the fantasy.

"Oh, yes," said Thelma. "I feel a failure, not at work, but sexually. I feel so much shame. Well, perhaps I could tell one of the versions of the fantasy. Sheila is 15 and away at boarding school. The teachers tell her she has to know their names, Miss This and Miss That, and if she doesn't get them all right, they can do things to her," Thelma paused, ". . . like take her clothes off. She can't remember their names but she'll do whatever they want. So she lets them take off parts of her clothes—like her underpants."

Thelma now seemed deep in the fantasy, in a somewhat dissociated state. She was staring straight ahead, her hands stiffly in front of her as if she were supporting a baby's head with her right hand and resting the other on the chest. Later her left hand shifted position as if she were holding an erect penis.

*The telling of this fantasy was not at all erotic. It was disturbing to me to be there while she was gone and to hear how tiny her voice had become. I felt she was a scared child at the mercy of overwhelming sexual wishes or perhaps abuse.*

Thelma continued, "Then more of the teachers appear. One of them is called the house mother. And she makes Sheila go to the bathroom in her sleep and then makes her wear diapers. When she wets herself, they tell her that they'll do other things to her, like she'll have to ask her Mommy to lick her. That's all I can tell. They do the things to arouse her and they make her beg the Mommy to do those things to her."

It was near the end of the session and I asked Thelma to come back from her dissociated state so we could talk together before we had to end. Yves started crying. He said, "Oh, Thelma, this is so very painful. It ties in to my own stuff. But the main thing is the diapers on. Oh! Oh! That's awful for you."

## YVES' INDIVIDUAL SESSION

Yves talked mostly of his work inhibition. Obviously bright, verbal, and well read, he was gifted in languages and literature. He went to an excellent college where he proceeded to get A-plus grades and was promoted to harder courses. He felt he got in over his head and lost interest, but graduated halfheartedly with a B average in French. He tried other intellectual areas, including religion, but nothing held his interest. As he said, "I have a scholarly mind, and I love reading good stuff, not that I use it, I just like hanging out with it. Things get my interest and then they fizzle out—let alone plug into the real world and get a job. I clutch when performing in front of someone else. Like I can't get it. Alone, I'm incredibly persistent, precise, good at problem solving, but I don't wanna do it in front of someone else, or for someone else, or on a schedule." He was describing an anxiety-based learning disability and a performance anxiety as well as a problem of withholding his skills when pressured.

He went on, "So instead of being serious at work, I'm a clown. Maybe I was meant to be a comic. I don't know what career would suit me. I'm waiting for a career to drop like manna from heaven, or for someone to spot me and say, 'You can be my chauffeur or companion for life and we can read books and listen to music forever.'"

I said, "This sounds like a woman wanting to be rescued by a good marriage."

"My mother raised me as a girl!" he replied, to my astonishment and his. "She didn't really, but that thought just came into my mind, so I said it." His out-of-the-blue thought made sense of my original fantasy of him dressed as a woman. He explained. "Their first child was a boy and I've always thought they wanted a girl. I've wondered whether I'm straight or gay, it's a lingering nag. I'm emotionally attracted to men and I did once get close enough to a man to almost have sex but I freaked out to think I might be gay and he wasn't a good person to explore that with. That was fifteen years ago. I think I'm primarily heterosexual. I get turned on by body-builder types but I would never think of masturbating with a picture of a man."

I asked about his parents. "My mother's a cold fish, lives by what's proper, very conservative. She emigrated from France to marry my father after his year in the Paris office of his firm. I was her favorite, because I did well at school, the right thing to do. But my dad's a soft guy, friendly, jokey, chatty, and warm. I have an inflated image of him that's inhibited my rage at him for all the guidance he never gave me. He was one of the tax lawyers in a big firm with lots of West Coast clients, and he traveled a lot." Yves went on to talk of getting a draft deferment for studying in Europe as a divinity student. "I would've killed somebody if I had to be in the army. I wouldn't want to wear a hat or have to salute somebody. I don't take things seriously—careers or myself. I just get little sparks of enthusiasm that die."

This suggested to me that Yves had a murderous level of rage at his experience of his parents that he had turned on himself. His previous therapy, individual, group, and spiritual, had not touched this. I asked how he would feel about intensive individual treatment.

"Like psychoanalysis? Yeah, heavy. What good does it do? I'm never gonna get help. Look at Thelma—she's just idolizing her therapy and it's beyond me. Where's the big change? I guess I'm not a very hopeful person."

## THELMA'S INDIVIDUAL SESSION

Thelma began by telling me how needy and greedy she felt, but she had thought that Yves was clamoring for something from me, too. Anyway, now that she was here alone, she wanted to tell me more about herself but she was afraid she'd be too much for me and that I'd be overwhelmed. She brought a number of things with her—a photo of her family: her parents happily sharing a picnic beside her two brothers enthusiastically fishing at a pond on Hampstead Heath. I noticed that her mother was much smaller and rounder than Thelma. In separate oil miniatures, mother as an adolescent looked sad and remote, while Thelma, whose facial resemblance to her mother at the same age is striking, looked similarly unhappy. As I looked at them, Thelma told me her mother was a histrionic woman, self-deprecating and suicidal. Her father was also suicidal and once locked himself in the attic with a gun. He was unreliable and unsuccessful. Her parents seemed to hate each other and often got in terrible fights that could be dangerous. Thelma as a child had once called the police and by the time they came her parents had got it together and said she was mistaken. She never saw her parents happy as in the photo. Of the paintings of her mother and herself, she said, "I felt possessed by Mum. I'd look in the mirror and see her face, her wispy blonde hair. I don't like the way I look. My face doesn't seem to be my own. And I feel too tall."

She had been blamed for being the reason her mother had to stay alive. Thelma had identified with her mother's suicidality and also her need to stay alive, but through therapy had been freed from the constant preoccupation of feeling and trying not to feel suicidal.

Thelma then showed me a photo of a teddy bear wearing a canvas apron and a cook's cap. This did not look like a snugly, cozy animal at all. It was curiously rigid, a gruesome sight with one eye, matted fur, and dirty stuffing bulging out of the ripped seams. She had battered it. Then Thelma said, "From another place I could say it's a representation of myself—messy." I said, "And if not from that other place, what would you say?"

She said, "I could say she feels stiff and cold and uncared for. I feel stiff and self-conscious. Here, I wrote this music."

I began to feel, as she had predicted, overwhelmed. I said, "You want to give me so much, so many things, I think, to take the place of you in case I would not want you, yourself."

"I want to give you a picture of me. My mother didn't have that. My therapist does. You've talked about the importance of holding. I had the fantasy of her and you talking, to merge you. It's jarring to me the ways you are not her."

Here was a fantasy wish that Thelma's therapist and I could experience what happened to Thelma and her mother. A more progressive view of that fantasy might be that her therapist and I would be extending a shared holding capacity, separately contributed to by us with our individual differences, much as a father and mother provide a shared context for their child.

## THE COUPLE'S SESSION

In the next couple session, I used this sense of her longing to be held. Thelma began by mentioning a dream in which she had gone looking for a set of building blocks and forgot that they were in my office. Helped by remembering the image from her first dream of the little boy who was doing a puzzle with me before her session, I said, "You wish to be a child here." She cried with relief that I understood and could allow for that.

Yves had also had a dream.

*I'm always grateful for dreams that can take us to a deeper level of understanding. But here there were almost too many dreams. There seemed to be an element of competition between Yves and Thelma to bring me something I would value.*

Yves described his dream in the present tense as follows.

"In the dream there is both me and a father. I see him take a pair of pliers. He's hiding in a pantry and he's going to kill his daughter with them. I warn her not to go in, 'cause she'll get killed. Then she's a woman with a round, pretty face, with a high Elizabethan forehead, and a bunch of packages."

*I wondered if this figure of a British woman with a high forehead represented me.*

"I see my mom going down the alley. I'm supposed to meet her and have dinner. I run out and meet up with her in the main street. We are going to the restaurant, now there are six or eight of us. It's a nice restaurant with white tablecloths. Suddenly my dad arrives. I say, 'Dad, What are you doing here? This is a dinner for Mom.' A waiter in his underwear is helping us to find a bigger table; we try one, then another, and I suggest adding another leaf. Then he spreads open yet another table. A guitarist is playing and talking in a foreign language. There's just not a lot of emotional tone to this. I woke up and thought about it for awhile."

Yves continued to associate. "I liked the tragic element. Reminds me of Hamlet. And some other tale—Yes! In one of Dostoevsky's books, the middle son has killed his father and a servant with a pestle! Well, in my dream it's murder by pliers!"

*When I work with couples' dreams, I like to hear both partners associate to the dream. I cannot hope to get as thorough an understanding of the individual's intrapsychic situation as in individual psychoanalysis or therapy. Instead, I am trying to correlate what is revealed of the intrapsychic with the interpersonal situation before me. This time I did not have to ask for associations.*

Thelma said, "First you said it was a little girl then an adult."

Yves replied, "Yes, it was his daughter, then a woman. And there was an inside/outside dimension to the dream and the identities were confused, as in a play by Shakespeare. We saw *A Midsummer Night's Dream* last weekend. Oh! I love the substance, complexity, emotionalism, overblown romanticism, the humor, and the wonderful writing."

*I thought to myself, "Why is this man selling houses?"*

Thelma, returning to the domestic aspect of his dream, continued, "I was thinking that putting a new leaf in the table has to do with our relationship. And spreading the table sounds sexual, like spreading my legs open."

"Well," said Yves, "the dinner was only for me and Mom and I was surprised when Dad showed up and I needed a bigger table."

Thelma continued, "I'm still struck by the little girl and the woman who were going to get killed. I have wanted to kill the little girl in me but it was frightening that you would want to kill my little Sheila."

"What? It wasn't Sheila to me."

"Then who was it?"

"I don't know. A woman of low character who is a rival between the young man and the father."

"How was she a rival?" I asked, confused.

"They are both rivals for her love," he replied.

*I began to get a sense that this girl/woman in the dream had a shared meaning for Yves and Thelma of an oedipal child who wants to steal the mommy and who should be killed for such guilt. For Yves, I thought the girl should be murdered by pliers so that the boy need not be killed or castrated but could freely run off with his mother, knowing his father was preoccupied.*

Yves went on to say that when Thelma interjected her thought about Sheila being killed in the dream, he remembered that he had had fantasies of molesting little girls. He'd been turned on by a cute, naked little 2-year-old. Yves and Thelma agreed that they shared a fascination for hairless vulvas. Then Yves panicked and froze. Soon he continued. He told of having murderous fantasies "when thwarted by some asshole." I got the idea that he used murderous fantasies to defend against incestuous or otherwise unacceptable sexual fantasies.

Then Thelma reported another dream, about my not being there because I had gone to a hospital to have another baby. My husband left Thelma in charge of our older baby while he came to the hospital to see me and the new baby. She felt bad for the baby being left with an unknown person. She also felt bad about a lamb chop she had left in my refrigerator, because it was expensive and she had let it rot and it was poisoning my refrigerator.

Thelma went into much more detail than this and Yves did not interrupt. Thelma was maybe getting to the end now. "And in the last part of the dream," said Thelma, "my Norwegian friend Britt was there. I mentioned your name and she said, 'Scharff, that's Norwegian too?'" Thelma continued to associate. "But I know it's German. That's why I called you rather than your husband because I know you are Scottish. Lamb chop, Lamb of God, blood of Lamb in the Passover keeps the angel of death from killing the firstborn and I'm the firstborn. I've been well versed in the Holocaust. Nazis are a big part of my dreams, and—"

I ventured to interrupt in the name of the transference. "Scharff is indeed a German name. Does that put it on the Jewish or the Nazi side?"

"Oh, on the Nazi side," she replied without a moment's hesitation. "The Scots defended the Jews. Our family spent our summer holidays hiking in the Scottish hills. I love Scotland—the flowers, the people; I felt safe there. I pretend I'm not Jewish, to be safe. With my blonde hair, no one guesses. I've never had a Jewish boyfriend. Yves isn't Jewish."

I asked Yves if he had any comment. "No," he answered. "I'm thinking about work." Returning to the present interaction, he offered, "Well, the name Scharff I heard as sharp, smart, like a weapon."

"I had those connections, too," Thelma concurred.

So Yves hadn't given as much attention to Thelma's dream as she had to his. She was worried about an abandoned baby, poisoned food supplies, and her own murder. I noticed that she was preserving me as good by splitting off my "Scharffness" into my husband, while I, the safe Scot and Brit, was identified as her friend and compatriot. Yet I was being perceived by both of them as someone whose insight could pierce or kill them. In his dream, Yves himself was not being murdered; instead, some girl was to be killed. And in both her readings of Yves' dream and her own dream, that's what Thelma expected to happen to her.

# FORMULATION AND RECOMMENDATION

Perhaps Yves and Thelma shared the problem that each felt more special to mother than did father, she because she gratified her mother by looking so like her and he because he was so successful at school. Each had a father who was looked down upon, hers because he was unreliable and a poor provider, and his because he was a nice guy with no authority. Because of their guilt at being oedipal victors over father, she could not claim her life as a woman and he could only survive if a woman was his substitute victim. Even so, he was so identified with the victim that he could not claim his maleness sexually or professionally and became like his father, an affable worker with little sense of personal authority. She survived by thinking of herself as the spared firstborn son, which compromised her femininity. The unconscious fit had been perfect for them. But now Thelma was expecting more of herself after a period of individual therapy and this was putting pressure on Yves. To the extent that he responded to this by becoming more sexual, both were thrilled, but it then revealed her fears of penetration and his of being inside her. They could not create a loving, sexual couple in intercourse, presumably because they shared a fantasy of parents who were anything but such a couple.

I used these thoughts, along with the results of the questionnaires, as a basis for my formulation. I told them I thought that there were three levels of problem.

## The Sexual Relationship

At the first level, their relationship was hampered by conscious and unconscious assumptions about their own and the other's sexuality. Both were aware of homosexual elements in self and partner. These had been tolerated usefully but had not been addressed. Both used masturbation as their sexual release. Thelma's masturbation perpetuated her fantasy, while Yves believed he had no fantasy, although he used pornographic material. Both had similar expectations of desired frequency of sex, their preference being for once or twice a week. His unacknowledged resentment of her control over the mode of sexual expression had led him to stop making advances. Her incorrect belief that he did not like kissing or cuddling had prevented her from exploring a wider range of arousing techniques. But she was right in thinking that he disliked having his breasts stimulated, whereas he was wrong in thinking that she would not like to have her breasts stimulated. They had a mutual avoidance of each other's breasts and her clitoris during intercourse, which had become an event separated from the arousal phase. A further complicating assumption was that he thought she would like intercourse to last one to three minutes, whereas she had thought ten to twenty minutes would be good. I told them that one to three minutes would not be long enough for most women. Both thought that it would be fun to work toward a longer period of intercourse.

I said that they had presented their sexual relationship as the main problem and I had focused on it with them. There were, indeed, problems that could be addressed in specific sex therapy in a behavioral format, if they still saw sex as the main problem by the time we had finished this final session of the consultation.

Then I went on to the second level.

## The Couple Relationship

I said, "I feel that you bring your sexual problem for help much as you bring your dreams or music—as if this is something you can give of yourself that will be acceptable. It needs work but not to the exclusion of the problems in the couple relationship." Both were relieved by this. Thelma said she was grateful that I had noticed. I said, "You need help with communicating your wishes and ideas to develop shared goals appropriate to this phase of life. I think you could decide affirmatively to remain childless as a positive choice you could be happy with. On the other hand, I'd expect that work on your conflicts could free you to consider house-owning and parenthood as choices that could be made or rejected thoughtfully rather than as dreaded out-of-reach possibilities. You both reject the model of marriage you carry from your parents and you are needing help with what is preventing you from developing beyond that." I concluded, "Each of you is inhibiting the other's development in order to avoid anxiety and aggression. That could be addressed in couple therapy during which individual contributions to that shared inhibition could also be worked with, but probably not to the degree Yves might need."

Then I went on to the third level.

## The Individual

It was clear to me that each of them had individual problems that got in the way of feeling like a grown up dealing with reality and responsibility. Thelma was already addressing these in individual therapy and had made considerable progress to have given up her suicidal grasp on herself. Nevertheless, her individual therapy had become blocked because she could not free herself of the incestuous fantasy without work on the couple's relationship. I strongly urged Yves to consider the option of intensive individual treatment for himself, now or later, if it turned out that couple therapy could not reach his individual inhibition sufficiently. I thought it likely that he would need intensive individual therapy because of the castration anxiety, the shakiness of his male identity, and because previous less intensive therapy had not helped him.

The couple chose to continue with me in couple therapy, which would include discussion of their sexual issues. Later, if the sexual problems persisted, I would refer them for sex therapy or I could myself switch to a behavioral sex therapy format with them and then resume the couple therapy. Yves agreed to think further about the individual therapy recommendation and Thelma looked surprised and pleased, as if a secret wish had been granted.

## THE POSTCONSULTATION SESSION

Thelma began by saying that Yves had been very angry and depressed since the last session.

"I felt it the minute I got in the car," he said, "I was feeling murderous and I started torturing her by withdrawing. I wouldn't speak for hours. Finally I said to her, 'I just wanna torture you.' Then I walked away and started crying 'cause I'd been feeling so warm and loving before. She tried to talk to me about it and I said, 'I'm not gonna change. Fuck you! I'm gonna stay just the way I am. And if you try too hard, I'll hurt you.'"

I said, "You were taking it out on her. But I think you were mad at me. You felt I was asking you to change."

"Forcing me," he shot back.

"And I felt that you were desperately asking me to show you a way," I replied.

"Ha, ha," smiling, he admitted, "as soon as I expressed my anger, I thought that myself." Then angrily, "I just hated having myself thrown up in my face. I thought 'Oh, here we go again. I have to deal with all that man stuff.'"

*Immediately he became the charming clown, telling of how the bank wouldn't validate his identity, either. I pointed out that he had turned anger into a joke and that I would like to hear more about the anger he felt.*

"I was angry at Thelma. I wanted to take thumbtacks and put them through her thumbs and pin her down." With an intent expression, Yves reached out with his thumbs, in vivid illustration of his anger. "I feel I have a cold murderer inside me—it's a fantasy—if I get aroused. I don't wanna change most things about my life. I have a protected little circle and if I step out of that, I don't feel good. I don't want you, Thelma, to want me to change." He looked intensely angry, cold, and mean, and stubborn in a vigorous, active way that I experienced as frustrating yet I rather admired it. It came as a relief after his affable clowning.

Thelma was crying, "I just feel hopeless when you get like this. And I'd like to hit you with this book. Every time I've said I want us both to change, you've withdrawn. It makes me so furious. I feel it's nasty. I'm not happy with it the way it is." She was able to be much more direct about her anger than I had seen before. "I have waited and I haven't forced you. I feel you are being a *brat*!"

"Fuck you," he spat back. "I'm not asking you to change. What's all this expectation? I'm not gonna change. It's not my fucking nature."

Crying, she went on, "I feel so shut out when you do this. And I don't believe you. I do believe you're scared. I don't feel good about sounding so demanding. You want me to encourage you and you just deny that you might want to change."

I said that Yves was displacing his conflict about change from inside himself to between him and me and between him and Thelma. Yves replied, "I just wanna say 'no,' but I do also wanna talk about our experience of making love."

For all his protestations about not wanting therapy, Yves made very good use of the couple therapy. So I thought he was mainly anxious about leaving the circle it provided and going out on his own. Fears of autonomy were accompanied by a stubborn, withholding way of relating, a regression from the loving, giving state he'd been in, but in which he'd been anxious.

I learned this as Yves and Thelma began to talk about their sexual experience. Yves had not come to orgasm but had been able to tell Thelma how he would like his penis to be touched. She was glad to do this but felt detached. Later, when thinking of intercourse lasting twenty minutes, she felt desire and had a fantasy of Yves' penis touching her vagina. This was a sustained, pleasurable feeling. Both Yves and Thelma had been anxious but both had been able to relate through the penis, nevertheless. In Thelma's case, the fantasy of being penetrated was quite a shift from the fantasy of being touched and humiliated. But Thelma's original fantasy was still controlling Yves. He said that his penis was inside Thelma's vagina and he lost confidence. "It was a mental block," he explained, "so I stopped and offered to kiss her. I thought, 'I want to be a woman not a man?' It was a relief to start kissing her instead of fucking her. Thelma, you said I was like a woman because of the way my legs were spread when you were touching me."

"It was upsetting," said Thelma, "and so is the idea that I'd participated in not treating you like a man."

"Until now," I said, "there's been a good fit between your fantasies of each other as not fully male or female and your views of how to lead your lives. But now things are changing and you are afraid that if you don't change together . . . ."

Thelma filled in the rest. "We'll break up. I haven't wanted it to end and that's why I haven't spoken up. It's felt safe for me. But I have felt so confined."

In this case the couple's resistance to treatment was split off from the couple therapy and expressed by Yves' reluctance to have individual therapy. It was also operating in their focusing so intently on sexuality when issues of aggression in the form of rage, money, ambition, and life goals were just as important. For many couples, resistance to treatment is expressed through a reluctance to deal with sexual material. Yves and Thelma were unusual in being so explicit so early in the treatment. This, however, was evidence not merely of resistance to other material but also of their urgent need to deal with their disturbed sexual relationship. They continued with commitment in ongoing couple therapy. A few months later, Yves started psychoanalytic psychotherapy with a colleague, moving into psychoanalysis by the end of the year.

## CONFIRMATION AND EXTENSION OF THE ASSESSMENT FORMULATION DURING THE MIDPHASE OF SUBSEQUENT THERAPY

Over the months of therapy, Thelma and Yves experienced their fears of sexuality and of commitment to marriage. These fears came to a point in the transference when Thelma was afraid I would show up late, miss an appointment, or cancel, while Yves dreamed of being unable to get up to my office because of a prickly bush blocking the driveway. Through these individual communications they told me of their shared wish to be held by me and to enter me, and their fear of my being inaccessible or downright castrating. Work on understanding this in the transference enabled them to move on to more intimacy and sexuality. In conclusion, we present a midphase session in which successful sex is linked to love and, at least for the moment, dispels the inhibiting fantasy of the dead internal couple.

The couple talked about a lovely day they had had doing things together. When they got home, they spontaneously had sex even though there were no sheets on the bed, and it was wonderful.

"I felt more passion than I've ever felt," enthused Thelma. "I was aroused from Yves' touching my clitoris but mainly from kissing a lot and touching his penis. When he entered, I felt discomfort as usual but he was able to slow down when I asked him to, and then it was so nice for me. I enjoyed the passion of it and the way he stopped and started."

"Well, I need to remember to slow down, slower than slow. No trouble. I really enjoyed it too. Afterwards I had an interesting experience: I thought of saying 'I love you.' . . ."

"Did you?" beamed Thelma. "I don't remember that."

"Yes I thought it, but I couldn't say it. Oh, I said it the next day—and I felt it—but at the time I couldn't. It was like it would be scary to say it because of the consequences."

I repeated that Yves had had a loving feeling and got scared of it. "Because of what consequences?" I asked.

Yves corrected me, "No, I didn't feel it. I thought it. What I felt was that something was missing and the thought came in my mind that 'I love you' would fill the gap. You see, sex and love aren't together in my mind."

I replied, "I believe you turned it into a thought because you got scared of feeling it. The next day you did think it, say it, and feel it when it wasn't amplified by the physical sensation. So back to the question of the consequences."

Yves immediately responded, "I'd be trapped. It would have implications: love, marriage, family—demands, demands, demands. Another thought just came in my mind. My father's advice. His sex talk was: 'I suppose you've noticed that men and women are built differently?' That was it! Then he said, 'Yves, women will find you attractive. Don't let them get their hooks into you.'"

"And at that moment *he* got his hook into you," I said rather more forcefully than I meant to. "You've been living by that line ever since." Yves looked stunned. Thelma looked deeply preoccupied.

"My comment has hit you rather hard," I said.

"It's true," said Yves. "I've been controlled by that advice. I think he felt trapped in his marriage."

"You've been living on his advice and maybe on his behalf," I said.

"Oh," he sighed. After a long pause, he said, "I'm really struck by that. On his behalf, not getting trapped. I've a rumor—no, I mean to say a memory—of Mom saying if it hadn't been for Susie, the mistake, they would've gotten divorced. That reminds me of a dream of a woman smoking a cigarette walking away saying, 'Don't blame me if this family falls apart.'"

I said, "If Susie, the child after you, kept them together, could it be that you were worried about your being the cause of their falling apart?"

"Except that I was the favorite," Yves rejoined. Suddenly he held his head.

"Oh, what was that covering up!"

"Talk about cover-up," added Thelma. "I've thought that I wanted to be

married and have a house, but it must've suited me to be in this relationship where Yves didn't want to marry me for eight years and still won't
buy a house. To me marriage means destruction. My parents were killing
each other. Yves' father's line was 'Don't let her get her hooks into you.'
My mother's line was 'You can't live on love.' But I feel I am really married.
I could never have an affair. I would like to feel that my marriage could be
a good one for children, but I can't imagine it."

Thelma and Yves both wanted a love relationship unlike their parents' relationships. They were afraid that if they had a house or children they would re-create their parents' marriages. They could not
enjoy their sexuality because intercourse had carried with it the fantasy of recreating the dead internal couple. Thelma was afraid Yves
would never give her the commitment she wanted but feared. Yves
was afraid the woman would get her hooks into him and bind him to
her. In his fantasy, the hooks were located in the vagina where they
would take possession and destroy the penis. Once some work had
been done on Yves' fantasy as it emerged in the transference through
his fear of the prickly bush blocking my driveway, the couple was able
to engage in intercourse with pleasure. This provided a healing experience that got them out of the grip of the dead internal couple.

# Chapter 6
# THE TECHNIQUE OF
# COUPLE THERAPY

Object relations couple therapy is a way of working that is based on principles of technique informed by the theories of object relations, small group process applied to the dyad, and psychosexual development. Our focus is on the relationship. We observe it, primarily, through noticing the way the couple deals with us, but we are also interested in how the spouses interact with each other. We are concerned not just with the conscious aspects of their bond but with the internal object relations operating through mutual projective identificatory processes in the couple's unconscious.

In keeping with this focus our technique employs nondirective listening for the emergence of unconscious themes, following the affect, analyzing dream and fantasy material and associations offered by both members of the couple, and exploring the family history of each spouse as it relates to the current couple relationship. We point out patterns of interaction that tend to recur and look for unconscious forces that drive the repetition. Gradually we become familiar with the defensive aspects of these repeating cycles. We do this over and over, covering the same ground and making inroads into defended territory, which we find particularly accessible at times when the couple's transference has stirred a countertransference response through which we can appreciate the couple's vulnerability. As trust builds, we can help the couple figure out and face the nameless anxiety behind the defense. Our help comes in the form of interpretations of resistance, defense and conflict, conceptualized as operating through unconscious object relation systems that support and subvert the marriage. These interpretations are imparted after metabolization in the countertransference. Interpretation may lead to insight, which produces change in the unconscious object relations of the couple or may lead to increased resistance to the unconscious conflict. Progression and regression succeed each other in cycles as we work through the defensive structures of the marriage to the point where these are no longer interfering with the couple's capacity for working together as life partners, loving each other, integrating good and bad, and building a relationship of intimacy and sexuality that is free to develop through the developmental life cycle of the marriage.

What does all this mean in practice? Our technique can be explored through its components, as summarized in Table 6–1.

## THE TASKS OF OBJECT RELATIONS COUPLE THERAPY

### Setting the Frame

Our first priority is to set a frame (Langs 1976) for therapy. This offers "a secure and consistent environment in which highly sensitive, private feelings and fantasies can be expressed and explored

Table 6–1. Tasks of Object Relations Couple Therapy

1. Setting the frame
2. Maintaining a neutral position of involved impartiality
3. Creating a psychological space
4. Use of the therapist's self: Negative capability
5. Transference and Countertransference
6. Interpretation of defense, anxiety, fantasy, and inner object relations: the Because Clause
7. Working through
8. Termination

without the threat of actualizing the feared consequences" (Zinner 1989 in J. Scharff 1989, p. 321). The couple tries to bend the frame so that unconscious wishes can be gratified, but their efforts are frustrated by the therapist, who holds firm. The ensuing conflict brings into the treatment the issues that have been dividing the marriage.

How is the frame set in the first place? By being clear about the arrangements and by staying with the agreed upon treatment format. For instance we give a couple a recommendation or a choice of treatment modalities and then by mutual agreement settle upon a plan. Then we explain our policy of sticking to it, unless future experience dictates a shift that will not be undertaken except after thorough discussion and mutual agreement. So the frame is secure, but flexible.

Then we outline other policies, such as fees, vacations, and billing practice. Our billing practice is to bill at the end of the month and to have the couple's check by the 10th of the month. We do this because it helps us to keep in mind the moment when the bill was rendered and to focus on how the couple is dealing with the financial aspects of the commitment. We sell our time not by item of service but by long-term commitment, so we expect the couple to attend as planned. If they have to be absent, we are willing to reschedule within the week, but if that is not possible then we hold them responsible for the time. Unlike our work with families where we will see the family with a member absent, in couple therapy we do not work unless both members of the couple are present. Suddenly doing individual therapy with one spouse poses a threat to the therapist's neutrality and capacity to help the couple. Of course, in keeping with the flexible frame, individual sessions can be scheduled by plan and by mutual agreement, but not as filler for absences from therapy.

At the moment of moving from assessment to treatment, the couple is given the choice of accepting the frame or accepting referral to another therapist whose conditions seem preferable. Here is an example from such a session.

> Mr. and Mrs. Melville had both had previous individual therapies and now wanted to work with me [J.S.S.] in marital therapy. He was a successful organizational consultant who loved his work, enjoyed food, sports, and sex, and felt great about himself, except in his marriage, where he felt unloved. She was a good homemaker, mother of three little ones, and ran a small business selling jewelry from her home. She felt exhausted, unaccomplished, and uninterested in sex. Both tended to overspend and so short-term cash flow problems created financial stress in addition to their marital tension.
>
> I told them my fee, which was acceptable. They had no problem agree-

ing to my payment schedule. But charging for missed sessions was another matter.

"Do you mean to say this would apply to my traveling on business?" asked Mr. Melville.

"I'm willing to reschedule within that week if I can," I replied. "But when I can't, then I have to hold you responsible for the time, if we have agreed to meet weekly as I recommend."

"But I'm very punctual and never miss an appointment," he protested. "My previous therapist will tell you that. And she never charged me because she knew I wasn't acting out. This business travel is out of my control."

Mrs. Melville's concern was different. "Do I have to take vacation when you do? And when do you go away?" she wanted to know. I thought she resented being tied to my plans, but without saying so I answered her question.

"I tend to take three weeks in August, sometimes one at Christmas, and another in late March," I replied.

"Oh, good!" she exclaimed. "That's what I do. So it's not a problem. It's more a problem for him, traveling."

I said, "I see that you react differently to my policy. You, Mr. Melville, feel that since you are a good, responsible person, you do not deserve to be charged, which to you feels like a punishment and a rejection of your worth. You, Mrs. Melville, feel afraid of being trapped in the relationship with me. I assume these feelings also come up between you as you deal with the consequences of the marriage commitment."

"Oh, yes," Mrs. Melville rushed to concur. "I feel so trapped in marriage. I need my own space, and especially my own money, but he feels punished by that."

"I sure do," said Mr. Melville. "I feel punished for the way your first husband left you feeling destitute. I'm not like that. I insist on sharing my inheritance with you, even though you insist yours goes directly to the children."

"It's true," she agreed. "And you were very fair with your first wife. But you just don't understand how it freaks me out to think of merging our accounts. I feel I'd be losing myself. I never, ever want to feel financially and emotionally destitute as I did when my first marriage broke up."

"I've been through divorce and if it happened again and I lost everything to her I'd still know I could start over," he said.

She said, "But I'm terrified I couldn't."

He said, "But I'm not your first husband."

Quietly now, Mrs. Melville said, "You just don't know how afraid I am of losing myself."

In early transference reactions to the frame, the Melvilles revealed their fundamental problems. His self-worth was tied to his earning capacity rather than to being loved, because the former was more dependable than the latter. His willingness to provide for her could not assuage her sense of insecurity because it emphasized his independence from her and defended against love. How could anyone so apparently confident ever understand her terror of her dependency and her fears of annihilation? How could someone so generous be married to someone to whom it meant so little? The answer must lie in their mutual projection of the good, abundant, nourishing, energetic breast into him (as both had experienced their fathers, I later learned) and the shriveled, nonreplenishing breast, depleted by their neediness into her (an image that derived from their shared views of their mothers). As the therapist expecting to be paid, I was a replenishing breast to which they had to contribute in partnership, an expectation that threatened them in ways unique to each individual and jointly in reflection of their object relations set.

## LISTENING TO THE UNCONSCIOUS

At the conscious level we listen to what the couple is saying, which of the partners is saying what, and in what order and with what affect. We try to listen just as carefully to the silence and to the nonverbal communications in the form of gestures. Yet this careful listening is not as consciously attentive as our description sounds so far. Instead, we experience a drifting state of mind, at one level interacting, maybe even asking a question and hearing the answer, at another level not listening for anything in particular. Freud (1912b) described this as "evenly-suspended attention," the therapist turning "his own unconscious like a receptive organ toward the transmitting unconscious of the patient" (pp. 111–115). We tune in at the deepest level of communication to the unconscious signals from the couple, coming through to us as a theme that emerges from the flow of associations and silences, amplified by dream and fantasy, and resonating in the therapist's unconscious in the form of countertransference experience. From this experience, we can share in and reconstruct the couple's unconscious object relations.

## THE NEUTRAL POSITION

We maintain a position of neutrality with no preference as to one spouse or the other, as to life-style choices, or as to treatment outcome. Our attention hovers evenly between the intrapsychic dimensions of each spouse, their interpersonal process, and their interaction with us. While we obviously value marriage as an institution, we do not have a bias about continuation of the marriage or divorce. We are invested in our work with the couple and in the possibility of growth and development, but we do not want to invest in the couple's achievement. We want to hold a position described as one of "involved impartiality" (Stierlin 1977). Any deviations from that occur in directions that are quite unique to each couple. From reviewing the specific pull exerted upon us we learn about the couple's unconscious object relationships.

## Creating the Psychological Space

This willingness to work with one's experience demonstrates an attitude of valuing process and review. It offers the couple a model for self-examination and personal sharing, and creates the psychological space into which the couple can move and there develop its potential for growth.

We offer a therapeutic environment in which the couple can experience its relationship in relation to the therapist. Our therapeutic stance derives from our integration of the concepts of container-contained (Bion 1962) and the holding environment (Winnicott 1960a) whose points of difference are described in Chapter 3. Now we will simply present our integration. The relationship to the therapist creates a transitional space in which the couple can portray and reflect upon its current way of functioning, learn about and modify its projective identificatory system, and invent new ways of being. Through clinical experience, training, supervision and intensive personal psychotherapy or psychoanalysis, the therapist develops a holding capacity, the capacity to bear the anxiety of the emergence of unconscious material and affect through containment and to modify it through internal processing of projective identifications. The therapist contributes this capacity to the transitional space, which is thereby transformed into an expanded psychological space for understanding. The couple then takes in this space and finds within its relationship the capacity to deal with current and future anxiety. Once this happens, the actual therapeutic relationship can be terminated because the therapeutic function has been internalized.

## The Use of the Self

Clearly the use of the therapist's self is central to our technique. Learning to use ourselves in this way requires an openness to learning from experience, nurtured in training and supervision. For fullest use of the self in the clinical setting, we need to have had the personal experience of understanding our own family history and object relations in psychoanalysis or intensive psychotherapy, including couple and family therapy, even if our private lives do not call for it. This gives the therapist the necessary base of self-knowledge to calibrate the self as a diagnostic and therapeutic instrument. Its continued refinement is a lifelong task, accomplished mainly through process and review in the clinical situation, discussion with colleagues, and through teaching and writing.

NEGATIVE CAPABILITY

Once the therapist's self is cleared for use as a receiving apparatus and as a space that can be filled with the experience of the couple, the therapist is able to know, without seeking to know actively, about the couple's unconscious. Striving to find out distorts the field of observation. Instead we recommend a nondirective, unfocused, receptive attitude best described as *negative capability*, a term invented by the poet Keats, who used it to describe Shakespeare's capacity as a poet for "being in uncertainties, mysteries, doubts, without any irritable reaching after fact and reason" (in Murray 1955, p. 261). Bion (1970), expanding on Keats's term, urged the therapist "to impose on himself a positive discipline of eschewing memory or desire," (p. 31) that is, to abandon the need to know and to impose meaning. Negative capability, however, is an ideal state and we do not advocate irritably reaching for it. Instead it is a state to sink into, best achieved by not doing too much and allowing understanding to come from inside our experience.

## Transference and Countertransference

Negative capability fosters our capacity to respond to the couple's transference. The transference gives rise to ideas, feelings, or behavior in our countertransference. As Heimann (1950) pointed out, "the analyst's countertransference is an instrument of research into the patient's unconscious" (p. 81). The analyst must value and study his countertransference because "the emotions roused in him are nearer to the heart of the matter than his reasoning" (p. 82). This elaboration of countertransference stresses an understanding of the normal countertransference and its deviations (Money-Kyrle 1956) rather than emphasizing the pathology of the therapist's responses.

In studying our reactions to unconscious material in psychoanalysis, psychotherapy, and couple and family therapy, we have found that our countertransference experiences tend to cluster in relation to two kinds of transferences. These are the contextual and the focused transferences respectively (Scharff and Scharff 1987).

The *contextual countertransference* refers to the therapist's reaction to the patient's contextual transference, namely the patient's response to the therapeutic environment, shown in attitudes about the frame of treatment, unconscious resistance in general, specific conscious feelings, and behavior toward the therapist as an object for providing a holding situation.

The *focused countertransference* occurs in response to the focused transference, namely feelings the patient transfers to the therapist as an object for intimate relating. Usually the contextual transference-countertransference predominates in the opening and closing phases of individual treatment and throughout family therapy. In couple therapy there is often rapid oscillation between the poles.

Mrs. Rhonda Clark, a tall, angular woman with a short, burgundy-colored, spiked hairdo, stormed ahead of her husband, Dr. Clark, a short, round-faced, gentle-looking man. Although in her early fifties, she wore high-style black leather pants and a studded jacket, which she threw on the couch. He meekly laid down his own sheepskin coat and looked expectantly at her through his traditionally rimmed glasses that were, however, unexpectedly bright purple, an odd choice for a surgeon, I thought. She was emitting hostility but no words.

I asked if they were waiting for me to start. He said that she almost didn't come today.

I said, "How come? You, Mrs. Clark, were the one who called me and made the arrangements."

"I'm just mad, today, at him, the bigshot, Mr. Doctor God. You are *not* God! I just thought 'What's the use?' He's always berating me and belittling me. His nurses have no respect for me, he says, and that's just bullshit. They seem to have no respect for me because *he* has no respect for me."

"Well, after you've called the surgi-center three times in half an hour they get wary," he replied. "And I do blame her for having such a short trigger and causing turmoil in our life and at my office. All I ask is to be in a happy situation with a decent sex life and no ruckus. My friends think I should bail out, but I want to stay for the children. The youngest has four more years of high school."

"He's just selfish. Why be there for him sexually when he's putting me down? I'm a good person. I've got friends. He's just fucked up and dumps all his shit on me and makes me sound like a lunatic."

*I felt some revulsion toward Mrs. Clark. I felt ashamed to be thinking that she didn't look or act like a doctor's wife. My sympathies were with the doctor, calm and reasonable and not asking much. But I knew from experience that this was not an opinion, it was just a temporary reaction, not just to her but to them as a couple. For some reason as this couple crossed the boundary into the therapy space, Mrs. Clark seemed dominating, interruptive, and crude.*

I said, "I can see, Mrs. Clark, you are so angry as to feel therapy will be no use, but I think maybe you also feel anxious about what will come of it."

"Yes," said Dr. Clark. "She always acts this anxious way."

I said, "Is Mrs. Clark the only one who is anxious or do you have questions too?"

"No, I'm not anxious, but, yes, I do have questions. I want to interview you about where you went to school."

I told him my professional background and he was glad to learn that I had graduated from medical school in 1967. He had thought that I was a psychologist (which he would not like) and that I seemed too young. So he felt relieved that I had been practicing as a board certified psychiatrist for fifteen years.

I said I was glad to hear of his concerns, because until now it had appeared as though Mrs. Clark was the one that had all the feelings about therapy being no use. I said I had the impression that she expressed her anxiety by getting angry, but that he expressed his anxiety through her. Now, usefully, he was admitting to it. Both of them for their own reasons and in their individual ways were anxious about therapy and about their marriage.

In my countertransference I experienced a deviation from "involved impartiality" (Stierlin 1977), and realized that Mrs. Clark was expressing a focused transference toward me as the doctor (the same profession as her husband) and that this was a cover for the couple's shared contextual transference of distrust in the context of treatment. My task was to address the contextual transference with them so that as a couple Dr. and Mrs. Clark could modify their reluctance to begin treatment.

In an assessment interview, we do not deliberately focus on the details of the individual transferences. Indeed, they may remain subordinate to the shared transference throughout a marital treatment, but more commonly they appear from time to time. This example serves, however, to illustrate another idea that is helpful in work with our reactions to focused transferences, namely Racker's concept of concordant and complementary transference.

Racker (1968), described countertransference as a fundamental condition of receiving the patient's projections and tolerating them inside him as projective identifications. His reception of the projections was unconscious, out of his awareness until he subjected his experience to process and review. In Racker's view, countertransference is a fundamental means of understanding the patient's internal world, a view that we share.

Racker went further to point out that the therapist might identify with parts either of the patient's self or objects. Identification with the patient's self he called *concordant identification*. Identification with the object was called *complementary identification*. As marital therapists, we can now think of our therapeutic task as the reception and clarification of the couple's projective identifications with parts of self or object, followed by analysis of the interpersonal conditions under which these occur.

> In the session with the Clarks, Mrs. Clark experienced me as a contemptuous and rejecting object like the object she projected into her husband, and evoked in me an unwelcome state of mind in which I felt contempt for her. My countertransference was one of complementary identification to her object. Dr. Clark experienced me as a denigrated object like the one he projected into his wife, and then switched to seeing me as a part of himself, the wise physician. To him, my countertransference was one of concordant identification with part of his self. I did not experience an identification with his denigrated object, perhaps because my identity as a physician protected me from it, but more likely because I was tuning into an internal process in which Dr. Clark used his ideal object to repress his rejected object, which he split and projected more readily into Mrs. Clark than into me at this stage of the assessment.

## INTERPRETATION OF DEFENSE AND ANXIETY ABOUT INTIMACY EARLY IN THE MIDPHASE

> Aaron and Phyllis Robinson, an apparently well-matched black couple, both business professionals, consulted me [J.S.S.] when they seemed close to divorce. They had had a fulfilling marriage for ten years—until Aaron's 16-year-old daughter, Susie, came to live with them. Phyllis had raised their shared family without much criticism from Aaron, and without challenge from their very young son and daughter. She felt supported by Aaron in her role as an efficient mother who ran a smooth household and was also successful as a stockbroker. She felt loved by him and by her

dependent children. Her self-esteem was good because she was a much better mother than her mother had been.

But when Susie came to stay, trouble began. Phyllis had firm ideas on what was appropriate for Susie and, in contrast, Aaron was extremely permissive. So Phyllis became the target for Susie's animosity. Aaron saw no need for limits and indeed saw no problem between Phyllis and Susie. Phyllis became increasingly angry at Aaron. He bore the situation stoically only occasionally confronting the problem. Then he would tell Phyllis that she was being small-minded and awful because she was acting out her jealousy and "making his kid miserable." She was angry at that attack on her self-esteem and never did recover from it.

They saw a family counselor who verified the 16-year-old's need for limits, supported Phyllis's views, and worked to get Aaron's cooperation. Aaron turned around and in a short time his daughter was behaving well and Phyllis could enjoy her. To this day, ten years later, Phyllis enjoys visits from her.

This seemed to have been a spectacular therapeutic success. I asked Aaron how he conceptualized the amazing turnabout. He said that once the therapist had made the situation clear, he simply told his daughter "You do what Phyllis says or you're out." But Phyllis's anger at Aaron's ignoring her pleas until then was still there. Although she continued to enjoy sex with Aaron, Phyllis walked out emotionally for several years, in an equal retribution for the years in which she felt Aaron had walked out on her. The family counselor had treated the family symptom and its effect on the couple with a useful prescription that removed the symptom. But she did it so rapidly that the underlying problem in the marriage was not recognized. The use of the focus upon a problem child as a defense against problems of intimacy had not been addressed, and so the issue came up again in their second treatment opportunity.

The force of Aaron's ultimatum, "Do what Phyllis says or you're out," suggested to me that he had lived by the same rule himself for the preceding ten years. Then, however, he began to challenge Phyllis's rule, by expressing his alternative way of coping with children—with predictable results. Now the same old problem they had had with Susie was surfacing with their shared older daughter who was now 15. Because no work had been done on their differences, they had not developed a shared method of childrearing. Now that Aaron was challenging Phyllis, they fought about the right way to do everything, but nowhere so painfully as over the care of their children.

Phyllis went on to give an example that, however, concerned not the problem daughter, but their 11-year-old son. He had asked at dinner, "If I wanted to go out with a girl on a date, would that be all right?" Phyllis had promptly told him that this was inappropriate because he was too young. Aaron had immediately interjected, "If you want to take a girl to the movies, that's fine, I'll drive you." Phyllis told me that she had felt undermined. Aaron said that he had spoken up because he felt she was being unhelpful to their son's social development. I said that I could see that either position could be defended, but that the problem was that they had not discussed things to arrive at a shared position that met their anxiety about their 11-year-old's burgeoning social independence.

Phyllis was furious at me for a whole day. She felt I had been unaccommodating and controlling. But to my surprise, and to her credit, she said that she had had to laugh when it struck her that it was not what *I* was doing but what *she* was bringing to the session.

"I was angry at what you said, but the words could have fallen out of my own mouth," she exclaimed.

I realized that Phyllis was seeing me in the transference as Aaron saw her, and I was speculating on the origin of this projective identification and admiring her insight.

Phyllis returned to her argument. "I don't feel every decision requires a conference as you seem to suggest, Dr. Scharff. I wouldn't think dating by an 11-year-old was a subject for discussion. It's the same as if a child had asked, 'Can I cut off my hand?' and I had said 'I'll ask your father.'"

*I had three responses. I felt put down for having not a clue about an 11-year-old's social development. I felt I was being small-minded getting into the fight with them about a child, when I knew they had come for help not with child-rearing but with their marriage. My third response was the thought that dating, meaning independence and intimacy, was equated with severe damage and loss. Perhaps Phyllis felt that she needed her son close to her and could not yet face being cut off from him. Perhaps Aaron, while wishing to facilitate their son's date, was offering to drive in order to stay close to him too, or possibly to stay close to the issue of intimacy vicariously. I also wondered if dating signaled sexuality causing loss, but that was probably not the case since sexuality was relatively free of conflict for them. So I concluded that the loss referred to sexuality being cut off from intimacy in the rest of the relationship.*

I said, "I'm not really talking about whether or not an 11-year-old should date. I'm taking you up on the effect of sticking to alternative positions and not talking about them together."

Here I was confronting their defense of using a child to portray their conflict about intimacy.

Aaron said, "I feel cramped in every part of my life. I can't say what I feel at all because Phyllis is so vulnerable."

Phyllis said, "I don't wanna live like this. We now argue about stuff we agree on. These patterns are vicious. They're killing us. We can't share a job because each of us is instructing the other on how to do it right. We even argue over how to load the grocery bags. I say put the chips on top, he says put the heavy stuff together. I say, 'Okay, do it your own way— and you'll have smashed chips!'"

I said to them, "Although you argue about what is the right way, you actually share an assumption that there is a right way and that if you don't do it right, things will get smashed."

Phyllis said, "I see the marriage as something that got cracked and can't be repaired. It's irretrievable. When things get sore, I leave. I'm trying to give up that idea now. But I had to leave once, to get away from my family. My mother was a dreadful, intrusive person and I was very unhappy. I got out by being perfect, an overachiever. I'm proud of rising above that background. Having struggled so hard not to be evil like her, I was very threatened when Aaron said I was small-minded and evil. I felt so wronged. Never compare me to her!"

*Now I understood my countertransference response of feeling small and no-good as reflecting a complementary identification with Phyllis's internal maternal object and at the same time a concordant identification with Phyllis's most repressed part of her self. Using the explanation that Phyllis had worked out I was now able to make an interpretation integrating her words and my countertransference.*

My interpretation illustrates the use of the "because clause" (Ezriel 1952). Ezriel noted that transference contained three aspects: (1) a required relationship that defended against (2) an avoided relationship, both of which were preferable to (3) a calamity. We have found it useful in couple therapy to follow his interpretive model since it brings the avoided relationship into focus as both anxiety and defense.

I said to Phyllis, "Now I can see that you retreated from Aaron because you wished to keep your relationship together as the harmonious marriage it used to be and occasionally still is when you have enjoyable sex. You were trying to protect yourself and him from your becoming as horrible as the angry, intrusive mother spoiling the relationship, or else facing the calamity of having to leave the marriage to leave that part of you behind."

Aaron had not yet told me enough about himself to let me complete the picture. It was clear that Phyllis was still using projection and overfunctioning within the marriage to keep herself above being horrible. And Aaron, feeling cramped like the children, was finding her control just as horrible. When he suppressed his angry or critical feelings, as he did most of the time except in irrational fights, he also suppressed his warm affectionate feelings except when he and Phyllis had sex.

In this example, the sexually exciting object relationship was the "required" relationship being used to repress the "avoided" rejecting object constellation. Aaron's conscious suppression felt withholding to Phyllis, who longed for feedback and emotional involvement. Aaron's eventual outbursts against her led her to relentless pursuit for his attention, approval, and affection. The emergence of the avoided relationship unleashed the energy of the exciting object constellation, because it was no longer needed for repression. When Phyllis failed to get what she hoped for from Aaron, she then suppressed her longings and withdrew. Now the rejecting object system was repressing the exciting one. But when this happened, she appeared to Aaron to be pouting, and he withdrew. The cycle continued—their needs for intimacy defended against and frustrated by their mutual projective identifications. I could see this pattern, but would have to wait for more object relations information from him to clarify his contribution. Incidentally, we cannot always achieve the same depth or specificity in interpretation, but the because clause is still useful as an intention in which we can ask the family to join as we move toward understanding.

## WORKING WITH FANTASY AND INNER OBJECT RELATIONS IN THE MIDPHASE

Instead of taking a genogram in evaluation and telling couples what their relationship to their family of origin is, we prefer to wait for a living history of inner objects to emerge through our attention to object relations' history at effectively charged moments in therapy.

> Dr. and Mrs. Clark had been working with me for a year. We had worked on his passivity, his inability to earn her admiration of him as a successful, ambitious, caring man, and his need to denigrate her by comparison to the nurses at the surgi-center. We worked on her tirades and her outrageous behavior that alienated him, his office staff, and his family, and that left her feeling contemptible. Their tenacious defensive system in which she was assigned the blame and was the repository for the rage, greed, ambition, and badness in the couple had not yet yielded to interpretation, although Mrs. Clark was no longer on such a short fuse. I could see improvement in the diminution in the volume and frequency of her reactions and in the degree of his contempt, but the basic pattern was still in place.
>
> They had been discussing their concern about their teenage children's sexual activity and after interpretation had realized that this concern was displaced from their anxiety about their own sexual relationship, which was now coming into focus.
>
> Dr. Clark timidly beat around the bush as usual and eventually got down to business:
>
> "Getting down to the nitty-gritty, here," he began, "about my sexual fantasies: I told my therapist about them and he kept trying to reassure me they were just fantasies, but when I talked about them, he'd sit there and squirm." He sighed, "My fantasies are like sadistic and murderous. I don't have them all day, only during sex," he added as if that was not so bad. To Rhonda he said, "We talked about this, you remember."
>
> "Uh-Uh," she said, shaking her head. "You never told me this."
>
> "Well," he continued. "The objects of the fantasies are specific women

who have left me on bad terms or real bitches. Once in a while I'll use someone I like."

"Like who?" demanded Rhonda. "Because you don't like any women I know and you don't like me much."

"You come up as the object," he responded.

I started to feel uncomfortable for Rhonda, but what Arthur said next was quite a relief.

"I'll switch away in the middle of a sadistic one and say, 'Wouldn't it be nice to use you as a loving object?'"

Mrs. Clark smiled. "Twenty years ago, before we got married, you used to do real sadistic, kinky things. Then our sex life got normal, like you shouldn't do wild things when you're married."

Dr. Clark asked what she meant and they had a teasing sharing of reminiscences about some refrigerator. I had no idea what they were talking about and felt excluded from something pleasurable and secret. It turned out they were remembering the thrill of chilling and squeezing her nipples in the refrigerator door.

"I don't call that sadistic," said Mrs. Clark. "When I think sadistic I think knives and guns. This was in control."

I remarked that this was a mild expression of Arthur's fantasy life that Rhonda had been happy to go along with.

"Oh, she enjoyed it more than I did," he averred, "Because (a) I was afraid of it, and (b) it wasn't nearly as much fun as my fantasies, not as good, not as sadistic, not as murderous."

"Maybe that's why we stopped," said Mrs. Clark thoughtfully.

I noticed that Dr. Clark was warming up to his revelation. His voice had lost its usual hesitancy and he seemed more assertive.

"Okay, so here's what starts the fantasy," he said. "I wish we had more petting and kissing, but our sex always goes the same way. Rhonda plays with my nipples. That gets me aroused. It's like turning on a switch. The fantasy starts. It feels kinda good. We have intercourse. That's the end of it and I roll over. So the fantasy last night was with a former resident, who left me to switch to a less demanding specialty. She's married and has a coupla kids now. To get sex to conduct the rape, I bring in her 6-year-old to threaten her with. Then I bring in the grandmother. That's good, I can extort her. What I do lately is I give them the choice of me doing oral sex or intercourse and they go for the oral sex because it's better than the mad rapist."

*I was feeling quite uncomfortable, even though I had heard fantasies of this sort before. I knew that it was important that the couple together had access to this. But I was concerned about how Mrs. Clark was taking it. I looked over at her. She was listening with interest, and did not seem upset.*

Dr. Clark resumed, "When I climax, I kill them off."

"How?" Rhonda wanted to know.

"Crazily. This is where my fear comes from. My fantasies are just like that quiet guy who chopped up people with an axe in New York." Turning to me, he said, "You would understand that fear."

Excluded and put down, Rhonda retorted, "You said she would understand as if I wouldn't."

"She's a psychiatrist. She's heard all this before. She'll know I don't have any urges to do this in real sex," he replied.

Rhonda had a good point to make: "How does she know you're not gonna act those out? How do I know? Do *you* know? Because you seem really scared."

I said, "There is no evidence that Arthur will act out the fantasies in their murderous form. But there is evidence that he's scared they'll get out of hand. We also have evidence that you do sadistic things to each other in this relationship, not physically any more, but emotionally. 'Put-downs' you call them."

"Like what just happened here," exclaimed Rhonda. "Sure she's trained but I can understand it, too."

"Not that I'm gonna go out and do it," he reminded her.

"Right," she rejoined. "It's how you're gonna feel it. Arthur, I feel so relieved that it's not just been me. All these years I've been taking the shit for fucking up the marriage. Do you know, I feel so relieved. Finally, after all these years he's taking responsibility. Finally."

"But I already told you about my sadistic fantasy," he said.

"You never did. I'm not saying you never talked about fantasies before, but you never went into your real self, never in this detail. You've always said I'm this, I'm that. It's always been me. Now I see in our marriage that your fantasies are totally in the way. Now rape I could maybe see as exciting, but why do you have to picture murders? That is scary. And to think you would ever hold our daughter over my head if I didn't have sex. That's scary for me."

I said, "To some extent the threatening part of the fantasy is arousing to both of you. But by the end of it, Arthur, you are terrified of losing control, and Rhonda, you are frightened for your life." They were nodding, thoughtfully. I went on, "We're not talking put-down, here. We're talking put *out*. These are compelling and forceful fantasies. I notice when you talk about them, Arthur, you talk forcefully. You're not beating around the bush now or slipping away from the point. Rhonda, you seem to respond to Arthur with more respect and compassion. I think you have both been hurting from this aggressive force leaking through in verbally abusive ways. Arthur, from the worry that it would erupt and wreak havoc, you've held yourself back from asserting yourself at home and at work."

Rhonda replied, "I never thought about the way he is affecting his work. But why doesn't he have patients knocking on the doors to get in? He's a first-rate hand surgeon. Arthur, you have to work on that. This has been a big interference to you and to us. This is like what you would call a breakthrough for us."

I felt inclined to agree with Rhonda's evaluation. The longer Arthur kept the fantasy to himself, the more it seemed to be the real him, terrified of being found out, hidden inside yet demanding to be heard. Furthermore, the way it got heard was through projection into Rhonda, who identified with it: in her rages and attacks on Arthur she gave expression to that attacking, chopping up part of him for which she had a valency. Meanwhile, he contained for her the greater calamity of the wish for death, a wish and fear that stemmed from early loss of an envied and hated older brother.

## WORKING THROUGH LATE IN THE MIDPHASE

Following the revelation, the Clarks had a session in which Rhonda talked of her continued sense of gratitude that her husband had shared his fantasies with her. Although she felt a bit scared and tentative about responding to him sexually, she felt close to him and committed to working things out. For the first time she felt an equal level of commitment from him. Summer was approaching and she was taking the children to visit her family in Maine for a month as usual. Until now, she had viewed her annual summer trip as a chance to get away from his criticizing her and demanding sex of her. This summer, for the first time, she felt sad that they would be apart.

The sharing of the fantasy had been a healing experience. The couple could now move beyond a level of functioning characteristic of the paranoid schizoid position toward the depressive, in which there is concern for the object whose loss can be appreciated.

After the vacation, the session was dominated by Dr. Clark's concern about whether I had talked about his fantasies with his former individual therapist during a planned collaborative discussion about the course of that treatment. After much hesitation, he revealed his fear that the two therapists would concur that he was nuts. Rhonda got angry on two counts: first that her husband couldn't get to the point as usual, and second, that he was obsessed with his therapist and me, instead of with what she wanted to talk about.

"You'd never guess what the real point is!" she exclaimed. "Arthur was ready to up and out again last week."

I interpreted Arthur's defense of creating a judging parental pair out of the two therapists as a substitute for his concern over his being a couple with Rhonda. This interpretation meant nothing to him. He added that he thought I might really have wanted to ask the other therapist if it was safe for me to work with him in my office since it was close to my house and I had children around. Now I understood his concern better. He was afraid that, because of my fear of his murderous fantasies, which must be about me and my children, I would stop treating him and he would lose the therapy opportunity.

I said that I thought Arthur was afraid of this, but even more afraid that Rhonda would leave him. He talked of me and the other therapist, not, as his wife suggested because he "didn't give a shit about her," but because he could not face the thought of her leaving.

"Everything you say is so compassionate to him," complained Rhonda, "compared to how I see it. He . . . ." Interrupting herself, she turned to Arthur. "But you wanna deal with this thing about your therapists."

"No," he said, "that's finished. Go ahead."

I concluded from his response that the defense had been interpreted successfully in the transference and we could go on with the couple's issues directly.

Rhonda continued with her view of things, describing thoughts and feelings she had had when on vacation. She had got so much from the last session, it kept her thinking and working for four weeks. She reviewed her attachment to her family of origin and realized that she was now rooted to her family here with Arthur and their teenage children. She felt able to experience a fuller range of "grown-up" feelings. When Arthur spoke to her on the telephone, he expressed no affection. He did not even say he missed her. She felt hurt by this but not outraged as before. She realized that in some way he just wasn't there. He now admitted that he knew what she was talking about. He had had other things on his mind. I suggested that he had been unaware of feeling angry that Rhonda had left him alone for a few weeks and had dealt with it by killing her off.

"I was kind of pissed off at her being in Maine, getting to lie around on the family boat," Arthur admitted.

"He just cut me dead," Rhonda confirmed.

I said, "Well there's the fantasy of killing operating again."

"Right" Rhonda replied. "Do you get it, Arthur? Do you know, the reason we got in the argument on vacation when he joined me was he appeared like 'Here I am, Rhonda! What are you gonna do about it?' He doesn't realize a woman wants to be talked to or she doesn't feel like having sex. He says the only time we have good sex is when we're mad and in an argument. It's not happening because we're in an argument, it's because in an argument you are being direct, honest, talking to me and listening to me. So then I feel close to you and then I can give myself 100 percent to you." Rhonda continued, confirming what I could see. "These last two weeks, I've been able to have grown-up feelings. Even though he belittles me, I don't live in a world of little feelings any more. Like he came home and said, 'Why isn't the air conditioning on? Don't you know it's ninety degrees out there?' And I didn't get all defensive or feel belittled and accused. I didn't take it personally. I just said, 'Well it was a lovely day here and I enjoyed the fresh air and the light breeze.' That's a big change for me."

Arthur's revelation of his murderous fantasies had released Rhonda's capacity for growth, confirming that the silent operation of the unconscious projective identification expressed in the fantasy had been cutting her down and killing off her adult capacities.

## WORKING THROUGH

As we peel away layers of repression, we experience more resistance. Sometimes it feels as though the farther we go the more we fall behind. The couple is suffering from a defensive system of object relationships that are mutually gratifying in an infantile way inside the marital system. Until more mature forms of gratification are found within the system, it is going to resist efforts at change. *Working through* is the term Freud (1914) gave to the therapeutic effort to keep working away at this resistance and conflict. Sessions in this phase can feel plodding, laborious, repetitive, and uninspired. Resolution comes piecemeal, until one day it looks as though the work is almost done.

## TERMINATION

The couple has had some rehearsal for termination in the form of the end of each time-limited session and facing breaks in treatment due to illness, business commitments, or vacations. We work with the couple's habitual way of dealing with separations in preparation for the final parting. Our criteria for judging when that will be are found in Table 6–2:

Table 6–2. Criteria for Termination

1. The couple has internalized the therapeutic space and now has a reasonably secure holding capacity.
2. Unconscious projective identifications have been recognized, owned, and taken back by each spouse.
3. The capacity to work together as life partners is restored.
4. Relating intimately and sexually is mutually gratifying.
5. The couple can envision its future development and provide a vital holding environment for its family.
6. The couple can differentiate among and meet the needs of each partner.
7. Alternatively, the couple recognizes the failure of the marital choice, understands the unconscious object relations incompatibility, and the partners separate with some grief work done and with a capacity to continue to mourn the loss of the marriage individually.

The goals that provide the criteria for terminating are really only markers of progress. The variations on termination are endless and some of them are reviewed in the final chapter of this book. Couples decide for themselves what their goals are. Sometimes they coincide with our idea of completion and sometimes not. We have to let ourselves become redundant and tolerate being discarded. As we mourn with the couple the loss of the therapy relationship, we rework all the earlier losses and reprise the earlier phases of the therapy.

Chapter 7

# THE EARLY PHASE OF THERAPY

Between the time of making a recommendation and beginning the treatment plan, there is a potential space during which the newly made commitment to treatment, and therefore to the marriage, turns up new evidence. It reminds us of the shift that often occurs at the point of commitment in relationships themselves: the repressed bad objects turn up for full consideration only after the contract is sealed.

There is work to be done in this space to help the couple settle in. Some couples pass through this phase with hardly a pause or trace of anxiety. The request for help is much what it seems, and if the therapist's recommendations fit, then they agree on a plan and promptly proceed to therapy. But this is not necessarily so. Other couples exhibit a sudden increase of anxiety immediately after accepting a recommendation for therapy, and the whole project is in danger of foundering. For these couples, between the recommendation and the plan there is a phase of testing commitment to the therapy and the therapist. It is useful, therefore, to consider this "time-between" phase of initial adjustment as having its own discrete task: working with the newly reemergent rejecting object relationships, as they now appear in the contextual transference, so as to facilitate the couple's settling in to therapeutic work.

There are, therefore, some generalizations that can be made about the things to be done in this beginning phase. This is not to say that all early phase work is alike, but only that there are certain kinds of early tasks that need doing. Sometimes these are addressed by the therapist consciously and conscientiously, but often they do not require a specific focus because things go well enough that the same ground is covered without a hitch.

The beginning phase tasks are outlined in Table 7–1.

The tasks listed in Table 7–1 overlap. They add up to a careful and empathetic examination of the couple's contextual transference to the therapist, and the therapist's reception and processing of that as felt in the countertransference.

Table 7–1.   Tasks of the Beginning Phase of Therapy

*The Tasks of Getting Going*

1. Dealing with resistance in the contextual transference.
    2. Confirming and modifying the agreed-on tasks.
    3. Accepting newly emerging repressed bad objects, those kept out of the interaction during the evaluation.
    4. Allowing the buildup of painful projective identifications in the transference.
    5. Building a treatment alliance based on contextual holding.
    6. Widening the field of the couple's observation.
    7. Testing defensive patterns and balances that have kept projective identifications in place in order to see how much flexibility the couple together and each partner can develop.
    8. Testing the couple's and each individual's capacities to work with links and interpretations. How much interpretation can the partners accept and work with about themselves, and how much about each other?
    9. Investigating the contribution of each partner to the shared difficulty toward understanding how the individual patterns interlock through mutual projective identification.
    10. Moving toward the explanation of underlying hurts that cause the need for defenses—the "Because Clause."
    11. Beginning to rework repetitive patterns.

# AN EXAMPLE OF DIFFICULTY IN EARLY TREATMENT

In the following example of a case of inhibited sexual desire, a couple came in with words of strong commitment from the wife to therapy for their marriage, which was threatened by the husband's long-standing lack of sexual interest. But after the recommendation was made, it was the wife who expressed her severe doubts and spoke for the first time of a resentment that immediately threatened to derail treatment.

Horst and Ingrid Braun came after eleven years of marriage, referred to me [D.E.S.] by another couple therapist because, after three months of work with him, the idea had emerged that their sexual blockade was at the center of their marital difficulty. The Brauns had little sex after their marriage, but had even less after Horst had a few episodes of erectile failure. Ingrid experienced his withdrawal as his lack of interest without any awareness of his anxiety about his erections.

This was an extremely attractive couple. Both had been professionally successful with active social lives at the time they had met. Horst had been a lively bachelor with no thoughts of marriage—and with perhaps some aversion to being tied down—when, in his mid-twenties he met Ingrid. She had had a brief previous marriage in her native Sweden, to a man who she decided was just wrong for her—a man who seemed to have no integrity or ambition, but who had offered her a vigorous sexual life. She had divorced him within a year of their marriage, with tears at the time, but with no subsequent regrets. She had then come to the United States, at first as an au pair, and later had gone to law school.

Sex had been good for Horst and Ingrid, too, during the two years of their dating and living together. It had tailed off after they had been married about two years. At first Horst had trouble keeping an erection, and got anxious. But later, Ingrid felt, he simply lost interest in her. He did not find her body attractive, although he was not repelled by it. And yet, he said, he loved her. His physical feeling for her had just disappeared. He did not know why or how.

It was all the more painful from Ingrid's point of view because they had been able to have three children despite the sexual difficulty. Horst had no trouble performing on demand in order to have children. Ingrid promptly got pregnant each time, and they now had children who were 8, 6, and 3. Horst was a good father, even though he worked so hard that he had little family time. Nevertheless, the children adored him. The pregnancies and her absorption with the children had occupied Ingrid, so that she was less aware of feeling unloved. Coming for therapy had reawakened the hurt, which she was loathe to feel. Several years ago, she had passed through a period of feeling the hurt acutely. Having buried it, she did not know if she could stand having it reawakened.

During the evaluation, I met with them first together, then each separately, and then finally again together. Neither had had affairs. Although Ingrid wished she might in order to feel loved, she was committed to seeing if this marriage would work. Both of them said they were extremely open with each other and had nothing to say privately that they had not said to each other.

## Dealing with Resistance in the Evaluation

Nevertheless, Horst spoke differently in his individual interview. It was only there that he could give the details of the ways he found Ingrid controlling. She knew when she was right, and she held onto her position. I felt Horst's resistance to speaking of his resentment. With encouragement he slowly admitted he was just a bit resentful. He never felt that way at work, where, as a computer consultant, he could do as he pleased without having to take orders. His own father had been an immigrant from Germany, a blustering and arbitrary man at home, although respected in his field. But Horst had smarted under his father's erratic, Germanic authority, and determined never to be treated that way again. He said he did not hold Ingrid responsible for being demanding. In the main, unlike his father, she was entirely reasonable and he felt awful for giving her a hard time. She was beautiful and responsive, a lovely person, and she deserved better than he gave her. Occasionally she could be demanding, but it wasn't anything important. Of course, he would defer and demur. She was right that he often said he would do things later. Then she would be The Little Red Hen, saying "All right, then! I'll do it myself!" And so she would!

*Countertransferentially, this couple presented as a puzzle initially. Horst's loss of interest was shrouded in vagueness, in his bland assertion that Ingrid was a completely satisfactory mate, justified even in her complaints about him. It was in my frustration at the opacity of the picture he presented that I began to have a sense of what she was up against. The picture he presented was too good to be true. I felt that he must think she was more difficult than he said, but I would have to needle him to get at what he really thought. And so my frustration with him was the first clue in the countertransference of his resistance, of his refusal to encounter me. I felt considerable sympathy for Ingrid's complaint that she could not find the real him, and I formed a sense of a passive dodginess in his personality. My experience left me sympathetic to her irritation and anger, and, feeling this, I felt myself swayed to Ingrid's side. This clue that I was drawn from a neutral position led me to the tentative conclusion that they jointly needed to present Ingrid as the wronged victim, to put the bad object into Horst despite the superficial picture of his bland cooperation and her desperate anger. I also worried that his reticence to express his own anger at Ingrid represented a shared resistance I might soon en-*

*counter from them jointly, and I prepared for the possibility they might join forces in the contextual transference to wall me out.*

## Confirming—Then Modifying—the Agreed-on Tasks

Immediately after the initial evaluation, the couple agreed to my recommendation for sex therapy. I thought that on balance there was a shared commitment to the marriage. From my feeling of being excluded from the emotional tone of their difficulty by their shared tendency to suppress emotion, I guessed that Horst's withdrawal was an obstinate refusal to knuckle under to Ingrid, whom he saw as demanding. I did not think the erectile failure ten years ago had only resulted in a lingering residue of performance anxiety, but rather that the original trigger for the anxious withdrawal embodied in his loss of sexual interest was his perception of Ingrid as a controlling object. When he withdrew, she in turn had become increasingly anxious, and feeling bereft by his withdrawal, had increased her assault, trying desperately to get a response. But my formulation was even more speculative than usual, because neither of them could locate the events that might have produced this pattern. There had been no drama or trauma that they could identify during the evaluation.

Having agreed, we set up a schedule to start a couple of weeks hence. Horst immediately began to lobby me to offer a more flexible schedule. I usually set up a mutually agreeable schedule of twice weekly meetings, and ask the couple to make those regularly. I will reschedule meetings if possible at their request, but I cannot guarantee that I will be able to do so—and I do charge for missed appointments. Horst argued that his computer consulting work was at others' beck and call. He had to travel to work, and he could not count on being available. It was unreasonable, he said, to charge him if he was forced to miss sessions by business obligations beyond his control. I said to him that the times we had arranged were the only times I had available to see them. While I could recognize such difficulties as practicalities, I thought they also served as a hedge on his commitment. If he were able to take up this issue of possible underlying reluctance, he might well find he was able to make almost all of the hours. Certainly, I said, I would rather see him than have to bill him for missed appointments, and that I had found that with this arrangement, couples missed very few hours.

*As soon as the couple agreed to treatment, Horst escalated his resistance. Now I felt the task we had agreed on was under assault. I felt pushed into Ingrid's position, having to justify my policies, fees, and schedule. It helped to know I could survive without them. Such attacks, designed to produce guilt and doubt in the therapist, will get more quickly into the less experienced therapist than the hardened veteran. But they must be understood fundamentally as an attack on the task rather than as personal. Nevertheless, I felt attacked. Twinges of doubt and guilt (over fees, perhaps my own rigidity, my greed) made me momentarily vulnerable. In this mild barrage, I failed for a time to notice how Ingrid quietly avoided confronting Horst herself, leaving me to experience the anger and to fight her battle. In retrospect, I could notice that he partly waged a war of resistance on her behalf, and that partly she left me to take him on because she felt inadequate to the job. The battle formation between them was already being enacted in the therapy and in the countertransference. I had subtly moved rather close to Ingrid's position of angry resistance. Again, in retrospect, I could note the projective identification they put into me. By attacking the famework of our agreement, they were enacting the assumption that their contextual holding could not contain their shared fear of damaging each other in their obsessionally balanced relationship.*

## THE FIRST TREATMENT SESSION

The couple cancelled the first treatment session. Ingrid had a biopsy for a breast lump, and since the surgeon was going out of town for vacation, it had to be scheduled on the day we had arranged. I accepted that cancellation, done several days ahead, without comment and actually without an intention to charge them, and confirmed our second appointment.

On the day arranged for the next session, they arrived late, having called me from their car. I was seeing them in my other office, and they had gotten lost on the way. Half the session was gone. Ingrid said that she had almost not come anyway. But she had come to tell me that she wanted Horst and me to work without her. She was appalled by the idea of what the couple would have to do in the sex therapy I had recommended.

### Allowing the Return of the Repressed Bad Objects

Ingrid said, "I'm not going to be anybody's CPR [cardiopulmonary resuscitation] doll in those exercises. I won't be used by someone who doesn't care for my body." In a questionnaire I had given the couple, Horst had said he felt "neutral" about her body—that he found it neither appealing nor repugnant. "I know it's true," she said, "but I'm so hurt by it I can hardly stand it. It's not new. I've felt hurt like this before. But I got over it. And I'm not going to have this pain opened up again. So I want Horst to come to see you alone, Dr. Scharff, to work it out. Then maybe I'll come back if you need me."

*I was struck by her anger and her pain. But most of all I felt her controlling-ness, telling me what to do and deciding unilaterally that Horst and I should be paired to do what she had decided. I knew that I didn't want to do it, and I had a vague notion of why it was not a good idea. But mainly I felt violated and mistreated by Ingrid.*

Meanwhile, Horst sat in quiet compliance. He said, "I'll do whatever needs to be done. I care deeply for Ingrid and I'll do anything." Beyond that, he had little to say.

## ACCEPTING PAINFUL PROJECTIVE IDENTIFICATIONS IN THE TRANSFERENCE AND COUNTERTRANSFERENCE

*I now moved from feeling controlled by Ingrid to imagining that being consigned to sit in a room alone with Horst would be a fate worse than death. I imagined my inability to get him to talk, just as one frequently experiences with balky adolescents. I did not want to do it. I did not take my own response as a factual matter, simply meaning that I would refuse to do what Ingrid wanted. She could have been right, or she might not have been. Rather, I took my experience as a set of clues about their marital interaction at an unconscious level. I felt I knew almost immediately what Horst had been trying to tell me about the way he got his back up when Ingrid became controlling. I could feel my own spine stiffen: I wasn't going to be told what to do. I could immediately empathize with what I imagined was his not wanting to make love to her when she took over. On the other hand, as I sat with my own feeling, I came to a slower understanding of Ingrid's position. Horst asked her, over and over again, to accept him as he was—to surrender to his conditions. She felt repeatedly humiliated and used. Trying to accommodate him over the years, she had suppressed her resentment until it finally boiled over. Having moved to her side of the impasse, I could see the way she became more controlling as she felt more exposed to humiliation.*

*I now felt I had begun to take in the shared difficulty in holding and the impasse they had constructed together. Once Ingrid began to harbor more resentment than she could contain, Horst would withdraw, fearing that she was on the verge of erupting. Sensing his increasing distance, she would try harder to suppress the anger, but she would also be nearer to venting it. Since the couple shared the assumption that the therapy would recreate their bind, the solution she proposed on their behalf was to dissolve the couple situation and offer Horst to me individually.*

## BUILDING A TREATMENT ALLIANCE THROUGH WORK ON CONTEXTUAL HOLDING

After some time of working with my countertransference, I took the first step in trying to rebuild an alliance with the couple. I said to Ingrid, "Excusing yourself won't give your marriage its best chance. You have a lot to say, and the resentment you're now expressing in a new way—at least as far as I know—is part of the information I need to work with you and for you. I agree that Horst has trouble talking. And his own motivation about being here is still in question. He says he wants to be here, but I feel he borrows a lot of that feeling from you. It might eventually be a good idea for him to work individually in therapy, but I'm not convinced it's the way to start. However," I said, "We certainly shouldn't start with sex therapy. It can't be done 'over your dead body.' But we need you here to get started. Without you, the chances of therapy working are much less."

They left, having agreed to come back together at least for the next time. We had already significantly modified our plan, shifting, by agreement, to a marital therapy format to consider the issues that would have to come before any sex therapy.

### Discussion

Many couples come with reluctance and shared resistance, but the evaluating process had not settled the shared reluctance in this couple. Partly this was so because Ingrid had defensively disowned her reluctance—that is, had repressed it in herself and put it into Horst. Like all parts of ourselves treated this way, it could not be dealt with or modified when it was denied in herself while lodged in him. For Horst, denial served his need to split off his defense against being controlled by his objects. He denied the need to control others, and put that need into Ingrid, who became more angrily controlling and demanding. The result was that my experience of them was rapidly evolving, shifting so that I now became the victim of her controlling rage, feeling that, like Horst, I was being asked to perform under her conditions.

Using the knowledge that any sudden demand to break the frame is a problem, and my own frequent experience that feeling countertransferentially controlled by women is an expression of their fear of being controlled and exploited, I was able to hold fast with Horst and Ingrid, to resist an assault on the framework of the therapy, and to appeal to their shared situation.

## THE SECOND SESSION

They were on time for the second session.

*I wasn't much looking forward to seeing them, wondering what kind of confrontation was coming. I was aware, as I sat down, that I was unsure on a point of history I had obtained. Did Horst's erectile difficulty begin with some failures and his subsequent humiliated withdrawal—or not? Were there any precipitating causes for his sexual withdrawal or had the story been that his interest in sex and in her body had just faded? This was an important question, because a withdrawal from a humiliating failure would be more directed at avoiding shame in front of the partner, I reasoned, while an unexplained loss of interest would represent more fear of the partner herself and be prognostically less promising.*

*Actually, I knew that the two are usually interrelated and are rather inseparable, but I was here wrestling with the question of whether there was much hope for my work with this couple, and in so doing, I was highly identified with Horst and against Ingrid and her angry outburst of the last session. Under the influence of this countertransferential moment, I forgot some of the information of the evaluation, and was thrown into confusion. The question outside my awareness was around my withdrawal from them after Ingrid's outburst. In the countertransference, I was identified with Horst, losing my interest and hope for them, losing my therapeutic "potency" in my confusion. As I realized this during the session, I knew that I had absorbed some of their despair through introjective identification. And from this new perspective, I felt more hopeful for the therapy, that is, I could provide firmer contextual holding and was in a position to return their shared projective identifications in modified form.*

## Widening the Field of the Couple's Observations within the Envelope of Therapeutic Holding

Ingrid was calmer today. I asked them their condition after last session. It wasn't great. Ingrid said she just had to tell me she was resentful. As she whisked her long blond hair over her shoulder, her Swedish face was clouded by a long-nursed anger that distorted her beauty. She began with a tirade.

"You have to understand, Doctor, that Horst has been dreadful to me for a long time. I put up with it. I think that really, if this therapy doesn't work, we probably face the break-up of our marriage. Whereas if we hadn't done anything, I could just have kept going without having felt this pain again.

"For a long time, I was patient and tried to be a good wife. But nothing I did made any difference. He wouldn't have gone without tennis or football for this long! Why would he go this long without sex? Only once or twice a year. And then only when I set it up! We even went on a relaxed vacation last year. He had the gall to offer to make love on the beach, where it was impossible. But when we were back in the bedroom, he lost interest. And he doesn't talk! The man just doesn't talk! You don't know what that's like for me, to feel spurned and to not even know what I've done."

## Testing Defensive Patterns and Balances

*This time I felt more immediate sympathy for Ingrid. With more time and less pressure, with her having dropped her demand, as far as I could tell, that I adopt Horst and the problem, I felt I could listen to her sympathetically. So I turned to Horst and asked for his thoughts, his version of the difficulty.*

Horst said, "It's all true. I don't know why, but I haven't been able to mount any interest in sex."

Ingrid jumped in. "It doesn't bother him. He wouldn't do this kind of thing—ignoring me—to anyone else. He just doesn't care."

I saw Horst grimace, and hoping for an effective response on his part, I gestured to him for his input.

"It's not true," he said. "I do care. I care deeply. I'm not as emotional as Ingrid, and I'm not going to get that way. But I do care. This hurts me, and I'll do anything I can to not hurt her in the process."

*Momentarily, I thought I was beginning to get a sense of Horst trying to care from underneath something that blocked him, and that this was in the territory I wanted. But in the next few minutes Ingrid buried him, and me, again.*

"He doesn't care," she insisted. "And he never talks."

## Initial Testing of the Couple's Capacity to Work with Links and Interpretations

Attempting a first interpretation of their defensive pattern, I now said, "I'd guess that Horst's withdrawal is to defend himself. If so, we have to know what he's defending himself from. I have a feeling it's as though he's holed up at the bottom of a dark, deep pool. Any pebbles he thinks you throw at him are reason enough to stay down there, far away from the surface where he can't be seen. The trouble is, he's so far away emotionally that no one can tell the specific effect of what's thrown in at him. He's so far away, we just can't tell."

"Oh yeah!" he said. "I'm defended. I'm tight as a clam. I retreat and hole up, but she doesn't do anything really that justifies my acting like that."

"Ingrid must do something," I said. "There must be something she does which you react to, justified or not."

"Well, yes," he said. "She criticizes me and tells me what to do."

Ingrid cut him off. "I do not!" she said sharply.

"Ingrid," I said, "I think you just cut Horst off when he's finally starting to talk. I can understand that you don't like what he has to say, but we may learn what he's reacting to if we can listen."

"No, I don't cut him off," she protested. "I'm just right about this one thing. I really don't criticize him, and I won't stand for him saying so. And he doesn't talk!"

Horst sat in smiling withdrawal.

*I saw that if I pressed this point, I would lose Ingrid, who was now braced in a rigid self-righteousness. I had overestimated the amount of his criticism she could take, and she had turned on Horst and on me for exposing her to the criticism she could not stand from him. I was struck with her inability to listen to him, and felt we were close to the limits of her tolerance. I was also impressed how his insistence that she did nothing wrong was an accommodation to her intolerance for disagreement.*

"So you now get angry at him when he says these things?" I asked.

"Sure I do," Ingrid said. "I'm angry and every once in a while I let loose at him. But this all started years ago, before that was true. I didn't get angry until he had been like this for a long time. For years I was able to ignore it."

*I began to sense that her testiness arose from the idea that any of his behavior could be laid at her feet. I felt she would be wary if I made statements that in any way implied that she had a hand in his resentment. I took the warning that I had better retreat a bit.*

"I didn't say you had caused his withdrawal, or that it's your fault," I said. "All I asked was what you did that he now withdraws from."

*I could see that she wasn't buying it. And what I had said wasn't entirely true. I was beginning not to like Ingrid. It was the kind of dislike that is the result of a received projective identification, because it was occurring in a setting in which, basically, I felt extremely sympathetic to her being locked in a marriage with a silent, wordless husband who took her for granted and withdrew from her—another projective identification, to be sure.*

## THE RESISTANCE CRYSTALLIZES

Now, as I persisted in my line of reasoning, I ran into the first real roadblock in the hour. In a way, I had seen it coming, and it made sense of the previous hour, in which Ingrid had refused to go on.

I said, "I was trying to get to hear what Horst was reacting to: he must find something you did difficult or even offensive. We know that has to be true, but we need the details to begin to understand it.

"I want him to talk," she said. "He doesn't talk. Never! So I want to hear it. And I don't cut him off. I want him to talk. I'm sorry, but I don't do anything to him to make him withdraw."

"Don't you ever tell him he's wrong?" I asked.

"No. Well—about some little things—but basically I spend a lot of my time biting my tongue."

Horst was grimacing again.

"Well?" I asked him. "Does she tell you what to think?"

"Oh, she's opinionated," he said. "She knows what she thinks. But it's fine. I mean, it's not important. I can just put up with that. She's such a good person."

Horst was smiling at me, trying to persuade me, telling me contradictory things and resisting my saying things about her which would have justified his feeling bossed around and withdrawing. And he wasn't having any of my attempts to draw him out!

*I knew now that I was both in trouble and in working territory. But I felt that I had taken on Ingrid too directly and that that could backfire quickly. I had an image of her ire from the previous session. I felt we were right at the limits of her rationality.*

Ingrid kept defending herself. "For instance," she said, "there's the situation in which I ask Horst to do things and he says, 'Not now. I'll do it in twenty minutes.' So if it's important to get it done right then, I have to do it myself."

"That does happen," Horst acknowledged. "Not if it's to drive the children someplace. I do things like that right away. But it happens fairly often. But I don't stall on important things."

*How accommodating he was being here in the hour, I thought. He seemed entirely reasonable—well, almost entirely.*

Ingrid said, "Well, it's like the feeding the children. I'll ask him to help, and he'll say 'I'll do it in twenty minutes.' But the 3-year-old won't wait. So I do it."

## Investigating the Contribution of Each Partner

"I have to face it," Horst finally admitted. "Anything she wants me to do, I don't want to do. And it's to bug her in little ways. It comes from resisting my parents. I took the opposite position with them, and I do it with her. It's not her fault. I would do it with anyone."

*I felt relief. Horst's admission let Ingrid off the hook.*

Ingrid nodded. She was being vindicated. She said, "It didn't start with my resentment. That only came after his withdrawal and after almost ten years without sex. First he stopped being interested in me. I tried to live with it. I thought, 'Maybe this is just what I have to live with. He's a nice guy. Many women have it worse than I do. So I sat on it. But later I got angry in frustration. Sure! *Now* I can see that he withdraws from my anger. But I didn't start it. He did!"

*I felt quite clear that Ingrid needed for me to understand all this. If I couldn't, she would feel accused. Her plea was more than putting the record straight. It was a plea to be understood so that she could keep a shred of her dignity. I felt I was getting closer to being able to say things she could hear, working my way slowly back upstream from the distance I had lost in getting on her wrong side.*

I said, "I can understand what you're saying, Ingrid. You feel that the anger you have now came after feeling assaulted and ignored for years. I hear that, and we will try to understand how all this got started eventually. But for now, we have to start with where things are at this point—with Horst's withdrawal from you, and with the anger that has become a pattern."

"Yes," she agreed. "I can see that now he withdraws because I'm going to get mad. But I can't help it."

## Moving toward the Explanation and Understanding of Hurt—The "Because Clause"

*I had by now settled into a more comfortable vein, having finally realized I had to back off from Ingrid and stop trying to prove that she was a know-it-all who any reasonable man would resist. That let me fashion a more evenhanded statement.*

I continued, "I think your anger now is often an attempt to reach out to Horst. It comes from frustration at being ignored and not noticed. But he feels attacked and retreats further into that clamshell of his. (Here I was using his language.) So the two of you have worked it out so that Ingrid is good, right, and reasonable, and Horst is the bad, rebellious boy who resists through his passivity."

Horst nodded. "Oh, I'm passive all right. And it's to get my anger across to her." And now his grin had turned impish, let out from the closet.

I said, "The two of you find the familiar comfort of being able to come back to the understanding that Ingrid is good and is the victim, and Horst is bad and causes the damage."

They both nodded.


## A MORE THOROUGH ATTEMPT AT LINKING BY THE THERAPIST


"I don't do things to hurt him, though," Ingrid said. "Or at least I only get mad at him when he's done something to make me angry."

*We were back in the territory of Ingrid's defense, and I felt again just how forceful the shared projective identifications were.*

I said, "That goes along with the idea that you have to be the good one, or else the two of you together would feel this loss of that goodness. If Ingrid becomes the bad one, there is no goodness anywhere, because you also agree it's not in Horst. The problem with that way of keeping something good in your marriage is that it's at the expense of Horst's having to feel bad about himself. It makes me think of what's holed up inside that shell of his."

*I had a fantasy of Horst as a pearl inside an oyster, protected by coats of mother-of-pearl but likely to be forcibly extracted. Then I thought of the pearl as being like a drop of semen that precedes a full ejaculation. Of course Ingrid wanted him, his seed, and his sexuality, but her attempt to get the pearl made her an aggressive figure and turned him from an oyster that made pearls into a clam that held nothing but itself.*

I continued, "Ingrid, you see a pearl in his shell. And you have to batter him to get some of that treasure for yourself, because without it you feel that the real and loving Horst is missing. And that pearl is the place he keeps what little self-esteem he can gather, because the agreement between the two of you is that he's bad. So, since he has to have something good, he has to keep it encased in the hidden sexual feeling. Then you go after the pearl because you can't feel good either unless he can share it with you. But when you do, he feels under attack, like you'll take it away from him. He defends it more. So you feel rejected all over again, and the cycle continues. There has to be a way out of the cycle, but this is the cycle we see continuing."

## THE COUPLE ELABORATES ON THEIR DEFENSIVE PATTERN

Ingrid and Horst nodded, and were silent for a moment. Then Ingrid said, "I'll tell you the real thing we used to argue about: his driving! He is a horrible driver. His mother sits in the back seat. She won't ride up front with him. I used to yell at him, nag him. Two months ago, he agreed to stop tailgating and pushing the speed limit, jerking around, refusing to slow before corners, and it's been entirely different."

Horst was gesturing, turning up his palms to prove his innocence.

I said, "Apparently you disagree?"

Horst said, "I don't agree that I've been driving any differently. But she has relaxed and I'm grateful."

"Oh, my God!" said Ingrid. "We had a talk and you agreed. And since then, it has been different."

"When did this start?" I asked.

"He's always driven like this," said Ingrid. "When we were dating, there was one fight I got out of the car and threatened to walk home. But that was the only one."

Horst said, "I don't think it was as bad then."

"It couldn't have been," I said. "You each had to hide some of your resentment, and love and idealize each other in order to get married. Everyone does. Otherwise no one could get married."

*I was feeling a bit manic, throwing in everything I could get at them.*

Horst was nodding. I continued, "Once you got married, then you were trapped with each other. From your side of it, Ingrid, you were stuck with his bad driving. And you, Horst, were stuck with her telling you how to drive. It's then the resentment started to surface."

"Mainly, this is just not important stuff," said Horst. "I can put up with this. There are larger issues here."

"No. This is the stuff of life, of your life together," I said. "It's the little things—who fixes lunch for the kids, how your rides in the car go together, that are the 'vehicles'—so to speak—for your relationship." (Now Ingrid is nodding and Horst is looking dubious.) "So this is the place to hammer it out. I want to hear more about the car and the fights, and the little things at home. And I think now I'm beginning to get an idea of the fights which leave you each feeling battered and misunderstood, even though you each think they are too trivial to matter. They do matter and they matter deeply. I expect through exploring these to understand the larger issues such as the assigning of goodness to Ingrid and badness to Horst."

It was time to go, and as I confirmed the appointment time for the end of the week, Horst said that he could not make it. A new client was pressing to have him at his office in Des Moines. I offered one substitute time, but he could not take it. He pressured me to try to fill the hour so that he would not have to pay for it.

*I felt the kind of pressure I had felt with this argument during the evaluation, and I now felt like something was hanging over my head. I said I would try to fill the hour, which is not my policy. After all, Horst had said my fee was worth it to him, this was the most important thing in his life. He had said he would be facing divorce if this did not work. And I knew that was part of the pain that Ingrid had spoken of early in the hour: if this did not work, they faced the breakup of the marriage. And yet, even in the face of this, he pressured me to accommodate to them, facing my resentment in doing so.*

I accommodated to Horst's request verbally.

*After I left the hour, I realized I had been subjected to an unconscious manipulation, which had got a grudging agreement out of me that carried with it my certain resentment. I felt the bind of the situation as I imagined the alternatives of filling the hour and not charging them, ignoring what I had said to them, or even the fantasy of acting dishonestly. Slowly I realized that they had gotten inside me once again, having insinuated themselves around the frame and my standard way of working, pushing to bend me. Of course, I resented it. But I realized that this experience had to be like what happened inside their partnership. Ingrid was experiencing this all the time, and being forced to bind her resentment, becoming more controlling in response. And Horst, feeling her need to control him, resisted whatever frame she offered. I surmised that life inside this partnership was not easy.*

I could tell by now that we had not yet fully turned the corner. I was upset at feeling manipulated. As really effective assaults always do, this one came at a vulnerable point on the frame of treatment. It stirred my lingering doubts about the justice in charging for missed appointments. I maintain a "working ambivalence" about this. It is an internal openness that lets me work best. I have a halftime practice and do not want to be trying to fill cancellations with the resentment that it carries. But I also sympathize with the couple that feels hard pressed. So I try to rework my own ambivalence with each challenge in the light of the specific transference of each patient or couple. Here I considered that they had been eager to work with me knowing my policy of charging for missed sessions that could not be rescheduled. I felt they were joining to batter the frame—and my commitment to it— as they each felt the frame of their marriage was battered by the other.

## THE THIRD SESSION: THE SPIRAL CONTINUES OF BUILDING PROJECTIVE IDENTIFICATIONS CALLING FOR RENEWAL OF HOLDING AND UNDERSTANDING

We still had a schedule of twice weekly sessions held over from the idea that we would conduct sex therapy. I felt, however, that the schedule was still a good one in this crisis, and perhaps for long-term work. I had thought of a discussion I recently had with Jack Graller on his use of twice weekly couple therapy as a way of intensifying the work and increasing the impact of the transference. However, as arranged at the end of the previous session, we had not met for the second session of the previous week, so this session occurred a week after the previous one.

### Working on Resistance Again

Ingrid began. "I just have to ask—I mean maybe you can't say—but I'm worried about the money. How long do you think this therapy might go on? Can you give me some guideline?"

I said, "You're wondering here at the beginning how this might go. I wonder if it's just the money, or are there other questions about whether this will help?"

She answered, "We're using our savings, and we've been doing this for eight months with other therapists, including the one who referred us to you for evaluation about the sexual things." She was crying and wiping her eyes as she spoke. "What we're doing here is important to me, but we're doing it out of savings now. And I'll have to do without domestic help as one way of paying for it. We don't have any insurance."

I said, "I would tell you if I could. If it were a format involving formal sex therapy, I'd say three to eight months or perhaps a bit longer. There might be other work afterwards, but that would be the approximate length of the sex therapy. But there's no defined limit on marital therapy. In a sense, if it goes well, it might go on much longer than if it doesn't."

Ingrid said, "So it's my fault. If I would just get on with the sex therapy, we could get it over with. Am I the holdup?"

I said, "I didn't say that. You can only proceed from where you're at. You can't 'submit' to the sex therapy the way you feel. There's work to be done first. But that being the case, I just can't tell you how long it will last. I may have a better sense later, and I'll be glad to monitor it with you. How do you feel about it, Horst?"

Horst said, "We are short of money, but this is the most important thing. I think we just have to do it. So I don't worry about the money. But then again, I never do worry."

"That's true," said Ingrid. "He doesn't worry. He leaves the worrying to me. He has no idea about the money."

I said, "You'll get an idea as you go whether this is being useful. It's not that you have to sign on indefinitely without any sense of how it's going. But I can say to you that it's useful to suspend judgment for a couple of months here at the beginning while we try to get an understanding of the issues here. Then we can more actively assess how the work is going and where it's leading as we go."

## The Couple Brings a Typical Disagreement into the Therapy

There was now a silence. As with many couples, the lack of observable structure initially left them floundering a bit. They did not know where to turn next. I let the silence go for a few moments, then decided to offer them a bit of a handle. I asked what was going on between them, and how they had felt after last week's session.

Ingrid said, "Nothing is going on. I mean it's no different. We left here and it's as though nothing had happened. We go on like good roommates."

Horst said, "One thing which is different this week is that I have been closer physically to Ingrid. I've been trying to be closer to her, to touch her."

"When?!" demanded Ingrid. "Tell me 'when?' You haven't been any different than you ever are."

"Well, I've been trying. I tried this week," said Horst.

"Give me one example. You were out three nights this week. We saw you between reading the sports section in the morning and bowling another evening."

"Well, I was trying," Horst said again. "But if you didn't feel it, then I didn't. I mean if you didn't think so, then it didn't happen and I'm wrong."

*Initially, I felt identified with Horst, then with Ingrid, feeling he was unavailable. I couldn't tell if Horst had tried something more, which I would have seen if I were there, or not. And I couldn't tell whether I would have identified with Ingrid in feeling his absence if I were there. It felt like two entirely different stories were unfolding. However, I was also struck with Horst's backing off in a way that I assumed meant that he would now suppress his resentment.*

I said, "This is not a way to leave it. If you say that, I won't know how you're going to manage resentment you most certainly have. Let's see if we can pursue this difference."

"Tell me one time you touched me," said Ingrid, "Just one time."

"Okay," said Horst. "Yesterday! Yesterday I sat on the couch with you."

"We just watched television yesterday," she said. "That wasn't anything. Well, yes, you sat on the same couch with me but you didn't touch me. I'm sorry. Maybe I should be grateful that you sat there instead of where you usually sit, in your own chair, leaving me alone."

"Well, see?" he said to me. "She didn't feel it, so that's it. It didn't happen. I thought I did, but I guess I didn't."

I said, "This seems to be a vulnerable area, the question of closeness. All I can tell so far is that both of you seem wary about it."

"No," said Ingrid. "I want him to be closer. I long for it! I would like it so much. But he didn't do anything. If he would just do anything! But it needs to be spontaneous, too. I don't want him to do something just because I tell him. I don't even mind if it's awkward. He's not very good at it, but I don't mind that."

*I felt we were back in the territory of Ingrid's unreasonable demands. She wanted a gesture from him, but it had to be just the right gesture or it didn't count.*

Ingrid continued, "I asked him to send me flowers. He used to send me flowers. I had fresh flowers nearly every day when he first met me, for two years. Now he can never remember to give me flowers. I dropped hints. I said, 'I would love it if you would send me flowers once in a while.' All he had to do was stop by the grocery store on the way home. It's right on his way. And he didn't. I haven't had flowers in years."

Horst said, "I did send flowers twice in the last three months."

"Tell me about it!" she said.

"I sent them from the florist for your birthday," he said.

"But that's it: you sent them from the florist. I don't want that. That's expensive! I told you what I want. I want you to stop by the store on your way home and get me a few cut flowers. You did it nearly every day for two years. That was incredible. And now you can't ever spare the time."

"That's not it," he objected. "I can do it that way if you want. But when we first went out, we were poor and I bought you flowers on the sidewalk. What I can get from the florist are much prettier. I like it that I can get you something nicer now."

"Anyhow, you only got me flowers because you were getting something for your secretary." Turning to me she explained, "She had done something nice for us and I told Horst he should get her some flowers. So while he's at the florist anyway, he gets some for me too."

"That's not it," he protested. "I got my secretary some from the grocery store, and I thought those weren't nice enough for you, so I called the florist."

"I like the ones from the grocery better," Ingrid retorted. "And I don't want you to spend so much on me. You see, Dr. Scharff, that's it. He doesn't do what I want, and when he finally does something, it's not what I want!"

*I felt we were caught in the same place we had been before. At this moment, I felt more for Horst and against Ingrid. But I had no conviction that he had managed any closeness during the week. Although I myself wouldn't be strong on daily flowers as a token of love, the flowers seemed to be an agreed on language between them. For years he had not gratified her frequent requests for a specific way of showing he cared, nor would he even act like he did. But then, when he did, she said he did it in the wrong way. With my own not caring much for flowers, it was easy for me to feel as though I were in his shoes and trapped there.*

*I knew, foremost, that I was finding Ingrid pretty impossible. I thought this feeling resided in a temporary identification with Horst, and was closely connected to his retreat. I wanted to urge him to a more direct expression of his response, which I imagined to be some form of outrage. I began with a question to Horst.*

## Trying Again: Enlarging the Field of Observation and Testing Defensive Patterns

"How do you feel, Horst, when Ingrid says you do it wrong? You say you did give her flowers, even if only on a couple of occasions, and she says, 'But not in the right way?'"

Horst turned to me and said, "I think the ones from the florist are nicer, but if she wants me to stand in line in the grocery and pick them up myself, then that's what she wants and I'll do it."

"Don't you get mad, even a little annoyed?" I persisted.

"No . . . well, a little maybe. Well, I can't say it. . . . Ingrid doesn't like being criticized." He looked at me, puzzled. "Do you want me to say it?"

Ingrid cut in. "I never know what he thinks or how he feels. He keeps everything to himself. This is Mister Stoic! So I can never talk to him."

*In this moment, I felt something different about Ingrid. Out of my sense of frustration with her cutting Horst off all the time, denying almost everything he did say, I had already developed a recurring discomfort. I had known from the previous hour that I could not keep confronting her. Saying she cut him off brought denial. I had already had the feeling that Horst could not tell her about his anger because he often didn't know when he felt it. Now I understood that he suppressed his anger for the additional reason that she couldn't stand it. Shaking off the distorting effect of the couple's projective identification and beginning to see clearly and with empathy the underlying motivation, I suddenly wondered what Ingrid was most afraid of. What was it that made her deny Horst's efforts and keep saying he was wrong? Having asked myself this question internally freed me to finally say something more sympathetic than anything I had managed in the last three sessions.*

## Making Links and Establishing an Alliance Again

"I think what gets you down the most, Ingrid, is the idea that Horst makes you so terribly mad. When he doesn't tell you what he feels, you get frustrated and angry. The less he says, the madder you get."

Ingrid looked tearful, and she paused. "Yes, I think that's right. I don't like to be an angry person. I wasn't used to that. And I hate it. I don't like who I've become." And she started to cry.

*I felt we were finally on the same wavelength for the first time since she had said she wasn't going along with "my plan." I could see her relax and she looked at me as though I had finally gotten something right. I glanced at Horst and thought he didn't look troubled by what was being said. I felt emboldened to go on.*

I continued, "And then you seem to feel humiliated by him—and that makes you furious, which is not the way you think of yourself. He takes away the you that *you* want to be and leaves you feeling you're nothing but an angry person. It's as though he robs you, not only of his love, but of yourself, too."

"I don't know about the humiliation, but I do find myself so angry when I don't want to be, and he's saying nothing. Like you said, 'It's all on me.'"

*I realized that she wanted to show me again how I hadn't quite got it right. Nevertheless, her disagreement seemed less defensive than before and more like the ordinary course correction a patient gives to what I have to say, mulling it over and deciding if it fits or not. I felt this was temporary disagreement encountered in working together. It was getting near the end of the hour, so I felt I needed to include Horst in on what I was saying.*

I said, "Ingrid, I accept what you're saying. And I want you to know that's why I am indeed encouraging Horst to speak more directly of his anger. I think he is angry at you. We have agreed that he can hardly stand to have anyone tell him *anything*, and you have so much resentment about all that has happened that you have a great deal to tell him. What he does with it is to clam up and go away inside. So you can't get to him or to his hidden pearl. That's what we were saying last week.

"Now on your side, Horst, the most important thing you are *not* saying is how angry you are. You let Ingrid know by clamming up, but when you do it that way, it puts the anger into her. She gets mad for both of you, but that's because when you are afraid to say it because she won't like it—and she doesn't—she feels even angrier."

"Well, I just don't think I should say it," he said. "She's a good person, so she deserves better."

"Look, Horst: You are mad quite a lot of the time," I insisted. "I've seen it in here when you look at me in a 'What-can-I-do?' way. But you don't say it! And having not said that, you have nothing else to say."

"Okay," he said. "So what should I do?"

"Yes," asked Ingrid. "What should we do?"

I said, "I don't think there's any advice I can give you except to keep coming in twice a week, at least for now. Speaking up in here will put pressure on you, and you'll need a place to deal with it so it doesn't go back underground. So, Ingrid, I want you to know I am asking him to speak up, not to hurt you needlessly, but so that you don't have to voice everything."

*It was a long speech, but they seemed to be able to listen. I felt that I had spoken to the mutuality of the projective system in a way that relieved them both just a bit. So I, too, felt some relief. Whether I was justified, we would find out in subsequent sessions. But I regarded it as a small breakthrough that I felt now on neutral territory, understanding both of them. It seemed a better beginning of a difficult therapy.*

"That's okay," said Ingrid. "I understand. It would be a relief to hear anything from him."

"And you, Horst?" I asked.

"Yes, I can manage that," he said. "In here, I can. If not at home. I'll try, though. That's why we're here."

"I'll see you Friday," I said.

"We'll see you Friday," said Ingrid, "if we survive 'til then!"

They were both smiling as they went out. I imagined it was with relief.

## DISCUSSION

This example of three initial treatment sessions shows a therapist frequently off balance, juggling countertransference reactions in a balder way than is often true later in a therapy. Here, before the couple and therapist settle in together, we can see the work of making an initial fit. Just as a new baby and mother struggle in the beginning to get the rhythms and crude signals of basic needs to work between them, so the couple newly in therapy has to signal their new therapist about their needs and about the most effective ways of getting them met.

Not all couples have such obvious difficulties at the beginning. Some may look as though they are so ready to work that there is no difficulty with fit, with how to communicate with them—no troubling countertransference imbalance that leaves the therapist identified strongly with one of them and against the other. But this apparently

smooth beginning may hide something just as tricky: an overly compliant pattern of shared holding that leaves the couple working together to hide the repressed bad objects from the therapist lest they
not be tolerated. In these situations, therapists will often find themselves enjoying the work, perhaps even idealizing the couple, and
unconsciously colluding in repressing the couple's shared
aggression.

These sessions demonstrate the tasks of the initial phase of therapy. They begin with the resistant wife saying strongly that she does
not accept the task or the way of working recommended by the therapist and previously agreed on. The sessions then lead through the
couple's resistance and the testing of defensive patterns to the beginning of more flexibility between the partners permitting the examination of mutual projective identifications.

On the way, the couple and their therapist have grown in their
shared capacity for mutual holding. An enhanced treatment alliance
has been accomplished through a slow widening of the field of observation and understanding and through the acceptance into the therapeutic space of previously repressed bad objects. Each of the partners
has contributed to the widening investigation, and their tolerance for
the contributions of the other has increased, although only by small
increments. Although the patterns of mutual projective identification
have been identified in a rough way, we should not have any confidence that this initial naming of them would do any lasting good by
itself. We do not yet know what patterns of resistance will emerge in
the wake of this early work, but it is a safe bet that resistance will
surface again and again. There has not yet been any substantial working through—a feature of the midphase of therapy where patterns
that have become familiar are retraced over and over as new variations and wrinkles are understood and worked on. But even in these
first three sessions we can see the spiral that is typical of therapy: the
same issues come up for consideration over and over. If the therapy is
going well, each rendition shows more and allows for a new reworking, but the basic pattern is often established early.

This example also illustrates the use of countertransference during
the first phase of therapy, the exquisite interplay of projective identification. The spouses trade off the role of speaking for resistance as
they join to confront the therapist with their shared defensive reluctance to join in the therapeutic process. Then we can see the therapist
following the subtle hints of hidden, repressed affect and object relations. Horst suppresses what resentment he knows about, and represses still more. Ingrid knows about her rage, but has suppressed
her sense of humiliation. While Horst's sexual desire is repressed

along with his anger, Ingrid has been working almost consciously to repress the pangs of her longing that threaten to awaken in the therapy. The sudden shifts in defense, in the pattern of projective and introjective identifications that express these themes, are gathered together in the couple's shared hedging of contextual transference, already fully operating here at the beginning of therapy. As soon as the commitment to therapy is cast, the relatively cooperative and eager stance of the evaluation period changed. Having wooed and won the therapist, the force of the couple's shared internal object difficulties surfaced, and the therapeutic relationship had to be tried on new grounds.

The countertransference is the proving ground for this work, the place where couple and therapist truly join, and where the couple gets inside the therapist just as the therapist must eventually get inside them if the therapy is going to be worth its salt.

The early struggle to scale the rocks of resistance of this therapy was tenuous, but seemed to progress through the shoals well enough. The couple continued for several weeks after these sessions, but did not return after the therapist's month-long summer vacation. They called to say they had lost their au pair for the children and would return after finding new help. They did not return. I thought of Ingrid's having been an au pair herself and I remembered that she had said she would have to do without help to afford therapy. But no coherent unconscious explanation emerged.

We cannot know exactly why this couple stopped. Interruptions to therapy are frequent after therapist absences. But the issues of resistance were expressed loudly by this couple from the beginning. We can do no more than work with them. Such early struggles are not always successful. The resistances that surface early have to be taken seriously and worked with toward understanding the deficits in contextual holding that threaten the work. Often this goes well enough for the therapist to survive and the couple to move into midphase work. Sometimes it does not.

Chapter **8**

# THE MANAGEMENT OF IMPASSE:
# MIDPHASE THERAPY WITH AN
# APPARENTLY IMPOSSIBLE COUPLE

Sooner or later, the marital therapist will be asked to help a couple of spouses who seem to attack their marriage at every quarter. Theoretically we know that it is the longing underneath the attack that keeps such couples together, but in the process of our trying to help them, they often turn from attacking each other to assaulting our capacity to provide a therapeutic context. In these situations, it is finally the capacity to survive that offers any possibility of a therapeutic change. The work is often painful, but it offers lessons that are infinitely helpful with less thoroughly destructive couples whose transferences nevertheless echo the one to be presented. The experience of impasse and impossibility in the countertransference that is illustrated here is a central feature of work with these couples.

Harvey and Anne Van Duren sought help for an impossible situation. He was a 58-year-old writer, raised in England, and she, at 42, a scientist of substantial and still growing reputation. They had been married for only eighteen months, but the marriage had been a stormy one from the start. They met in a long affair after Harvey had been invited to do a biography of Anne for a magazine. Both had been married at the time, but had essentially signed out of their marriages, with multiple affairs and little regard for their previous spouses. Harvey said that his first wife had been depressed and unresponsive except to their child, who was now grown. Anne described a marriage to a successful builder who had little interest in the family, and who left her alone with their son and daughter, allowing her to do as she pleased in raising them. Both first marriages had been calm, with no turbulence or remarkable fighting. Harvey had emotionally left his marriage many years before, and for several years had lived in an apartment in a building near his wife's house. Anne had taken the initiative in running her family while getting her emotional needs met elsewhere.

Their affair though hardly noticed by either of their spouses was passionate from the beginning. They each said they felt alive as they never had before, and they expended enormous amounts of energy planning to see each other. During the early phase of their romance, when their meetings were brief and surreptitious, the sex went well. But as soon as they declared their love, felt free to date openly, and to have longer times together, Harvey began to have intermittent erectile difficulty. They both explained this as being due to the stress of the relationship in forbidding circumstances, but the sexual difficulty persisted even when both were free to date. After their marriage, Harvey's difficulty with erections increased.

This was what Anne said was the chief reason for her anger. She could no longer face being married without a sexual life. Things were too difficult. She had to face difficulties with her children, who had repeated school troubles. She felt she got no sympathy from Harvey about this, but she could stand that. After all, she had always raised her children alone. What she could not face was that having had to handle everything herself, she then got nothing from him sexually. This she felt as an extreme rejection, and it made her feel uncared for in the way she had as a small child when she had suffered severe burns to her legs and lower body in a fire at the age of 5. She felt ugly and rejected. She could barely remember the fire, but as far back as she could remember, she had to spend long lonely periods in the hospital, times when she felt rejected and uncared for. The repairs to her skin and the related physical therapy had gone on until age 10. Surprisingly, slight scars remained. These ugly feelings came back with the sexual rejection she felt from Harvey. But that was certainly not all. Mainly, she felt he did not care what she had to put up with in her own daily situation. He was not there emotionally when she tried to manage her children, one of whom was anorectic, and the other who, although bright, was constantly defeating himself. The children were demanding, and in addition resented Harvey—and no wonder. He was self-centered and uncaring with them, and when he did tune in on them, he was often provocative or teasing, so that they dissolved into tears. Once the boy had attacked Harvey physically after Harvey had been scathing with him.

While Anne's round face was flushed with anger, Harvey's was pale and immobile. He sat quietly and dispassionately, a bit slumped in the easy chair, until she finished. Then he pulled himself up and began to defend himself. He was as distressed as she was about his impotence. He had intermittent trouble with it earlier in his life, but never as much difficulty as this. He did not feel unsympathetic about her troubles, nor did he feel unsupportive.

He was calm, rational, and well spoken, with a high-bred accent. Nothing about his demeanor would have seemed to warrant the tirade that Anne had launched. He expressed his hope that they could do something, and as quickly as possible, about the trouble with the erections. He would like to make her happy.

## THE TREATMENT

Work with Harvey and Anne was among the most difficult and discouraging I [D.E.S.] have done. Early on, Anne reached an equilibrium in which she would refuse to speak for the first part of the session. She was trying to control her rage and to force his participation. At first she said, "I'm not going to speak today. Harvey, you speak!" This soon hardened into a pattern in which he would look to me, and begin with whatever he could muster—an account of the week's activities, the fight that had preceded the appointment, or occasionally, an account of a relatively good week.

Sooner or later, Anne would cut in to disagree with his account. He had not represented her side of it correctly, she would say. Or he had been accurate in his account, but had failed to be understanding of her this time, as usual. The pattern that regularly surfaced was that although he did the talking, nothing he said mattered until she cut in. And the talking that he did by himself was a rational accounting for the time since I had last seen them, for the most part devoid of any emotion.

*My job was not made any easier by the fact that I regularly felt my position with them severely skewed. I liked his urbane wit, his upper-class English accent, and his patrician elocution despite his being relatively walled off from feeling. I found her shrewish despite her capacity for psychological mindedness. Overall, I felt that this couple constantly cut me off from my own wish to be neutral between them. I felt inside me the unwelcome wish to side with him and to get rid of her. In my struggle to be true to my principles and regain a position equidistant between them, I felt so frequently frustrated that I often wished to be rid of them altogether.*

The first task of the therapy was, on the one hand, to help them settle down enough that they did not burst apart, while, on the other hand, containing the fiery physical fights that had become a feature of their marriage. Neither of them had been involved in fights in previous relationships, but they had been fighting violently and frequently for the past year. The fights were echoed by Anne's flaming eruptions within the sessions when she would scream at Harvey with a ferocity I had not previously heard in couple therapy, even though I have worked with many desperately angry couples. The threat that this would erupt began to permeate every session, although the episodes occurred only every few weeks. At their request, I was now seeing them two to three times a week, and while the intensity of the rages seemed to have increased, they were now contained inside the therapy.

At first the couple gave me the impression that they were largely verbally abusive to each other. Because they felt trusting enough to tell me, it eventually became clear that the fights actually included physical abuse to each other. I found out that Harvey's social drinking was more than moderate. He reluctantly agreed when I suggested that this could be exacerbating their lack of control. I advised him to stop drinking—which would also remove alcohol's depressant effect on his erections—and said they both had to agree to stop the physical aspects of their fights. I immediately took the position that they had to stop hitting each other, because of the threat to fundamental survival, and without a measure of physical safety we could not work. They were able to virtually stop the physical fighting, with only a few recurrences over the next few months. This brought the strength of the difficulties all the more pressingly into the hours. Anne spoke for the brunt of the upset, while Harvey was the patient, but spare stoic. When they were at peace, they had a relationship where love was expressed through mutual teasing and sarcasm at an admirable level of wit and erudition. George Bernard Shaw might have written their lines of mutual cynicism about the human condition and each other's contribution to our common catastrophe. Their relationship was a constantly humbling experience for anyone who wished to remain optimistic about the possibility of humane marriage in a humane world.

A new pattern now developed in therapy hours. While either Harvey or I was speaking, Anne would declare without warning that she had had all she could take. She would start to cry, promptly leave the room, and slam the door. On the first such occasion, Harvey stayed and we tried to make some sense of what he had done to contribute to her retreat. But after the hour, she said that his staying had left her burning with anger, hurt, and fundamentally mistrustful of me. She could only assume he and I were ganging up against her. If that happened again, she really would never come back.

This declaration paradoxically gave me some hope for them, because until then I had felt that her leaving the room was close to her quitting the therapy. Her ultimatum let me know that she left when she was beyond words, but that she did not intend to end the work.

After that, when Anne left, Harvey would stir himself in a languid way, and, nodding at me in resignation, follow her out. Sometimes they returned together after a few minutes, and sometimes not until the next hour. On some occasions, Anne's departure would occur in the midst of expressing doubt about continuing the process at all. Then Harvey would have to leave lest Anne feel we were ganging up on her—and I would be left alone and often somewhat perturbed. But usually, when they returned for the next appointment, it was as though nothing had happened.

When they walked out, not knowing whether they would return, I felt shaken every time. I felt diminished, incompetent, and contemptible. I felt I was not smart enough for him nor steady enough for her. I began to hate them for making me feel this way and so there was also some relief each time they left. I could only work on this countertransference feeling by myself, because my attempts to use it in discussion of the transference to me were frustrated.

When I spoke with them about the way in which they left me shaken and wondering if there would be a tomorrow, only to return as though everything was fine, or at least no worse than the usual doom and gloom, Anne could be counted on to lecture me about Harvey's failures and unreliabilities. He was, she assured me, a truly terrible man, full of aggression and a bane to all who tried to be close to him, including his child and first wife. She felt sympathetic to his first wife, since he was so horrible.

I felt that it was unsaid that I was not far behind Harvey in my human failings, especially if I were measured by my failure to help them. I could tangibly feel her disappointment in me from her feeling, which I shared, that I failed to understand the depth of her unjustified suffering at his hands.

And yet Anne could also work in the hours with a capacity that Harvey could not manage. She drew on her previous psychoanalysis to link the marital difficulty and her role in it both to her early childhood and to her concerns as a parent of two adolescents. She clung closely to her children, she thought, out of her aloneness. In her previous empty marriage, when she had retreated to the children, her former husband had been glad to have her off his back.

*Early and late in this therapy I felt controlled by Anne's rages and subsequent nonchalance. I felt buffeted and turned on my head like a puppet with no brain. I often felt that my attempt to discern a truly shared contribution to the troubling relationship was merely lip service to my belief. I thought Harvey did contribute to their difficulties, but I could not find out how, because Anne's rages and demandingness were so ascendant. I tried to work with Harvey on the underlying issues in his treatment of her but always felt frustrated by a well-meaning but shallow compliance in his attempts.*

He would talk about his family history, but with little feeling. He told of his father, who was a high-level failure, a politician who had a startling early career, but who had suffered subsequent defeat. Although his father eventually became a widely respected elder statesman, he had always carried a sense of failure and disappointment with him, which Harvey had absorbed. Harvey's mother had become alcoholic during his adolescence, and she deteriorated, especially after the death of his father when Harvey was 18. He had an older brother and a younger sister. The brother was the father's favorite. It was the sister, however, with whom Harvey had the more problematic relationship. She had had encephalitis at the age of 3, and the subsequent attention from the family had left Harvey feeling both responsible for her and jealous of the attention she received from his parents.

Harvey could make the intellectual connections. He could say that Anne represented his unsatisfiable or unavailable mother and made him feel like his revered but failed father. He could agree that he was trying to goad her into a better opinion of him. But I never had the satisfaction of things hitting home with him. He admitted his affective disconnection. He lamented it. But he could not change it.

Nevertheless, things continued to improve slowly. From time to time, the couple began to report periods of well-being when life together was more tolerable.

Then Anne reintroduced the demand that something be done about their sex life. The lack of sex in a marginal marriage was more than she felt she could live with. Since thorough evaluation had established that Harvey's impotence did not have an organic cause, and Harvey said he was willing to work on their sexual relationship, we switched to sex therapy, in which I assigned homework using the format described in Chapter 9. They did the assignments dubiously, and reported on them with their typically contemptuous wit. Still, they made progress with them, and Harvey began having more reliable erections. The previous erectile incapacity could now be understood: it served to suppress rage at Anne as a controlling mother, while protecting her from the rage that would have been located in an invading penis. But at the end of three months of this work, they refused to "play by rules" and plunged ahead to full intercourse before I thought it wise. They told me they assumed that I had set up "my rules" so that they could triumph over me by breaking them.

I found it of interest, intellectually rising above my sense of being abused, to see what was possible therapeutically now that I felt treated by the two of them together the way they habitually treated each other. I told them this was happening, and while they took in my confrontation, they did not change. For some time they continued to have successful intercourse over my therapeutic dead body, and then the sex fell away again as their competitive rage resurfaced.

Now a new crisis emerged. Anne felt betrayed when Harvey took a drink while out with a mutual friend, an old girlfriend of Harvey's by whom Anne had always felt mistreated. Harvey had been effectively off alcohol for more than six months, and he said that he felt healthier, calmer, and considerably relieved. But on this occasion he had given in to their friend's urgent tender of a drink.

Harvey admitted that part of his motivation for taking a drink had been annoyance with Anne, and he explored his angry wish to get back at her through it, but nothing would satisfy her. She moved steadily away from him, berating him in almost every session. Her silent demand that he begin the sessions was stronger than ever. My interventions seemed to make less and less difference, because she now felt any focus on her was a weapon used against her, whether Harvey or I was talking. Because of this insistence, any focus on Harvey assumed a false air of being carried out simply to appease her.

*In this situation, all I could do was openly discuss my countertransference position. The couple had seemed impossible and now therapy seemed impossible too. I talked about feeling that I was helpless to make a difference, and I reflected on Anne's now avowed intention to end the marriage. I addressed the relentless spoiling I felt she led with that also was a characteristic of their marriage which, outside the sessions, both of them carried out. I spent many hours feeling I had nothing to offer. On these occasions, Anne would turn to me and say, "Why don't you talk, Dr. Scharff? What do you think about us?"*

*I would say, "I don't have any new thoughts about you. I'm not sure there is anything I have to offer because I can't say what I think." Having said that, I then was able to face what I thought, which was that Anne had the controlling lead in forbidding thought or feeling. I felt hamstrung, particularly by her, even though she had told me that was just what she could not stand hearing.*

Over time, Anne was hit by my confrontation. The first time I said this, not surprisingly, she walked out of the hour. I felt better mainly because I thought the agony of the work with this couple was likely to be over soon. But Anne came back with Harvey in the next hour, and acted as though everything was better. I said I was sure that Harvey did contribute to the problem fully, as she had said. But I knew from my experience of feeling hampered by her control on my thoughts that until she let Harvey off the hook, he would not be free to work. I noted that although she said he was impossible and that the marriage was not salvageable, she stayed. And I concluded that if she meant to stay, she would have to stop spoiling and blocking the work. Otherwise we would not be able to understand his contribution. Her fearfulness, for all the reasons we understood and many we did not, was keeping her from allowing Harvey to really speak despite her insistence that he fill the time. And her determination that it was not safe was the controlling factor, like it or not. She certainly had the right to end the marriage. But if she did not want to end the marriage, or if she did want to invest in the therapy, she would have to let go. She would have to make that decision.

They stayed, and after another four months, things began to yield. Almost imperceptibly, Anne softened and began to admit that Harvey was capable of standing by her on occasions. After my repeated confrontation, she rarely had to leave the room after I spoke, and so, with trepidation, I could mention that things were reported as better. During these months we could discuss the factors that threw them over the cliff so that we were not confined to experiencing the fall over and over without any added capacity for understanding.

And finally Anne began, now with full affect that caught my sympathy, to tell the story of feeling so abandoned by her parents during her long bout of recovering from her childhood trauma. The fire had happened in the night when she was asleep. She awoke screaming with her bed on fire. Really she had been lucky it was only her lower body that was badly burned, but what she chiefly remembered was the time in the hospital afterward. The burn had been excruciating, and required painful dressing and redressing. She had multiple surgical procedures, and to this day had bodily scarring. She found her nude body painfully ugly, although residual scarring was minimal. But most painful to her was the feeling that her parents had abandoned her to the care of the hospital. Later while she was healing, her father told her she would never fully recover—which to her had meant that she would never recover their affection. She felt that her treatment by doctors and nurses had gone on in the absence of her parents, who had apparently stayed away a good deal in reaction to their own fear and turmoil. That feeling had made her insistence that the treatment itself was a trauma all the more heartfelt, since the more searing the couple's therapy was, the more it reminded her of the fear and pain of the treatment for her burns.

But this time, her review of this material meant more to both Anne and Harvey. Although the reasons are not entirely clear, I think that my talking about my helplessness addressed her situation as a child, and that my confrontation about her leaving sessions and slamming doors against Harvey and me may have spoken to a childhood wish to scream at her parents for leaving her alone. I could now understand the shaken feeling I had when she walked out of the hour as representing how she had felt when left alone by her parents in the hospital to face the painful "assault" of the doctors and nurses.

Harvey thought of his concern as a boy for his sister, who similarly had a physically painful childhood hospitalization with his wish to take care of Anne. Now he lived out the same ambivalence about taking care of Anne that must have existed then about his sister: he both wanted to take care of her, and he was wordlessly envious of the care she received, even from himself.

## A SESSION

Finally, after just two years, their defensive structure shifted. On the day I am going to describe, they sat next to each other on the same couch, a configuration I had not seen in at least a year. Separated still by the middle seat in the couch, Harvey teasingly reached across to Anne and poked her in the ribs from time to time. Finally she said the poking really bothered her. Harvey smiled and said that he knew she really liked it, at which she shot him an ambiguously sweet grimace. Harvey began, as was still the mandatory procedure, by filling me in on the situation. They had a good week, despite extraordinary stress. Anne's son had been arrested mistakenly by the police, and her daughter had been in an automobile accident and taken to the hospital. Although she was all right, that had not been clear at first. And there was a house full of visitors including the daughter's live-in boyfriend. Nevertheless, Anne had been able to cope, supported by Harvey. Anne said that she did not know quite what accounted for the improvement.

*I was having the feeling of walking again on thin ice, having tried so often to speak to the forces of destructiveness that led them to spoil periods of good feeling. Yet I felt a bit flushed with some late-inning success. So I elected, in a way against my better judgment, to push on in this positive view, glad that today a new kind of work seemed possible.*

For the first time in two years of work, Harvey seemed able to respond. Anne took the lead in introducing the topic of Harvey's son Bill's recent request for financial support from them so that he could have psychotherapy. Harvey was disposed to give it to him, but he felt mildly abused by the request from a self-supporting 30-year-old. This led Anne to discuss Harvey's dreadful relationship with his son. Harvey agreed it was awful, but in the intellectually distant way he agreed about anything. In my experience of him, he was always emotionally out of touch with what he was agreeing to. His tendency to erupt irrationally at home in the enormous fights with Anne had not been betrayed in the hours, where even his anger would seem most reasonable.

But today, something yielded. Harvey said that he thought he felt resentful of his son because, in large part, he would like to give him so much. When Bill called, Harvey felt himself in the role of his father, the man he had longed to turn to when he had felt isolated or rejected. So the request from Bill stirred the urge to give to him, as he longed to be given to. Then the underlying sense of rejection loomed when, on the other hand, he felt he should not give to Bill because the request was unreasonable.

But another issue was nearby, one to do with his mother. Somehow, he said, he had a sense that she interfered between him and his father. How was it that she came between them? Here Anne chimed in to ask if it was his mother's alcoholism. Harvey thought not because she wasn't alcoholic until later, probably when he was already in his teens. But there was something in the way with his father, and he couldn't identify it, try as he might.

I said that although he could not find the information in his memory at present, perhaps he could learn about it from his interaction with Anne, in which he participated in and initiated relentless, recurrent fighting to which both of them were quite attached. I recalled what I had noted so often: whenever things were quiet, they seemed to share an urge to have some noise, and the quickest way to quiet the anxiety about peace was to fight. Their way of expressing intimacy was often to prod each other, just as Harvey had physically prodded Anne early in this hour.

Harvey, looking thoughtful, seemed to be following me. I thought he might find something to connect back to his parents' relationship and his difficulty in reaching his father. I continued saying that Harvey frequently prodded Anne verbally. Anne protested that she did not like that prodding either. Although she was a partner in the acerbically witty exchanges, I accepted her statement, and prepared to continue my review of their relationship. But Anne was off and running. She said that however much this might be a part of her, she did not relate this way with anyone else. She could see that it expressed her resentment. The resentment was an old one that we had discussed frequently, stemming from the period of her childhood convalescence when she was so resentful of the pain and the expectations of her, and especially, she now added, of the insult added to the injury when her father said to her that since she was scarred and no longer beautiful, she had better develop her brain in order to get along in this life. This was the father she was trying to reach, even while resenting him, when Harvey was busy prodding her. But, she noted, here we were in the hour focusing on her again. And she resented that. She resented it that Harvey could duck out, partly to be sure, because she was so ready to pick up the work and focus it on herself. But she was tired of that.

*I agreed, I thought that this was an example of the two of them working to take the emotional focus off Harvey, just when he had begun to move into it. I was feeling that the slender thread of their working together without Anne wading in or storming out would break in my grasp—or perhaps that I had no hold on it at all. It was in their hands. It was as if the thread had wound around me, not enough for me to pull on it helpfully, but only enough for them to pull on it and spin me around in the process. Feeling here today that they were beginning to work, I felt again the sense of therapeutic helplessness and of being only one step away from their familiar maelstorm. On the other hand, I would see that she was right on the theme of connecting their relationship to the problem of reaching for a parent, in her case the father and, in the transference, me.*

I now wondered aloud how Harvey and Anne had joined to keep Harvey from continuing to investigate something about his early life with his parents. Perhaps it was something painful to both of them that threatened to emerge at the point they had switched away from Harvey. Could he go back to that?

In his evenhanded and overly reasonable way, Harvey said that he would try. It was a dim impression, but he thought his mother must have made demands on him by which he felt constrained. Many times his father would be trying to placate his mother, when he could not, therefore, get his father's attention.

I wondered if things were not rougher in the early relationship with his mother than he had been thinking. The evidence in the relationship with Anne was that he was extraordinarily wary, and yet at the same time he was prodding her. That behavior, so destructive of what he said he wanted with her, was a persistent and repeated pattern. Anne was busy nodding from her chair, about to speak and challenge him herself. I imagined she would do so aggressively, and so I asserted myself and continued my direct work with Harvey to model a check on *her* prodding of him.

*I was countertransferentially experiencing the mutual prodding that was a feature of the way they, with their anxious holding relationship, experienced calm or peace to be absence and rejection. Mutual prodding was their attempt to get compliant surrender or a nonthreatening sign of life from each other. My heightened activity occurred without my quite being aware of it, in order to substitute my empathic questioning for her invasive relationship.*

This sense let me suggest to Harvey that his mother may well have been, in her depression when he was 4 or 5, difficult for him to get to. In his attempt to bring her to life, and to focus on him, he must have had to prod her, and must have been willing to do so even at the expense of angering her.

"I think that's true," he said. "I can remember her being depressed. Probably she did drink some then, maybe more than I remember, just as I used to drink more than I thought. As we talk about this, I do have a distant feeling, one of loneliness, a quiet without walls, stretching in front of me and all around. It's eerie. And this relates to my father somehow. To a feeling that if I could just get to him, I could get some comfort. So even right now, I have a sense of missing him terribly. But where is he? And then, there is the sense that he's a failure. And the one way I can be with him is to risk being a failure myself. But I think the failure here is not just about the failures he felt in the later years, which were many. Yes!" he said, his eyes unexpectedly filling with tears, "Here, I think it's mainly the failure to help me with my mother, and the sense of sorrow that he, too, could not breathe life into her."

The room was quiet, in an unusually sad and full way. I felt we had given birth to something. Since it was close to the end of the hour, I turned to Anne to ask her response.

Anne said that she felt moved. There was something tentative, perhaps grudging in her acknowledgement, but she did not interrupt, and she looked concerned for Harvey. It made sense, she said, of his prodding her, as though she were the depressed, rejecting mother who he had to jolly into life, but with whom it was preferable to fight if that's what it took to get through to her. She could see the loneliness behind it. Until today, she had never felt she could penetrate the fog that always seemed to separate

Harvey from her and in which he blamed her for nearly everything. But this helped. And challengingly, at the end, she added that she hoped there would be more of it.

## DISCUSSION

We chose to present this work because it illustrates the therapist's struggle in the face of the couple's assault on the therapist's capacity to provide a therapeutic context that stems directly from the couple's devastatingly flawed holding. They attempted to compensate for their fears for themselves and for each other. For Anne, there was the fear that she would be engulfed in the flames of her original burn and abandoned to pain without support. In the face of this she became enormously controlling of Harvey and the therapist. Harvey's experience with a depressed and later volatile mother and an absent father had led him to be rigidly walled off. His controlled personality felt like a continual, maddening rejection to Anne, so they came together mostly in aggressive outbursts, at which times they felt closest.

We have outlined the way in which the countertransference reflected the couple's flawed holding capacity, expressed in their dubious contextual transference. Both of them had internalized the experience of enviable but rejecting parents. Harvey and Anne had somewhat different constellations of exciting and rejecting parents. Both were focused on their fathers as exciting figures. For Anne, father was also the rejecting figure. She had few thoughts of her mother at all: functionally, no mother seemed to exist, leaving her with little model for an accepting mother. For Harvey, good and bad were mainly split between father and mother, but the cost of identification with his father was the internalization of the failed father— probably as reinforced by his mother's accusations. For both of them, however, the parental couples had been disappointing and yet envied.

In the countertransference, the therapist was often absorbed in his own doubts and feelings of failure as a therapist. It was a daily experience of feeling deskilled and dismissed, separated from his own operating principles and self-esteem, and joined with them in a style that he felt attracted to, and yet which gave him considerable self-loathing.

It was through being willing to absorb this couple's destructiveness, their mutual spoiling and envy, their condescension and contempt, and through becoming someone he did not like in small ways, that the therapist was able to understand their internal experience of trying to reach each other in endlessly frustrating ways. With them he felt that he was in the presence of enviable but persecuting parents, ones who would not let him in. What resonated in him was his own rejecting internal couple, just as it was in sharing a projective identification of rejecting internal couples that the couple so badly abused each other.

This therapy demonstrates, more than anything, the power of survival of the therapist. Here the holding and the experience of trying to provide the holding has none of the softness or mutuality of the mother and the baby. It has the immediacy of coping with assault by an automatic weapon that fires repeatedly at point blank range. It is the therapist's duty to survive the aggressive attacks just as parents must. The triumph of survival is therapeutic because that is what the couple's relationship cannot do until the partners experience it with us.

Meanwhile, it is not fun. The spoiling in the holding between the couple has to be fully, and emotionally, leveled at the therapist, and probably felt quite fully inside the therapist, before it can finally be taken back inside the couple. Without this kind of work, couples like this face a life of continued mutual battering. Some of them may choose to separate, while others will stay together. Certainly, in the middle of therapy it seems that they would be better separated. A therapist is tempted to advise them to separate in the middle of the storm, but it is not up to us to cut their options. Many such therapies do indeed founder before a turning point of the kind described here, but some turn the corner to a different kind of relationship.

In the middle of this, we may decide *we* can go no further with a given marriage, but we cannot make the decision that such a couple should not be together. Barring the case of continued physical abuse or threats of death, it is not up to us to decide which marriages are over and which are not. Those decisions are too important to be decided by the therapist, who in the end does not have to live with the consequences of the decision.

Therapeutically transforming this experience was a longer, slower haul than for many couples. It often felt beyond the outer limits of possibility as the therapist frequently felt overwhelmed with hopelessness! But it is precisely such couples who make the point that this kind of difficulty can only be worked with if one is willing to absorb and suffer the inner objects, the mutual projective identifications, and then to slowly work one's way out of them. It is a most uncomfortable process, for these aggressive and hating couples have almost given up on being loved for themselves, and they can do no other than bring this difficulty to us.

## THE COUNTERTRANSFERENCE OF IMPASSE

The turning point of this case centered around the therapist's absorption of the sense of impossibility from the couple—a thorough introjective identification that accumulated through the months of work. It was not a conscious decision but a feeling there was nowhere else to turn that led to his sharing the countertransference with them. Only then could the destructiveness of their work be understood and worked with as deriving from their shared early experience of unreachable parents, absent holding, and anger in place of loving support.

For us, this experience of hopelessness in the countertransference is not uncommon. We have learned that it is often the central experience in couples who use massive splitting and repression, and who fear confrontation with their own mutual destructiveness. Work with such countertransference cannot be "faked." Therapists cannot interpret it until they experience it in cases at hand. They must have absorbed it in the current clinical experience for such interpretation to be honest and effective. But they can be on the lookout for such countertransferences when they encounter difficult couples—and for milder similar versions of countertransference with many couples.

Part III

# The Treatment of Sexual Disorders

They originally required couples to stay in St. Louis for two weeks of intensive work in isolation from their home environment and its distractions. Initial medical, psychological, and sexual evaluations were performed, followed by an interpretive round table session for giving feedback to the couple and recommendations for treatment. Then sexual interactive exercises were prescribed in a preset order, for the couple to perform in privacy. The graded series began by excluding the genitalia and the woman's breasts from the interaction, and by restricting verbal communication. The initial exercise was called pleasuring rather than massage, in order to emphasize the emotional rather than the physical focus of the work. Over the 2-week period, components of the sexual relationship were added back in discrete increments. Then the physical exercises, which were done in private, were reviewed verbally in the psychotherapy sessions.

This de facto dissection of sexual interactions allows the couple and therapist to examine where sexual and interactive difficulties tend to occur, and to confront ingrained attitudes and defenses. It also offers an opportunity for instruction and education—something foreign to most analytic psychotherapists. Masters and Johnson originally used a co-therapy team of a man and a woman, as have most sexual treatment programs in the beginning of their work. They did so with the idea that understanding is improved if both members of the couple have someone of the same sex in their corner. The treatment team working with David Scharff at Preterm, in Washington, D.C. in the 1970s, also used co-therapy in developing their work, but later found its use no more necessary than for marital therapy. At this juncture, we think that co-therapy can be useful, especially for teaching and learning, but that it is generally an expensive luxury.

The essential modifications of sex therapy used by David Scharff have been based on the method of Helen Singer Kaplan (1974), with modifications and additions in subsequent publications (1977, 1979, 1983, 1987a, 1987b.) Her method relies on the behavioral interactive framework defined from Masters and Johnson's (1970) original model, but psychodynamically derived interpretations are used frequently. Different workers have employed various modifications of technique, with differences in frequency of sessions, and in the use of co-therapists, some more psychodynamic and some more behavioral (Lieblum and Pervin 1980, LoPiccolo and LoPiccolo 1978). Kaplan and her group have tended to focus on the sexual symptomatology more strictly than is our preference. They use fewer sessions and do not necessarily move toward the more general issues of the marriage unless the couple indicates a need to do so. Lief (1989) has presented an eloquent integration of approaches, establishing the place of all elements of an approach to treatment, beginning with education and support, specific behavioral approaches to dysfunctions, marital therapy for interpersonal conflict, and dynamic psychotherapy or psychoanalysis for those issues we have described as stemming from internal object relations.

Our own preference is to assume that most sexual disorders are part of a larger marital difficulty unless proven otherwise during evaluation. Some couples come to us assuming this to be true, while others would prefer to define their sexual complaints as isolated to the physical aspect of their bond. The thorough evaluation we employ helps us locate the role of the physical sexual disorder within the overall marital bond. Then, in an interpretive session with the couple, we can present our understanding of the situation leading to a recommendation for sex therapy, marital therapy, individual therapy, or a combination.

Our current procedures are as follows. When a couple seeks help and sexual difficulty plays a prominent role, a sexual diagnostic evaluation must be done in addition to the general marital diagnostic evaluation. We give a questionnaire concerning sexual attitudes, practices, and desires, particularly focused on sexual transactions and on each partner's understanding and estimation of the other partner's wishes and experience (LoPicollo and Steger 1974). We begin with one or more joint interviews with the couple. We also include individual interviews with each partner, during which each may feel freer to discuss certain matters, especially any extramarital affairs. At the end of the evaluation, the consultant meets with the couple jointly to share conclusions and recommendations, but also to explore further their experience in the light of the unfolding process.

Assuming that no medical or physical cause underlies the difficulty, recommendations for therapy range broadly from formal sex therapy, marital therapy without specific focus on sex, to individual psychotherapy or psychoanalysis. An individual or group educational program centering on masturbation may be recommended for orgasmic difficulty in the woman (LoPicollo and Lobitz 1972, Herman and LoPicollo 1988, Barbach 1974, 1975, 1980). On occasion, if for instance the couple is separating, there may be a recommendation for no treatment for the marriage.

The diagnostic category is relevant to the therapy recommended, but there is no one-to-one correlation. For instance, the finding of a disorder of sexual desire, which Lief (1977) has estimated accounts for 40 percent of couples seeking help for sexual difficulty, may indicate a preferred role for individual psychotherapy or psychoanalysis, but Kaplan (1979) has established that these disorders can at times be treated with conjoint sex therapy as well, and this has been borne out in our experience, a^ described in several illustrations in this volume. A recent volume, *Disorders of Sexual Desire* (Lieblum and Rosen 1988), deals extensively with the application of sex therapy to this most deeply seated set of syndromes.

We follow the classification of sexual disorders introduced by Kaplan (1974, 1979). She differentiated between "proximal anxiety" caused by the more immediate or superficial factors in the sexual situation, and "distal anxiety" caused by underlying factors associated with object relations issues. The disorders are also divided by categories corresponding to the triphasic model of sexual response: (1) desire, (2) excitement, and (3) orgasm (see Table 9–1).

Before sex therapy can be undertaken, a thorough evaluation must be done. This part of the evaluation is so specialized that referral to a sex therapist for further assessment may be wise. With some exceptions, the evaluation should include medical, urological, and gynecological examination in addition to our interviews. For erectile problems, a sleep EEG (electroencephalogram) with measurement of Nocturnal Penile Tumescence is crucial in deciding on the contribution of organic disease. Vascular or hormonal evaluation may be re-

Table 9–1.  Classification of sexual disorders (modified from Kaplan 1979, 1983, 1987b)

| Phase | Male/Female | Disorder |
|---|---|---|
| I. Desire | 1. M&F | Inhibited sexual desire (ISD): low or absolute lack of interest. |
| | 2. M&F | Phobic avoidance of arousal or coitus, including panic disorders. |
| | 3. M&F | Unconsummated marriages. |
| | 4. M&F | Hyperactive sexual desire: rare unless due to heightened general anxiety such as obsessive-compulsive disorder. |
| II. Excitement | 5. M | Erectile dysfunction, total or partial; absolute or situational; lifelong or late onset. |
| | 6. F | General sexual dysfunction: lack of enjoyment with or without desire. |
| | 7. F | Vaginismus. |
| III. Orgasm | 8. M | Premature ejaculation. |
| | 9. M | Retarded or absent ejaculation: absolute or situational, e.g., with a partner, only in coitus. |
| | 10. M&F | Total anorgasmia (far more frequent in women than men). |
| | 11. F | Situational anorgasmia with partner and/or in coitus. |
| | 12. M&F | Dyspareunia associated with organic conditions or genital muscle spasm. |

quired, especially in the older patient. Medical evaluation may not be necessary in certain cases, for instance in premature ejaculation for which no organic cause is known, or for disturbances that are situationally variable. The possibility of organic pathology such as neurovascular causes of erectile dysfunction, and of that psychopathology which is best treated by medication, must not be overlooked (Kaplan 1983). Kaplan (1987b) has written extensively on the place of medication and of modified psychological treatment for aversive, panic, and phobic disorders that appear in the form of sexual symptomatology. The clinician must also consider the role of medication in causing erectile dysfunction, of depression in reducing sexual interest, or of declining hormonal status in menopausal women in producing dyspareunia or loss of sexual interest. Often medical treatment can be usefully combined with the methods described here.

Assuming that sex therapy is recommended and accepted, the consultant doing the assessment can then move into a behavioral sex therapy format if trained to do so. If not, the couple is referred for sex therapy with the understanding that the marital therapist will be available later for marital therapy if that is required. In our practices, David Scharff moves into the sex therapy format, while Jill Scharff refers to a colleague for specific sex therapy. What follows is an account of the sex therapy method developed and used by David Scharff.

The partners are assigned the first of the series of graded home exercises that have the aim of reducing their sexual interaction, beginning with a nonthreatening, nongenital level. When they have mastered each step, a new component is added. Meetings are best arranged twice weekly to allow for the detailed reporting and work of therapy. Couples are asked to carry out the exercises at least twice between each meeting, so it is clear that they have to make a considerable time commitment. Unlike more behavioral approaches, sex therapy from an object relations perspective tends not to shortcut the program, because of its focus on the totality of the couple's interaction, not only on the physical parts of their sexual life.

Whenever any level of exercise does not progress smoothly, it is repeated. New components are not added until the current level is mastered. Therapists learn most from such failures, and accordingly, the couple is encouraged about learning from setbacks. Encouragement, support, and direct advice are combined with our interpretive approach, which focuses both on depth and surface matters, that is, on those "proximal anxieties" that begin relatively close to the surface as well as those "distal anxieties" traditionally taken up in intensive psychotherapy. An example of surface anxiety is the so-called "spectator anxiety" in erectile failure, in which the man is essentially outside himself, watchirg over his own shoulder (Masters and Johnson 1970, p. 11).

The interpretive work that deals with projective identification and object relations issues relies, of course, on less conscious material. Superficial anxiety usually sits on top of the more profound sources of anxiety, and the two can be related. The interpretive work draws not only on the report of the exercises, but on the usual sources for psychotherapy as well—verbal exchange, free association, dreams as understood first by the dreamer and then the spouse, transference and countertransference experience.

## TRANSFERENCE AND COUNTERTRANSFERENCE

In much of the writing about sex therapy, transference is not mentioned or specifically rejected as not useful. Perhaps this stems from Masters and Johnson (1970) who wrote,

> . . . from the start of the clinical program, the Foundation has taken the specific position that the therapeutic techniques of transference have no place in the acute two-week attempt to reverse the symptoms of sexual dysfunction and establish, reestablish or improve the channels of communication between husband and wife. Anything that distracts from positive exchange between husband and wife during their time in therapy is the responsibility of the therapeutic team to identify and immediately nullify or negate. Positive transference of sexual orientation can be and frequently is a severe deterrent to effective reconstitution of interpersonal communication for members of a marital unit, particularly when they are contending with a problem of sexual dysfunction. [p. 8]

They also see their program as minimizing opportunities for development of countertransference, which they see as an interference. "By design, [co-therapy] team interaction will minimize or eliminate specific elements of countertransference clinically detrimental to the marital relationship or to a positive prognosis for therapy" (p. 29).

The beginnings of sex therapy cast the use of countertransference not as a useful analytic tool but as an interference, echoing Freud's original description of transference as an interference to treatment (1895, 1905a, 1912a, 1912b). Although in the literature countervailing voices speak for the use of transference, many have not spelled out the specifics of its use (Kaplan 1974, Lieblum and Pervin 1980, Schmidt and Lucas 1976). Others, however, have addressed the issue. Levay and colleagues (1978, 1979) wrote of the importance of understanding both negative and positive (or excited) transference for the safeguarding of the behavioral program, and for the integration of sex therapy with the psychodynamic psychotherapy. Dickes and his colleagues (Dickes and Strauss 1979, Dunn and Dickes 1977) wrote about the need for awareness of countertransference issues—especially those involving excited and sexualized countertransference—as interfering with therapeutic judgment. None of these writers, however, advocate transference and countertransference as a major aid in the therapeutic armamentarium. Our need to employ all the tools of psychotherapy, including those of transference and countertransference, developed as the couples we try to help have come with increasingly complex difficulties. We have taken the further step of promoting transference and countertransference analysis as the most crucial technique in complete therapy (Scharff and Scharff 1987). Examples that illustrate this technique are given throughout this volume.

The sequence of exercises and the issues that may emerge during the various steps are given in Table 9–2. Their early assignments are standardized, while the later ones are tailored to the couple, to the specific sexual difficulty, and to issues as they unfold. Many therapists often omit the early exercises in treatment of some specific syndromes. It is better to begin with them because they invoke the early experiences of safety and reciprocity between a child and parents. They are often the most difficult and the most fruitful for couples, and generate a great deal of information while offering an opportunity for solidifying a therapeutic alliance.

At the end of the sequence, couples are encouraged to extend the range of their sexual expression and interaction, and to try new positions and variations that they may like. Capacity for orgasm during the shared experience and especially during intercourse is developed.

A final phase of sex therapy takes up the termination issues important to any therapy. The partners' anxiety about the end of the therapy usually shows up as they approach the integration of orgasm with containment. They realize they are approaching the capacity to have full intercourse in a new way, and that this achievement will mean the end of the therapy. Anxiety about stopping may bring a return of symptoms. As in other therapies, this offers an opportunity for review and reworking. This is also the chance to work with the loss of the therapy as a holding environment, and to look at the couple's fears of being unable to provide a safe sexual context without the support of therapy.

During the termination phase, visits typically taper off to support the couple's progress in integrating what they have learned into their

Table 9–2. The Sequence of Sex Therapy Exercises

| Title | Method | Communication |
|---|---|---|
| 1. Sensate focus 1: non-genital. | Massage or pleasuring of whole body in turns with oil or lotion, genitals and woman's breasts excluded. | No verbal or nonverbal exchange except in case of pain. Focus on self-directed experience, giving pleasure to self. |

Object relations issues: the other as environmental mother allowing self to develop and "be," with pleasure in the self developing while held in the "arms around" situation.

| Title | Method | Communication |
|---|---|---|
| 2. Sensate focus 2: genitals included. | Genitals and breasts included *in passing* in pleasuring. Arousal not to exceed mild state. | Verbal and nonverbal (hand-guiding) feedback by recipient about what is more or less pleasurable. Focus on getting and giving pleasure. |

Object relations issues: self in pleasurable interaction with primary object within envelope of safety. The couple now cooperates to maintain the holding environment while forming images of self and other, but still in units of interaction that travel only in one direction at a time, i.e., one partner gives pleasure while the other receives it. This also allows the giver to experience the pleasure of giving.

| Title | Method | Communication |
|---|---|---|
| 3. "Clinical exam" of genitalia and breasts. | Detailed exam of self and other. Speculum, instruction manual, and educational material about sexual anatomy and the sexual response cycle provided. | Full informational cooperation and exchange encouraged. Arousal not encouraged here. |

Object relations issues: this is a central ego-oriented exercise, enabling the couple to ground their knowledge of each other in the facts of each other's sexual response and anatomy. It demystifies sex, and encourages central ego growth and communication between central egos.

| Title | Method | Communication |
|---|---|---|
| 4. Self-pleasuring and masturbation (concurrent with other exercises). | Each spouse, in private, pleasures self and masturbates. May add vibrator for women, lubrication for men. | Communication with self. Understanding of own body enhances communication to other. |

Object relations issues: knowledge of self, both central self and the excited/longing aspects of self, in preparation for improved relationship to other. A more realistic knowledge of self decreases the demand on object to make up for longings, and at the same time improves ability to empathize and to give to the other. Developmentally, this has the standing of infantile and adolescent knowledge of own body and masturbation as preparation for move from self to an object.

Table 9–2.   The Sequence of Sex Therapy Exercises (continued)

| Title | Method | Communication |
|---|---|---|
| 5. Genital sensate focus 3. | Pleasuring now focused on genitals and breasts while still including whole body. Arousal, while not required, is encouraged to moderate degree, but not to orgasm. | Broad communication verbally and nonverbally during moderately heightened bodily state of arousal. |

Object relations issues: this exercise allows full intimacy and expanded cooperative object relating, still without the threats of penetration and interpenetration. Safety and lowered anxiety are maintained.

Here the exercises diverge according to specific sexual disorders and the progress and issues of the couple. The general direction involves slow progression toward full intercourse, with continuing emphasis on the whole body and whole person relationship of the couple. Some or all of the following will be prescribed depending on the couple's needs.

| | | |
|---|---|---|
| 6a. For vaginismus. | Insertion of fingers or progressive dilators into vagina during woman's self-pleasuring; then of penis in shared situation. | Tolerance of own anxiety leading to nonthreatening tolerance of penetration. |

Object relations issues: fear of penetration is built on defensive encapsulation of repressed bad object in the genitals, protecting both self and object by psychosomatic muscular contraction, which prevents penetration. Building of safety allows release of bad object from encapsulation during arousal.

| | | |
|---|---|---|
| 6b. For premature ejaculation. | Semans (1956) stop-start technique: woman stimulates man almost to climax. At his signal she stops until arousal diminishes. Repeated two or three times, then proceeds to orgasm.<br><br>and/or<br><br>Squeeze technique (Masters & Johnson 1970): Woman stimulates man to arousal, then uses thumb and first finger, squeezing just below coronal ridge. Repeated. | Self-knowledge and communication of man's knowledge of ejaculatory precursors and control. |

Object relations issues: man's fear of engulfment by object and of harmfulness of penis results in confusion of anxiety and arousal. Exercise sorts out difference between arousal and aggression, separating excited and persecuting self and object.

Table 9–2.  The Sequence of Sex Therapy Exercises (continued)

| Title | Method | Communication |
| --- | --- | --- |
| 6c. For erectile disorders, and absent or lowered male interest (ISD). | Woman stimulates man's genitals, then moves to other areas whether erection occurs or not, returning periodically to genital stimulation. | Nondemand stimulation lowers man's anxiety in shared setting. |

Object relations issues: anxiety about the persecuting object, and about the effects of the harmful self on the woman, dominate object relations in Inhibited Sexual Desire and many erectile dysfunctions. The nondemand situation allows familiarity with the bad self and object to tame them, leading to improved central object relations.

| Title | Method | Communication |
| --- | --- | --- |
| 6d. Absent or lowered female arousal (ISD); dyspareunia of psychological origin; absence of female orgasm in shared setting. | Man alternates stimulation of woman's genitals and moving away in nondemand format. Lessons from woman's solo exercises applied to shared setting. | Nondemand pleasuring reduces woman's anxiety; learning transferred from solo to shared setting. |

Object relations issues: rejecting and persecuting object issues dominate in Inhibited Sexual Desire (ISD) and dyspareunia of psychological origin. These are mollified by the nondemand stimulation, allowing tolerance of arousal, and sorting out of aggression from arousal.

Absence of orgasm in the woman is usually a learning problem about the self, best treated by instruction and support of masturbation. Several programs involving education, support, and therapy have been developed (Barbach 1974; Herman and LoPiccolo 1988). The transfer of orgasm from masturbation to the couple's shared setting involves work to decrease fear of the bad object and diminish confusion between excited and aggressive aspects of the object and the self.

The next step is shared for most formats and disorders:

| Title | Method | Communication |
| --- | --- | --- |
| 7. Containment 1: without movement. | Woman seated astride man, inserts penis, remains immobile. Man is passive. | Mutual reassurance in previously anxious situation of penetration. |
| 8. Containment 2: with increasing movement. | Slow movement added first by woman only, then by both. Arousal increases until orgasm allowed. | Mutuality of control and nondemand. |

Object relations issues: interpenetration of physical and object relations builds excitement and trust in tolerable increments. Building toward full cooperation and intimacy.

| Title | Method | Communication |
| --- | --- | --- |
| 9. Optional for ejaculatory and orgasmic disorders: manual stimulation by woman of man, man of woman and/or either of self (the bridge techniques [Kaplan 1987a]). | Stimulation of self and/or other before entry and during containment. Modifications of position to facilitate manual stimulation during containment. | Communication of patience and cooperation in place of demand. |

Object relations issues: full, whole object relations that tolerate each other's needs, build concern for the other, and lead to confidence in the object's concern for the self. Intimacy and excitement are fully integrated with the capacity for full genital pleasure, but not at the expense of the rest of one's own body or of the other person.

ordinary life without the support of the therapist. Sex therapy usually takes from three to eight months, but there is no fixed time table.

It is worth noting that Kaplan's methodology of treatment relies heavily on the introduction of fantasy, both the patient's own and that stimulated by erotica, as an adjunct to sex therapy (Kaplan 1974). In sex therapy based on object relations theory, fantasy and erotic literature have been introduced to a limited degree in many cases, but the main focus is on psychodynamic work around the themes that interfere with normal fantasy life.

Before or during sex therapy, couples who are naïve or uninformed about sexual functioning and the emotional issues involved are advised to read about sexual anatomy and the response cycle, and about the issues involved in sexual distress. Books such as Levine's *Sex is Not Simple* (1988), Raley's *Making Love* (1976), and Comfort's *The Joy of Sex* (1972) are used as aids to the process at various stages.

One-third to one-half of the couples seen primarily in sex therapy initially, later request further couple treatment or individual psychotherapy to deal with therapeutic impasse reached in sex therapy or new areas for exploration opened up by success in sex therapy. A small proportion request family therapy for family issues that they now see to derive from difficulty in their marital relationship (D. E. Scharff 1982). Psychotherapy afterward has included continuing marital therapy, family therapy, and individual therapy ranging from a few sessions to psychoanalysis.

The outcome of sex therapy is variable, partly depending on the type of disorder, and partly depending on the ambition of the undertaking. Masters and Johnson's (1970) original report of 80% success with only a 5% relapse after five years has not been upheld in the field (Zilbergeld and Evans 1980). Early reports indicated that follow-up of apparent successes found much higher rates of relapse than had been thought (Levine and Agle 1978, Althof et al. 1988).

Kaplan (1974, 1979) notes that disorders of the orgasm phase—premature ejaculation and primary anorgasmia—do well with treatment, while erectile disorders are more variable. Some cases of erectile difficulty, those due to relatively superficial anxiety, act like the disorders of orgasm in meeting with a high rate of success, while those caused by deeper anxiety are often refractory to sex therapy. Kaplan (1987b) concludes that disorders of inhibited desire are the most difficult to treat and most often require intensive psychotherapy or psychoanalysis, although a small percentage of these cases respond surprisingly well to sex therapy. Disorders with a panic or phobic component to the sexual aversion run an intermediate course, responding best when psychotherapy is teamed with medication.

Those clinicians wishing to familiarize themselves more thoroughly with the practicalities and technique of behavioral sex therapy would do well to look at Kaplan's original work *The New Sex Therapy* (1974) or at its briefer rendition in her *Illustrated Manual of Sex Therapy* (1987a). Our intention in this chapter has been to give a sufficient framework for understanding the method used in cases where we describe examples of sexual exercise assignments and the ensuing therapy sessions in which they are reviewed. The combination of behavioral aspects of sex therapy with an object relations approach paves the way for integrating sexuality and marital issues without the exclusion of either from treatment.

Two examples of unfolding sex therapy will illustrate the interplay of behavioral and analytic psychotherapy.

## OBJECT RELATIONS IN THE EARLY PHASE OF SEX THERAPY

Nate and Cynthia Ornstein, in their late twenties, had married after years of on-again-off-again courtship, trying out other partners and always coming back to each other. They were an attractive couple, athletic and energetic despite Cynthia's mild congenital limp due to one leg being slightly shorter than the other. Nate had lost interest in sex with Cynthia, withdrawing to masturbate to fantasy material. They came to one of our students for sex therapy. After working successfully with their resistance, he now felt stymied.

In the first nongenital exercise Cynthia felt exceedingly bored. She reported when she was active doing the massage, "I did things I hoped he would do back to me." It sounded as though she were trying to send Nate a message.

The therapist said, "You're focusing on Nate's experience instead of your own, and you're able to get your own enjoyment only if he treats you in a certain way—which you are spending your energy trying to signal him about. Does this echo a way you may have felt treated as a child?"

Cynthia was thoughtful for a moment, and then said, "I think I spent a lot of time trying to guess what my parents thought, and I was nervous about it. I would feel I couldn't enjoy something unless they approved, so I'd be doing things to get their approval. That may be the way I'm treating Nate. I'm watching him to see if he approves."

In subsequent sessions, Cynthia was slowly able to be active on her own behalf, to let a sense of pleasure grow from inside her. As she did so, Nate said that he could feel her relax, that he felt less obligated to reassure her, and freer to enjoy what she did to him without feeling responsible for her experience.

"It lets me off the hook," he said. "My mom used to be watching me. I felt responsible for her feeling all right. It's a relief when Cynthia backs off."

Here the exercise revealed a mutually reinforcing pattern in which Cynthia's attempts to communicate her needs interfered with her empathic reception of Nate's needs, while Nate's capacity to detect Cynthia's needs was blocked by his defense against his mother's demand for support.

Despite their improvement, the couple found excuses. A week later, Cynthia was still bored and reluctant although continuing to do the exercises. The therapist reported his countertransference: he felt rejected by Cynthia's ennui and sensed continued denigration of the process. All motivation was left to him. He asked more about her history of difficulty in enjoying things for herself. Cynthia described how her mother had discouraged her initiatives as a child. She would take music lessons, sports, drama, and then drop them, feeling a lack of encouragement.

"But I try to encourage her, to tell her I love her or I like the way she looks," said Nate.

"He bothers me. He *stares* at me," she said with a sudden force.

"What is it about the staring?" asked the therapist.

"People used to stare at me because I had a deformity. I hardly notice my limp now," Cynthia said. "But until it was corrected, I'd dread exposure to other kids and would isolate myself. At a party recently, an orthopedic resident came up to me to ask about one of my legs being shorter than the other. It brought back all I felt as a child, and I was upset for days. People used to look at me, strangers, people on the street, friends' parents. My parents tried hard to protect me, but they couldn't completely."

Exposing herself fully to Nate and reporting exercises in therapy sessions to the therapist was the equivalent of the unprotected gaze of peers, strangers, and doctors that she had fled. Sex therapy—and marriage, too—had meant being stared at and exposed. In supervision, we encouraged the student to make this link in an interpretation aimed at the resistance to active engagement in treatment.

## OBJECT RELATIONS IN EARLY AND LATE PHASES

A second couple illustrates the emergence of repressed object relations from both early and later stages of sex therapy.

Rebecca and Quentin, described in Chapter 1, came for sex therapy with David Scharff because of Rebecca's vaginismus and aversion. It later developed that Quentin had difficulty ejaculating inside her vagina. Before the formal sex therapy even began, Quentin asked for an individual session to share a fantasy he was fighting, and that he feared would hurt Rebecca irreparably. When they had sex, which was infrequent, he would help bring himself to ejaculation by fantasizing intercourse with a friend of

Rebecca's mother. But recently the fantasy had changed to Rebecca's mother herself. I [D.E.S.] urge revelation of this fantasy in accordance with the principle that any charged secret continues to exert subversive influence, as elaborated in Chapter 12. I suggested doing so before beginning the exercises. Quentin told Rebecca, trembling and hesitant. Rebecca said she did feel hurt, but that she wasn't going away over it. She recognized that Quentin had problems to deal with, and it made her think he needed individual therapy.

This cleared the air for the first assignment of the sex therapy, where it became clear that Rebecca feared full bodily exposure to Quentin as much as he had feared exposure of his physical self and fantasy. While he said he loved her, he criticized everything she did. Growing up, his own critical mother leveled endless rapierlike critiques at him just like the ones he now leveled at Rebecca—saying she couldn't do anything quite right for him. The exchange established the presence of his mother as an object who returned from repression to haunt him and them on an almost daily basis. Rebecca's valency to accept these critical assaults and live in retreat from them came from her experience with her own intrusive, commanding mother whose drive to possess Rebecca's body had taken the form of intense interest in her eating. We could quickly understand Rebecca's vaginismus as an attempt to keep Quentin—as her mother-with-a-penis—from invading.

Quentin's fantasies of Rebecca's mother quickly faded away and the sex therapy moved slowly on as he recognized from the exercises that he treated Rebecca as though she were his forbidden and exciting mother. He dreamt of sessions with me and Rebecca—but his mother was there, too. Then under the influence of therapy, she was transformed into a favorite aunt—the mother he wished he had. He was angry at his father for not intervening more between him and his mother. Both he and Rebecca agreed I was now keeping both their internal mothers at bay as the exercises brought the new threat of invasion from within—and Quentin finally shed tears as he said that in his head his mother no longer came between him and Rebecca. As he felt this, he could *feel* what she did to him in the massages and what he did to her for the first time, no longer completely withdrawn to a schizoid and narcissistic preoccupation.

The progression of exercises went slowly in this anxious and phobic couple. Three months later, they were still at the Sensate II stage, massaging each other including the genitals and breasts with only a moderate level of arousal allowed. They were also working exercises on communications—telling each other exactly what they liked and did not like the other to do. Their tolerance and mutual enjoyment were growing along with an acceptance of their own and each other's bodies. Rebecca had a dream: "We were waiting in an old building to see you. A fat man came up and took a group of little children. Quentin said, 'That's a therapist.' I asked him how he knew. He said, 'All therapists are fat.' A mother said to her child, 'Wash your hands.' I felt dirty because I had touched Quentin's penis without washing my hands.

"The frightening thing was," Rebecca continued, "that in making notes on the dream, I wrote therapist as 'the rapist.' I don't know if 'the rapist' is you or Quentin."

"Who would you say then?" the therapist asked.

"Probably both of you," she said.

Quentin added, "My association was to the idea of a 'pedophile.' I was angry that Rebecca sort of told you about the last session, asking you to set me straight like a teacher taking a kid to the principal. It's like you're a pedophile watching and scolding us, getting aroused, and we're like a couple of children in here."

The transference elaborated in association to the dream then led them to see that their wariness about exposing themselves came from their own voyeuristic curiosity and repressed sexual aggression. Until now, they had jointly blamed the assaultiveness on Quentin, but they now saw their mutual invasion of their own holding echoed in the transference to the therapist, who had been feeling as he pressed on with the therapy that he might be harming Rebecca.

Three weeks later, the exercises had progressed so that Rebecca was inserting the glans of Quentin's penis gently into her vagina while sitting astride him. She still had some pain, which then subsided as she sat still, and she was able to tolerate her anxiety. Doing this exercise, she became aware of a fantasy that Quentin's penis was a sword, an association to her father, who was a marine. She said, "My father was obnoxious, and proud of being in the military. Did I tell you that some days he'd strip to his shorts and undershirt, buckle on his dress sword, and drink beer? I try not to think about him."

She also now remembered a dream about the therapist. "We were on a bus in Washington but ended up in Jacksonville—my other home. It was summer, but you were wearing a herringbone tweed jacket. You seemed handsome and I liked talking to you. We walked down the hill and you dropped me at my parents' house and went to your own house further on."

The jacket linked the therapist to Quentin, who has one like it. She thought the therapist handsome. The day before, a handsome, likeable neighbor had gotten too close for comfort, kissing her on the neck. Quentin was upset at her dream. He felt she did not see him as providing enough safety. He thought the dream was about a date, and remembered that growing up, the word "bus" meant "kiss." Rebecca denied knowing that. The therapist said that the dream did present Rebecca's emerging erotic longings as aimed at him, but that the herringbone jacket bound him and Quentin. The therapist was providing safety for a new way of romantic and previously unsafe feeling for them.

"That's true," said Rebecca. "I just thought that Washington and Jacksonville were my two homes. Jacksonville is mostly where I grew up, and where I was sexually uncomfortable—too hot really. That jacket—I think it means now those feelings that were too hot for comfort now feel like an old, comfy jacket.

The therapist added, "And your new comfort with Quentin and with me is like the new comfort your vagina has with his penis. It used to be too hot to handle, but it seems to be cooling to comfort."

These sessions provided a sense of the complex issues that emerge as the sexual anxieties are faced in a steady sequential way through the exercises. Then the ordinary complements of analytic psychotherapy—associations, dreams, understanding of the interpersonal situation, transference and countertransference—all become useful in understanding the internal object relations that emerge on the projection screen of bodily and genital interplay. In this way, sex therapy from an object relations perspective points up the difficulties in the couple's psychosomatic partnership and paves the way for new understanding and working through.

Chapter **10**

# A COUPLE IN SEX THERAPY WITH CONCURRENT INDIVIDUAL AND FAMILY THERAPY

The following case example, given in this chapter and the next one, allows us to examine the process of an unusually extensive and integrated treatment, from which we can learn about the interlocking of individual, couple, and family processes, and the mutual influence of the three treatment approaches. This chapter details the evaluation of both couple and family, and then describes the treatment of the couple. Then the following chapter describes a phase of the family therapy that sheds light on how couples' sexual distress influences their children.

> Lars and Velia Simpson, described briefly in Chapter 2, came to consult me [D.E.S.] one December some years ago for help with their sex life. The consultation began with a dramatic announcement from Velia: "I hate sex. That's all. What more do you want to know?"
> Lars added, "And I have premature ejaculation."

"How long do you last?" I asked.

"Two or three minutes," he responded.

I turned to Velia and asked, "Is that what you hate about it? That Lars doesn't last long enough?"

Before she could answer, Lars quipped, "No! That's four minutes too long for her!"

Velia concurred. "I just don't like sex. I never have."

In fact, she later said, it was not quite accurate to say that she had *never* liked it. There had been a brief period of pleasure five years before, when she was in therapy for depression, after the birth of their second child. During the last few months of her treatment she found herself longing for sex for the first and only time in her life. Sexual activity had led to arousal but with no orgasmic release, so her pleasure led only to aching longing and eventually to resentment. Her psychotherapy had stopped when the family was transferred to another location, and Velia's interest in sex had disappeared, leaving her both disappointed and relieved.

Now she would merely tolerate Lars' demands. "I can feel his vibes," she said, "and I know the thing to do is to get it over with. But it makes me mad, and sometimes, I just go downstairs and scream at the kids or at anybody."

"What makes you angry at these times?" I asked.

"Just the sex," she said. "The fact of the sex is all it takes. It isn't that Lars does anything wrong. It's just that I hate it. I hold my breath and wait for it to be over. I don't blame him for wanting it. But it's just more than I can stand!"

Velia was able to give an extensive history of her experience growing up. Her father was verbally abusive to the children, and occasionally physically abusive of her mother. He was probably alcoholic. She was angry at her mother for failing to protect the children. Looking for love and kind authority, she had "played doctor" with her older brother. Her vague memories of this body play left the uncertain suggestion that sibling incest might have occurred at that time. She did recall quite definitely a few episodes of sexual interaction with her brothers in pre-adolescence. She remembered them as partly traumatic, but also as offering more love than she could find anywhere else in her family. Sex had assumed a threatening yet beckoning quality for her.

Velia remembered wondering about sex as an adolescent: where were the wonderful romantic feelings that she read about in the novels she devoured? Slowly, her hopes and feelings had faded. Then at 19, she met Lars when they were both enrolled in a special summer program at college. They had a brief courtship, with a great deal of newfound cuddling and rubbing. She had a spurt of physical longing, but they agreed to postpone intercourse until marriage, which occurred three months after they met.

Sex was difficult from the first. Penetration was impossible until Velia had a hymenectomy. Thereafter penetration was possible, but Lars had premature ejaculation, emission occurring after intercourse lasting from a few seconds to perhaps three minutes. Velia became reluctant to have sex, although she tried to give Lars what he needed.

Lars began to regret the forcing of his wishes on Velia, preferring to protect her from the invasion she felt. He felt that his sexual needs were an assault on Velia. When he first spoke to me individually, Lars asked if saltpeter would help him to curb his own sexual urgency so that he could protect her. He accepted my suggestion that they search in therapy for an answer.

Lars' own history, as given earlier in Chapter 2, was brief and his forgetting impenetrable. He could not give any details of his childhood, remembering only his father's arrest for homosexual solicitation, and the ensuing breakup of the family when Lars was 17. Thereafter he had an attenuated relationship with his father, although he continued to see his mother and felt reasonably close to her. He had not dated much in high school, so Velia was his first serious love and his first sexual partner. In response to my query about other, nonsexual difficulties, Lars spoke of his persistent difficulty with memory, a problem which he thought was "organic" and with which he would like help.

Both Lars and Velia thought that divorce was unlikely. Even if they could not get help with sex, they would carry on somehow.

## THE CHILDREN'S EXPRESSION OF THE PARENT'S SEXUAL RELATIONSHIP

In the first couple assessment interview, Lars and Velia had mentioned that Alex, the middle of their three children, was symptomatic. He was disruptive at home, and he soiled and wet day and night, without any clear pattern to his enuresis and encopresis. When he was born Velia suffered postpartum depression, which was the occasion for her psychotherapy. She said that she got depressed for two reasons. Shortly after Alex's birth she felt accused and guilty to learn from Lars that he was masturbating because of the lack of sex. The other trigger for her depression was her disappointment in having another boy. Their first child, Eric, now 7½, had been a source of pleasure and was doing well, but Velia desperately wanted a girl, and was profoundly disappointed when Alex was born.

Now, aged 5½, he had been difficult from the first, a hyperactive baby who was difficult to soothe. He had continued to be difficult throughout his development. Recently, his kindergarten teacher had spoken to them about his high activity level and distractibility.

Two years later, their third child was born, the longed-for girl, who, they agreed, had brought light into everyone's life from the beginning. Jeanette was a delightful imp who gave hugs and kisses freely, and who was as easygoing as Alex was difficult.

The couple readily agreed to a family assessment interview, which occurred some weeks later in January. This family interview is of special interest because the children were able to express in their play their understanding and incorporation of issues arising in their parents' sexual difficulty. This play, along with the parents' open responses to it, enriched our understanding of the marital and sexual disorder.

## The Family Assessment Session

In the family evaluation, Alex demonstrated a combined picture of hyperactivity and attention deficit disorder. The oldest son, Eric, aged 7½, seemed to be a normal latency boy. And the youngest, Jeanette, aged 3½, had immature speech—not unusual for her age—and a sexualized way of interacting. I thought that she was often as disruptive as Alex in the play, but she got away with it, coyly playing on her charm. Where Alex was impulsive and bumptious, she was sly and charming—but to the same disruptive effect. Sitting with this family, I quickly began to sense an excitement and sexualization of Jeanette's personality, which made me think that this charming 3-year-old carried the excitement and sexuality that was fearfully held out of the parental sexual relationship. It seemed to have been put into her, where the parents, and perhaps the family-at-large, could feel it would be more safely lodged and responded to.

Early in the family interview, Lars and Velia spoke obliquely about their sexual relationship in a way appropriate to the presence of children. Velia said, "Our fights happen when Lars wants conjugal relations and I don't." Lars laughed anxiously and agreed. As they talked, the children played out the issues they were discussing, and with a clarity that no conversation could have achieved.

First 5-year-old Alex took wooden blocks and built an elongated tunnel, which he said was a firehouse. Jeanette took a firetruck with a ladder that could be raised and lowered, and promptly pushed it through the firehouse, which broke apart. I immediately called this juxtaposition of the children's play and the parents' discussion to the attention of Lars and Velia. Velia responded, "The firetruck wrecked the tunnel. I guess that's the way I would see it, too." And Lars' laughter seemed to say, "I think that's what their mother is afraid of, and it's as if they know it." When I questioned the children as to which drivers in the family would wreck things, 7-year-old Eric offered the opinion that his little sister would always cause this kind of wreckage, while Alex, the boy, could drive more skillfully.

This play seemed to me to represent the children's understanding that phallic sexual activity was felt to be fundamentally destructive to Velia, and was therefore to be avoided just as the parents were now seeking to avoid it at all costs. However, Eric's comments indicated a different idea: that girls were more destructive sexually than boys—a view not consciously shared by Velia or Lars, but consistent with Jeanette's impulsivity and Velia's barely concealed anger and Lars' fears of invading Velia and his habit of ending intercourse early.

Later in the session, the children played out the way a father doll could "drive a ship" by lying down, that is by passivity. They explained to me that that was the best way to control the ship, except that the father doll immediately got buried, encased in a wooden box. Without any questioning from me, Lars grimaced in recognition of the emotional message of the play. He said that he often felt he got buried by events in the family, even while he struggled to "steer the ship." Sometimes he just gave up and "lay down on the job." It was then that events were especially likely to bury him. A short while later, Alex played at inserting the father doll into a cement mixer, grinding it up, and unceremoniously dumping it out.

While all this action was going on in the center of the floor, Eric knelt calmly at the play table and drew pictures of interstellar wars in which the good guys fought off horrendous attacks from the "gold and silver enemy." He continued to comment on Jeanette and Alex's play, until I asked him to explain his picture to me. He said that the good guys, who "had a humongous home base," were under attack from the "gold and silver enemy." He explained the strategy of their defense against surprise attack. He pointed out the launch pad for their counterattacks on the enemy ships from outer space. And he reassured me that the good guys would win. Eric seemed to be the "good" and "well-adjusted" child. I was aware of my identification with him as the oldest boy interested in aerospace and the mediation of good and bad. (I was particularly interested in this initial impression a year later, when on reevaluation I discovered another part of Eric. On that occasion he played with a Superman action figure who wreaked havoc on innocent victims. In playing this theme, he demonstrated that there were internal object relations in which a part of his self was identified with persecuting objects, something that had not been observable initially.)

Jeanette's main preoccupation was with the large baby doll whom she said was the mommy. She took some colored blocks and built her a comfortable "spaceship" that looked like a bed. She put the tiny father doll alongside her. The mommy seemed safe as she dwarfed her partner in her spaceship-bed, but it was not long before Alex came over to fracture the structure and scatter the dolls. Jeanette objected, but took the dolls to safety and went off to play elsewhere in the room.

## USING FAMILY INFORMATION TO FORMULATE THE COUPLE'S DIFFICULTY

From the couple's initial interview and from individual interviews with each of them, I had understood that the parents' sexual dysfunction represented the net result of their individual histories. Although Velia's history was much clearer, I guessed that Lars, like Velia, had grown up in a family in which hopes for love were frustrated and in which aggressive, but sexualized relationships with parents were substituted. The resultant fear of sex was something they shared, even though both carried hopes for emotional intimacy, mutual support, and a decent sexual life. Velia's openly acknowledged fear and hate of sex was matched by Lars' unconscious fear of sex. In trying to rid himself of his own sexual wishes in order to protect her, he was, through projective identification, trying to protect himself from a "bad father." It was clear that the couple shared a fear of sex and an idea that a mother would be harmed by a bad father and specifically by his penis. I would only learn the contours of Lars' internal bad father from him directly later in the couple's sex therapy.

For now, the image of the bad father and the danger in the couple's relationship were more clearly expressed in the children's play: the destruction the phallic firetruck did to the vaginal garage, the fragmentation of the father ground up and spit out by Alex's cement mixer, and in the following years, the viciousness of Eric's portrayal of Superman.

Similarly, the family's preoccupation with protecting the mother was spoken for in Jeanette's play, as she built the safe spaceship and balanced the huge mommy doll with the tiny, unthreatening father. Even so, Alex came to disrupt the play, and symbolically, to destroy the safe space and the sexual relationship Jeanette had arranged for her internal parents.

## THE FAMILY'S INTERNALIZATION OF THE COUPLE'S SEXUALITY

Sexual tension between the couple affected the whole family. As the children shared in the family anxiety about the well-being of the couple, each of them incorporated different elements of the parents' difficulty in their own growth. The children would often quarrel to draw attention from a potential fight between parents. Eric, the oldest, tried to be good, to use the rational defenses appropriate to his stage of development to combat the forces of evil in the family and the universe, located by him on behalf of his family in masculine characters with whom he also unconsciously identified.

Alex, the middle boy, had attempted to stay his development in order not to grow into a destructive man, but intolerance for aggression, taken from both parents, led him to soil his pants whenever he might otherwise have become angry. I thought he also had a constitutional difficulty, confirmed afterward by psychometric testing, which yielded the diagnostic classification "Attention Deficit Disorder with Hyperactivity." Nevertheless, he also had a thematic interference with his maturation. Throughout his development, he fell back on anal techniques of relating—holding things in or pooping them out aggressively—instead of advancing to phallic or oedipal phases. Thus he could disguise his strivings for his mother, and his rivalry with his father. Instead of competing directly with his father or brother for his mother's attention and affection, he maintained a kind of innocent infantile impulsivity and random destructiveness that attacked the relationship between the parents and the overall family structure.

Finally, Jeanette had been seen from the first as the child who could give to everybody. She had, however, a precocious seductive quality that, as Eric noted, caused wrecks frequently, but without drawing the kind of blame earned by Alex's masculine recklessness. It was Eric who noted the danger in the female role in the family, and who alerted me that there was an aggressive attack on the structural integrity of the parents' relationship in Jeanette's play too, a threat that was largely overlooked by the family.

In these individualized ways, according to their different developmental stages, the children had incorporated aspects of the parental problem and were now, in turn, affecting the family. Alex's gender had triggered mother's original depression, and emphasized her sexual withdrawal. Jeanette's oedipal development was bringing an insidious danger by sexualizing the family despite their fear of sex. And Eric's latency defenses were relied on too heavily by his parents as they tried to get him to set things right in the family to compensate for their own hopelessness about being able to do so themselves.

The sexual difficulty of the parents followed from their individual and combined internal object relations. Their resulting relationship formed the holding context for the family and provided the object relations material that determined the shape of the developmental pathways and troubles of the children. The deficits and vulnerabilities in their relationship were felt by the children, and were reflected in their development, each of them in different ways. The dynamic connections between these elements were demonstrated and interpreted in this family evaluation, and later in sex therapy and family therapy. While the facts of dissatisfaction with their sexual life could be noted in the family setting, the specifics of their sexual difficulties were appropriately not addressed with children present.

## THE COURSE OF THERAPY

I initially recommended a combined approach to the Simpson family. Optimally it should have included individual therapies for Velia and Alex, family therapy to address the children's internalization of the family's difficulties, and sex therapy for the couple. Lars was referred for evaluation of his memory difficulty, which psychological testing confirmed to be both neurotically and constitutionally based in a learning disorder not unlike Alex's. However, the resources for all these therapies were not available. Velia, who felt most in need, began intensive individual therapy first. During the process, her therapist, who was a child psychiatrist, also evaluated Alex and attempted to treat him. He confirmed the diagnosis of attention deficit disorder with hyperactivity. He prescribed stimulant medication, and there was prompt improvement in Alex's school behavior, but not in his enuresis or encopresis, nor in his immature, jealous, or disruptive behavior. After a trial of play therapy, he concluded that Alex was not motivated or especially competent in individual play therapy. Alex's continued needs were one of the reasons for recommending family therapy again a year later.

We will not detail the course of Velia's individual therapy here, but it is of interest to give some flavor of it. Her therapist described a rewarding, intense, committed psychotherapy characterized by stormy oscillations. He found Velia to be a strongly motivated woman struggling against severe depression with marked borderline features, who worked hard in therapy and viewed it as a potentially lifesaving opportunity. Her depressive mood swings responded to antidepressive medication, which also steadied her capacity to work in psychotherapy. She formed an intensely adhesive transference in which the therapist became the center of her life. With him, she worked on her insistent dependency and her rage at both parents, but especially at her father. It became clear that she had turned to her brother for love and understanding she could find nowhere else, and that she had done so in a sexualized way. The therapist survived feeling battered and mauled and so succeeded in containing the raging and loving transference.

After less than three months of individual therapy, Velia became interested in sex with Lars. They resumed attempts to have intercourse. But the restoration of her desire frustrated her immediately, since Lars's premature ejaculation was so severe that it left her painfully hanging without release. She would then retreat in bitter agony, chancing sex again in a few days. This unsatisfied longing left Velia frequently depressed. Lars, too, felt that the sex ought to go better, although he was thrilled that it was now possible to have a sexual relationship that Velia no longer found fundamentally assaultive.

At the end of a year of individual therapy, she again asked for help with her sexual dysfunction and with Alex. At her therapist's request, I reevaluated them, both as a couple, and as a family. I thought that with Velia's progress, the chances of success for sex therapy were greatly improved. The need for family work was still pressing, and perhaps more so following my reassessment of Eric. Alex, now 6½, and on the stimulant medication, was better able to pay attention but he was still disruptive, immature, encopretic, and enuretic. His behavior frequently disorganized the family. Jeanette, now 4½, was positively coquettish and her development had become more obviously sexualized. Eric, now 8, was still articulate and well organized, but now showed an identification with brutes who harmed others. Velia and Lars were somewhat more able to cope as parents, but they still wanted, and warranted, help with parenting and other family issues.

I offered sex therapy and family therapy, each weekly. That constituted a compromise plan. While I usually see families at weekly intervals, I almost always conduct sex therapy by seeing couples twice weekly because I find that the intensity of the anxiety generated by the exercises is difficult for them to bear for an entire week without the holding environment of more frequent sessions. I explained to Lars and Velia that this schedule would put more demand on them to contain the anxiety aroused by the sex therapy. Nevertheless, this was simply all the time I had available. In making the recommendation, however, I considered the fact that Velia was continuing her intensive individual work, seeing her therapist three to four times a week. I hoped this would help with her anxiety and offer a place to deal more thoroughly with the issues raised in the couple and family work. Lars was also seeing a behavioral psychiatrist for his memory and learning problems, and these sessions were helping him manage his anxiety.

The family therapy was instituted in January without much difficulty, but Lars and Velia gave multiple reasons why they could not start the sex therapy then. Lars felt he couldn't get away from work more than once a week. He was frightened. After one session the couple broke off the sex therapy, although they kept up the family work.

That June, Velia reported during a family session that she had had to be briefly hospitalized while her psychiatrist was away because she had been terribly depressed at his absence. Before going to the hospital, she decided, "I'll just make love with Lars although I don't feel any desire for it myself." It was to be a farewell gift to him. She thought that "he could just pop it in and it wouldn't bother me." After this thought, she sank further into a frustrated depression.

The hospitalization, which was brief, spurred her individual work. The couple seemed to strengthen around Velia's realization that collapse was not the answer. With this general fortitude, they asked to begin the sex therapy again. They felt that they could now "at least tolerate it," and began at last, in late summer, a year and a half after their initial application to the clinic.

## TECHNIQUE OF SEX THERAPY: A BRIEF REVIEW

The sex therapy conducted with Lars and Velia proceeded along regular lines as described by Kaplan (1974) modified by D.E. Scharff (1982), and described at length in Chapter 9. The couple is given a series of behavioral assignments, each of which applies to restricted phases of the sexual response cycle. The couple's sexual relationship is conceptualized as a "psychosomatic partnership"—that partnership which is like the earliest relationship between mother and baby in being entirely physical and at the same time entirely psychological. (Winnicott 1971).

The couple is asked not to have intercourse and to go no further physically than the level of assignment they have achieved. Beginning with the first assignment—to alternate in giving each other pleasurable massages while omitting the genitals and the woman's breasts—the couple is slowly given back increasingly wide areas of sexual interaction: first the breasts and genitals in passing without arousal; then breasts and genitals in a more focused way; then alternating arousal and relaxation, "containment" of penis in vagina without movement; adding slow controlled movement; adding manual stimulation to the genitals, with special attention to the woman; and finally full intercourse.

Along the way, there are ancillary exercises: masturbation and pleasuring of the body for each partner privately; a "clinical examination" of their own genitals and each other's for informational and demystification purposes; and work on the details of communication during and between exercises. in addition to the standard framework, other techniques may be used to address specific problems: progressive dilators for vaginismus; a vibrator in addition to masturbation exercises for women whose orgasmic capacity is more refractory; visual or written erotic material to aid in fantasy; and techniques to help delay ejaculation—the "squeeze" and "stop-start" techniques to help delay orgasm and ejaculation—or to promote orgasm and ejaculation—the "bridge technique" (Kaplan 1987a). Positions that help with some of these processes are suggested when relevant, and other advice is freely given.

All exercises occur in the privacy of the couple's home, and are then reviewed verbally with the therapist at the next therapy session, with particular attention to the points at which difficulty is experienced. Each stage of the therapy tends to focus on different developmental levels. Thus the early stages of nongenital pleasuring bring up issues that can be understood as reflecting difficulties in basic trust, the holding of the mother–infant situation, and of bodily integrity. Later stages involving mutual feedback reflect the reciprocity of the mother–infant situation, but also involve issues of separation and individualization. To put that in Fairbairn's language, we are working on the mediation of internal object relations in the transition from infantile dependency to mature interdependency between two whole people who are involved in genital interaction. In the midphase of the sex therapy, issues of the mediation of good and bad object relations can be seen in action during the artificially framed sexual interaction.

The emotions elicited in understanding the experiences and especially the setbacks during the couple's attempts to carry out the exercises at home, lead to some powerful sessions. It has regularly been my experience that the impact of therapy sessions during the conduct of sex therapy is similar to that of a particularly moving psychoanalytic hour. Issues that have been deeply buried are brought forcefully to the surface by the pressure of the physical interaction, by its successes and by its failures. The couple is asked to associate to these events, to bring in dreams that occur in the course of the therapy, and to work with them in this focused and accelerated psychotherapy. The therapist works with the couple interpretively to understand the material dynamically.

## SHIFTING OBJECT RELATIONS DURING SEX THERAPY

Sex therapy with Lars and Velia was unusual in several respects. I [D.E.S.] have already mentioned that I saw them weekly, when it is my usual practice to see couples twice a week. Also, this was the only instance in my practice when I have conducted sex therapy concurrently with *both* family therapy and intensive analytic psychotherapy. Thirdly, some of the family sessions were videotaped, which allowed for extensive review. For these reasons, and perhaps because Velia was emotionally so labile and expressive of transference material, the information available was considerably richer than usual.

Once we finally began sex therapy, Lars and Velia were cooperative about the therapeutic regimen. But they suffered deeply with the agonies of the inhibitions imposed by the sex therapy framework. Lars would press to break the 'rules' and ignore the prohibition against genital touching. Even when he maintained the prescribed restraints, he longed for more.

Surprisingly, so did Velia! Mutual heightened excitement emerged for both of them from the beginning. In retrospect, I could see that behind Velia's original hatred of sex was a barely repressed, raging longing, a denied excitement. This illustrates Fairbairn's theoretical description of the way in which the rejecting object constellation launches a hostile attack on the exciting object and ego, deeply repressing it. Velia's initial psychotherapy had changed her internal balance, so that now she and Lars were at the mercy of the return of previously repressed ruthlessly exciting internal objects that they had struggled for years to keep at bay.

Now, despite the fact that the assignments of mutual pleasurable massaging excluded genital and breast contact, Lars tried to French kiss Velia. That felt to her like an intrusion on her safety, but at the same time she urgently longed to respond. This longing which the exercises released constituted a further sense of danger to her. Lars and Velia could hardly stand this agonized, irritable, hyperexcitement which now went on without release.

At this point, I assigned solo exercises to them. They were to spend time working with their own bodies including masturbation, which could give them individual sexual release while that was still prohibited in the shared exercises. This private pleasuring was difficult for both of them for different reasons. Velia had never masturbated and never had an orgasm. She had a great deal of learning to do, and meanwhile was left hanging with the painful sense of frustration she now most feared. Lars felt that in the past he had suffered from an addiction to masturbation which he rigidly suppressed. He could hardly bear to chance trying it again because he found the idea of masturbation threatening to his self control.

## A PRODUCTIVE REGRESSION

In early October, three months after the beginning of the sex therapy, Velia had a second hospitalization of three days. This had three determinants: (1) her upset after reviewing in sex therapy her adolescent sexual activity with her brother, (2) realization of rage at her father for physical abuse she now began to remember in her individual therapy, and (3) her anxiety and rage at me for being absent from family therapy that week.

After reviewing her rage at my absence and her need for hospital doctors to care for her, Velia returned to the anxiety-laden area of her turning to her brother for love. During sex therapy she recovered the experience of adolescent arousal during sexual play with one of her brothers. She had fondled his penis on several occasions and had longed for it. She could now recall the urgency of her longing for the penis, and the ensuing years of repressed longing and revulsion. Although she feared Lars would be disgusted by her revelation, he was patient and sympathetic. Then, she remembered that one of her brothers did have intercourse with her when she was 13. She was aroused as she remembered it in therapy, but she was unsure whether she had been aroused at 13. A great deal of shame accompanied the revelation.

## THE TURNING POINT

About a month later, in late November, Velia showed up in a frilly blouse, looking not at all depressed. Lars looked irrepressible and impish. The exercise that had been assigned to them was to have been a pleasuring massage that was to include the breasts and genitals, but only in passing and without any attempts at arousal.

In this exercise, Velia said, she had felt an urgent ache to touch more and to be touched. She said, "When he touched my vulva and his hand went away, it was like dying inside." She fought back the tears and felt frightened. As she said, "When we finished, I had Lars hold me in his arms because I needed to feel safe." She felt the continuing "breast and genital hungering." She had worked on tolerating the intensity and therefore had felt in better control in the following three exercise sessions.

But, then, in the next exercise session, Lars had put her hand on his penis. Suddenly, she "felt everything went to pieces."

I asked, "What did 'going to pieces' remind you of?"

She responded, "It reminded me of the times with my brother when we were 13. We were in his room, and he would unzip his fly and pull out his penis and have me touch it. It didn't feel good. It was hard. The top looked rubbery with ridges on it. I didn't want to touch it."

I asked, "Did you also feel drawn to it?"

She said, "No!" Then she paused and said, "You know, I don't know if it is 'No,' I didn't, or 'no' I don't want to admit it. I think this ties to something else. For years, without remembering this, I've seen an erect penis in everything, not connected to anything, but floating in the air like my brother's penis. Just sticking out from his pants without testicles."

I asked Lars, "What do you feel, listening to Velia?"

Lars said, pulling on his eyebrow distractedly. "I'm sad that she had to go through that. But when she told me that at home this week, it brought something up for me that I hadn't remembered. It was the time my father molested me!"

This was complete news to me. It had never been mentioned before, although I had been working with them as a couple now for nine months and had known them on and off for almost two years.

"Tell me about it," I said.

"I told Velia about it this week," he continued. "It happened when I was 12 or 13. My father had stopped working because of his double hernia. He couldn't lift anything. So Mom was working to support us. I don't know how we got onto the subject, but one day at home I remember asking my father what it was like to have sex. He said, 'Here, I'll show you.' He performed anal sex on me. That was the only time that happened. But later on I was talking about it with my brother. I fondled his penis, and then I did it to him twice when he was asleep—or pretending to be asleep."

"Was that all, or was there more?" I asked.

"Well, later, we were coming back from Boy Scouts with my dad and three other kids in the car. When two of the kids went into a store, I told my father what I had done to my brother. My father didn't say, 'That's not right!' He only said, 'You've got to be careful when you say things like that!' There was another kid in the backseat of the car, so I got the idea that my father and that boy must have had sex together.

"I was so naïve that everything must have not connected for me. So I was as surprised as I could be when I was 18 and I found out that my father was a homosexual. None of this seemed to have made me think of that before. And although somewhere I knew about it, I just never thought about it."

Lars was visibly uncomfortable talking about this. He continued, "To say my father had relations with me, that's hard to tell anyone. Once I had a security clearance examination to go overseas for the State Department. Although they're not supposed to ask, the man asked if I had ever had any relationship with men. I said, 'No, but my father molested me.' But I was too uncomfortable to go further."

I said, "This is quite a different story than the one you told me at the beginning, that the first thing you knew about difficulty for your parents was when your father was arrested. Do you think you have always consciously remembered what happened with your father?"

"Yes, I think so," he said. "But I didn't remember the business with my brother 'til after Velia told me what happened with her brother."

I discussed briefly the relationship of these events to Lars's difficulty with sex, and to the prominent memory problems that long hampered his work, for which he had obtained behavioral treatment.

I said, "Your loss of memory for your entire childhood seems to have been caught up in a massive attempt to keep from knowing these painful things. But that effort has taken a big toll on your being able to remember a lot of things. As you said, you didn't think about the link between the sex with your father and your parents' divorce, and that is a model for your trouble linking thoughts and remembering."

His memory was improving rapidly, for he soon related these events to his masturbation.

"I used to have a habit of using the end of a toilet plunger in my rectum when I masturbated, he said, with a full red-faced blush. "I feel embarrassed to think I ever did that! I think it comes from what happened with my father and brother, though."

"I also think it is why you've had so much trouble with the masturbation exercises," I said. "They threaten you with the return of these memories and also with the longing for your father and his penis."

I now turned to Velia to ask her reaction to Lars's memories. She said, "To use his words, I feel sad for him. It explains his difficulties with sex. It makes them somehow understandable now. It's so hard for him to have control. Now I understand why our memories are so embarrassing. The part of us that feels responsible morally for our conduct is so appalled by what we did that it is hard to imagine anybody hearing what we did without condemning us—because we condemn ourselves! How could you ever tell someone you did that, and have them think that you were a decent human being again?"

Velia's face turned red and she was leaning heavily on the arm of the couch. She went on, "I just re-asked your question if I felt any desire toward my brother's penis. I know the answer is "YES!" but I don't want to remember it, because . . . I don't know why!"

I said, "Perhaps you do know *something* about why."

"I don't know," she spat out. "When I've let myself remember it happening and I feel the desire now, then I remember whose penis it is and I don't want to feel that way. And then I can't remember."

I said, "The danger of not remembering has been that you've had to continue fighting the buried memory. After all, you were a child when all this happened."

She said, "I told my doctor that I had prostituted myself once for companionship."

I said, "Both you and your brother were children. And your parents didn't provide safety. There must have been something missing in the provision of safety and of caring by your parents that set the stage for this. Both you and Lars still need safety. When you don't have safety, you both feel bad and frightened, and then your worried longing takes this intense sexual form. But getting your sexual longing met immediately brings you to the moment of feeling violated and unsafe."

They nodded. Lars added dubiously and half teasingly, "So you think my problems with memory are based on this, too?"

"I do!" I said quietly. "These stories of both your childhoods share the theme of invasion by the penis leading to a painful, excited, sexual way of longing for love. It's a pain you share as molested children. And you've tried to help each other with it without knowing how."

Velia said, "That makes sense to me."

And then as we tried to set up a time for the next appointment, Lars got very confused. He shook his head and he said, "This 'confusion!' It's my problem everywhere!"

In the next session, which occurred in the first week of December, Lars and Velia were able to discuss the longing in more detail. The exercises had now clarified the way in which Velia felt so threatened.

She said, "You said it was important to remember these things that I find so painful because they're still causing problems. I was able to feel the arousal and the longing that I thought was so frightening in the past. Remembering it was threatening again."

During one exercise, Lars looked at the clock and saw that only one minute was left during his turn to be active. He had said to himself, "I'd better get my jollies in now," and he began to kiss her feverishly.

She began to cry. She said, "I cried because I couldn't keep myself from getting aroused. The impulse to kiss him back was so compelling I couldn't stop, even though I wanted to."

I said, "You said you kissed him because 'you wanted to.' But really it was being driven to *have to*. It was the longing you used to feel for your brother. When there was no one you felt loved you, you turned to your brother with a kind of arousal, a hunger you couldn't control."

Velia shook her head. "I can't make that fit into a memory."

Lars said, "What about the one you mentioned to me after the last session? You said you didn't necessarily long to touch his penis, but you were desperate to have somebody touch you. Do you remember that?"

Velia now was able to remember instances of boys trying to touch her breasts and her own frightened longing. She went on to say that although she had not allowed that, as far as she knew she had done all the touching with one of her brothers. The other brother had done the touching of her. As she talked about this, her face flushed with a beet-red blush. She said, "There's a feeling of familiarity about the longing to be touched that reminds me of that time long ago." Thus Velia had split the longing to touch from the longing to be touched.

The therapy to this point had been a struggle, one centered on the beckoning, shared, seductive exciting objects, which also threatened fundamental harm and abuse. The slow protected pace of the behavioral sex therapy demonstrated over and over the threats contained in sexual excitement. The recall of the memories of childhood instances of invasive sex represented a culmination of this work, and led in turn to a new foundation of mutual understanding. From there we could begin to see how, for instance, Velia had split the longing to touch from the longing to be touched, controlling an urge to merge sexually with a brother by dividing feelings between the two brothers. Lars had handled his own longings to be touched by a repression so dense that it damaged his capacity for thinking, for making links at all.

## SUBSEQUENT COURSE OF SEX THERAPY

Over the next weeks Lars and Velia struggled with the rules and the limits that embodied safety from their mutual yearning. Velia said that the threat was that she felt her longing would still bring her to those painful memories that she didn't want to emerge. The pain was almost physical, although Velia could tell "it wasn't a real physical thing."

She said, "I'm feeling angry at you for pressing the issue of childhood memories. I don't want to discuss them. Leave me alone."

I said that her present anger was close to her longing for touch. I wondered if she could tell me more about being mad at me. She had a momentary fantasy of saying something rude to me, something that wasn't in her usual vocabulary. Lars asked if he could guess at it, and guessed that it might be "fuck off." Velia said that it wasn't that bad. It was only "You son of a bitch, leave me alone."

I asked who it might be that she would be telling, "Leave me alone."

"It was my father!" She began to sob, saying, "I don't know when it was."

"Was it a fantasy of longing for your father—for his touch?" I asked.

She slowly nodded. She said, "I just remembered, when Lars and I first got married. I would feel so good when he would hug me. He had a habit of tapping my back three times before he stopped. It got to the point that I would be in agony thinking, 'Don't tap your hands on my back.' I didn't want him to stop. It was like if the hug ended, then I was all alone again. There was no way to know he still loved me, because I couldn't feel him anymore."

I then spoke of the relationship between her longing and her years of loneliness. This brought up her fear of needing attention—physical attention. She was afraid it would disappear forever. I thought that she must also be telling me something about a yearning in the transference, but at this time I dealt with it only in the displacement.

As we closed the session, Lars said offhandedly, "By the way, I thought you would like to know, I find I can study and remember new material for my promotional exam. It's the first time I've ever felt that way."

Over the next weeks, Lars was able to understand the mixture of feelings of longing for and prohibition against the stimulation of masturbation, the repressed fantasy of his molesting father, and his longing for help from his mother as well. But the main struggle between the couple was one of control. Lars tended to take the role of the aggressive, intrusive object, and Velia tended to feel much safer if she had set firm boundaries and guidelines. As he was able to hold back, seeing that it brought them a safer mutual arousal, Velia was able to allow arousal to build gradually. It became clear, however, that when this occurred, Lars felt Velia was like a prudish controlling mother. This was an image he could not locate in his mother, but which Velia felt definitely fit the image he always portrayed of her, a cold woman from whom he had felt little affection. As these insights accumulated, they slowly moved to levels of excitement that gradually built between them not impulsively, anxiously, or one-sidedly, but with the safety of mutual arousal and control.

## THE THREAT OF SEPARATION

In March, after the sex therapy had been going on for about eight months and the family therapy about fourteen months, I told them I was planning to leave the university where I had been seeing them free of charge. Velia was devastated. Despite my assurances that I intended to see them for whatever they could afford, she could not believe that I would actually be willing to see them for the pittance that they could manage.

All progress in sex stopped. Velia felt devastated. By this point, they had moved to the point of "containment" in the sex therapy, the step in which Velia inserted Lars's penis into her vagina while she controlled all movement. Not only did Lars ejaculate quickly, but she now found trouble with sustaining her own mounting arousal. As soon as they introduced genital movement into the exercise, Lars's tolerance was as short as ever. They struggled with the question of my availability and its relationship to their own sexual regression. During this phase we were able to see that, in their devastation, the issues once again spilled onto the children in famil- iar ways, which had not been happening recently. (The family session de- scribed in detail in the next chapter is one in which the sexual issues be- came prominent. It comes from this period.) Only slowly, as the couple regained their trust in the integrity of the relationship with me, and began to feel I would be there for them, could Lars build tolerance for arousal so that he could begin to last for a number of minutes.

## THE FINAL PHASE—WORKING THROUGH IN THE TRANSFERENCE

A final problem lasted over the whole summer. Velia was still unable to move to orgasm individually or in the shared situation. She felt that sex was now too much work. She was once again increasingly resentful and worried that she would never be able to achieve orgasm, and that sex therapy and couple's work would never end. I interpreted that her fear of not finishing masked a fear of letting go of her sexual arousal, which was linked to her difficulty in letting go of therapy. The threat of success was even more acute because things were also going so well in the family work that termination was being considered there also. After working on their ambivalence about concluding and their grief over the loss of therapy, they pushed on, even trying oral sex for the first time and finding it mutually pleasurable.

Finally, Velia gradually began to experience orgasm. At first, in mastur- bation privately, she had what was a general pelvic vascular release, a kind of a slow, leaking letdown. But with continued manual stimulation during masturbation, she began slowly to get a more satisfying orgasm, one which was not intense but was more pleasing. Slowly, it became more of a sensation of warmth spreading into her pelvis. And she was able to decrease the time that it took her to reach orgasm in masturbation, from more than 40 minutes to 15 minutes or so. Although Velia was still frustrated at not being able to have orgasms in intercourse, even with added manual stimulation, she was now pleasantly aroused when Lars shared his own fantasies with her—fantasies, for instance, of intercourse with a woman in an elevator. And he was able to feel less embarrassed in telling her. She was able to hear his fantasies about women friends of theirs.

Encouraging the sharing of these fantasies does not imply a reinforcement of them. The common fantasies partners have of other sexual partners represent isolated repressed objects. Like any repressed objects, they are more likely to exert divisive unconscious influence if they are repressed or even consciously suppressed. With sharing, the wishes and fears they carry are more likely to be integrated into the central relationship.

I said that these fantasies, on both sides, represented in part holding the idealized relationship out of the marriage. Talking about these fantasies based on ideally exciting images brought these split-off objects into their sexual relationship where perhaps they could metabolize them and then have them revitalize the impoverished relationship.

Velia now said that since they had been able to share these fantasies, she hoped Lars could tolerate her saying that she had fantasies about her individual therapist and about me. We had alluded to transference issues often, but Velia was now able to discuss her feelings more openly.

She said, "Yes, the fantasies do hold something that I haven't been able to feel I have in our relationship. Something about you, Dr. Scharff, rather than about a lover or husband. It's a missing element in reality. It's what I feel I don't have. My ideal fantasy is that I could be seductive and that I can move, touch, and act sexy without any repercussions and without something bad happening. I told my individual therapist about a feeling that 'nobody would understand that I feel dirty for my fantasies.' I was terrified because I was sure this one thing at the core was going to be revealed: everyone would see how dirty I am. He tried to get me to see that there wasn't anything dirty. I'm like my own prosecuting attorney with circumstantial evidence, one who threatens a surprise witness that's going to condemn me. But there isn't any such witness. My doctor was able to help me understand that I have a fantasy of a sexy person inside me. But I have a hard time admitting I can be that sexy person because she's dangerous and dirty."

"Are there more specific fantasies?" I asked.

"I don't really want to tell you," she said, "but well, they're about you. I imagined having sex with you." Blushing, haltingly, she continued. "In my fantasy, you were able to do all the things I wanted, to make my body work the way I wish it would."

*I glanced at Lars, wondering how he was taking this material. I felt Velia's attention on me to see perhaps if I could take her excited fantasies. She seemed oblivious to Lars, riveted on me with an embarrassed desire. I felt an assault, not so much in her fantasy—for such eroticized fantasies are not uncommon in sex therapy—but in a quality of telling that seemed to demand a response. I felt we were in the emotional clutches of her excited object, an incestuous demand. I wanted to beat a hasty retreat—she had put into me the rejecting object, which feared the sexual excitement her fantasies embodied. Realizing that in the heat of her excitement also lay the seeds of her fear enabled me to speak to the transference.*

"You're worried about these fantasies, Velia, because you feel them so urgently, and therefore you fear I might act on your fantasy, feat it will get out of control, and fear it will alienate Lars."

She burst into tears. When she recovered she said, "I think it's the same kind of feeling I had for my brothers—longing, sexual longing, then fear and disgust."

As it was the end of the hour, I asked Lars, "How do you feel, hearing Velia's sexual fantasies about me?"

"It's okay," he said. "I know she has them. I wish they were about me, but I know her feeling for you."

"These urgent sexual feelings Velia has may seem to be about me," I said.

"But the important part of them is not so personal. It's the urgency to find a supportive, loving parent, but with sex as a way of getting it because nothing else worked. And Lars, she's speaking for something that is true for you, too. In a way, she's doing it for both of you. It's also what you want from each other, but you're afraid the sex will undo it."

In this session, Velia and Lars brought their shared longing specifically through Velia's focused transference. This helped me to feel the urgency of longing and fear that penetrated their holding, and allowed me to join emotionally in their experience.

It was now September. Termination had begun and the family had agreed to relocate to Seattle in December because of a particularly good job opportunity for Velia, which would also offer an opportunity for Lars. At the time they did so, I was in agreement that the family work was nearing an end, and it looked as though the sex therapy would be likely to be done by then, too. But since then, Velia had felt increasingly depressed that she was never going to manage orgasm during intercourse.

Then in mid-September, Lars opened a session by saying, "Our only problem is sex."

*Velia then said, "The trouble is that it's impossible for me to have a satisfactory orgasm unless Lars is whispering a fantasy in my ear. It is upsetting to have to have that. It's okay when we're together, but it makes it harder to have an orgasm when I'm having my solo exercise."*

*I blinked, surprised to learn of her achievement in this negative way. It quickly* emerged that in this week Velia had had her first completely satisfying orgasm during intercourse with added manual—and fantasy—stimulation. I congratulated them on their achievement, which I knew would give them great relief, although they had announced their success as though it were a complaint.

Velia laughed. "It's true that I still can't do it alone. I need Lars and, partly, I need his fantasies." But with mild chagrin, she acknowledged, "I guess I've finally managed to get just what I always wanted."

I said that there was plenty of learning for them still to do in refining their sexual relationship, but that now they could do it themselves. This final movement had occurred with the context of the threat of termination, which had spurred their final growth and release.

The final phases of the work over the next two months produced more freedom and reliability of orgasm, although there was considerable anxiety about whether they would really work out everything they needed to before they left. Lars's ejaculatory control also improved markedly. By the beginning of November, they felt that their sexual relationship worked well most of the time, suffering only from the occasional setbacks stemming from ordinary difficulties encountered in their life.

## DISCUSSION

This case presents the unfolding of a couple's object relations history through the course of a therapy. It illustrates how the behavioral framework of sex therapy can promote the focused uncovering of these issues, facilitated by attention to the transference.

As the therapy evolved, we could also see the combined pattern of projective identifications. Velia had taken over the bodily vulnerability for both of them, and Lars the strength and protective burden. The sexual interest had been lodged in Lars. This also meant that when Lars failed to contain the sexual urgency, he became the bad and persecuting object for both of them. Velia then withdrew and protected herself, but on many occasions, she became the raging father she was attempting to suppress and to cure by placing a more benign father in Lars.

Bringing their sexuality to life threatened both of them with the revival of the bad and invasive fathers of their shared longing. The original solution was to join in repressing any possibility of actual sex between them. But this inevitably led to the return of the repressed sense of rejection, which they each felt in different ways: Lars in the sexual rejection, and Velia through Lars' suppressed resentment and continued intermittent pressure. And in her own urgent although unconscious way, Velia missed the physical sexuality and the closeness she longed for, the image of an ideal father she could never have.

In another way, both of them embodied the mothers who had failed to protect them. They became protective of each other in exaggerated ways, while they both also assumed disabled roles—Velia in her depression, irrational rages, and sexual disability, and Lars in his occupational problems and his passivity. These handicapped roles seemed to embody the mothers who could not function to care for each of them as children, but the identifications with their mothers were not discussed as much as the ones with their fathers.

The couple brought shared longings to be loved and cared for by a good parent who could respond to a child's sexual interest without acting incestuously. This wish was expressed on their behalf by Velia's focused transference communicated through her sexual fantasy about the therapist. When he experienced personally an incestuous discomfort in the countertransference, he was able to understand from within himself their shared deficits in holding. Finding space inside himself to contain his countertransference created a new psychological space for transitional relatedness (Winer 1989) in which Velia and Lars could experience themselves as sexually interested and interesting without violation of the transitional space by an excited, rejecting, defensively neutral, or exploitative response by the therapist. This piece of work was critical in resolving the couple's sexual inhibitions.

Sex therapy was successful in restoring a functioning, enjoyable sexual life to the couple, and in improving their capacity for holding both for their marriage and for their children. But at the end of the treatment, Velia also knew that she had continuing individual needs for therapy, which she planned to pursue in Seattle.

Concurrent with their sex therapy and Velia's individual therapy, the Simpson family was in family therapy. In the next chapter we describe a family session from the late phase of their family therapy that illustrates our finding that the parents' sexual relationship influences the development of their children.

Chapter **11**

# TREATING THE FAMILY RAMIFICATIONS
# OF SEXUAL DIFFICULTY

In the last chapter we traced the interrelation of the individual, sexual, and marital difficulties of a couple called Lars and Velia Simpson. In this chapter, we will look at the ramifications of those issues for their children, through illustrative sessions from their family treatment. Family therapy may be at the periphery of attention for the couple therapist, but this illustration is included because it is important for couple therapists to understand the influence of sexual and marital disorder across the generations.

The Simpsons were willing to re-create their family life in the treatment setting. Deeply concerned for their children, they brought an unusual capacity for looking at the interface between their own issues and those of the children.

## AN EARLY FAMILY SESSION

In a session in the first months of the family therapy, the oldest boy, Eric, now 8½, was playing in a controlled way at being an "Incredible Hulk" with his brother and sister. Tension developed between Lars and Velia, and suddenly Eric's Hulk lost all concern for others and ran rampant. Velia immediately lost patience and lashed out verbally at Eric, saying she hated him when he was like this. He collapsed in despair at his mother's anger. To my questioning, she was then able to say that his behavior reminded her of her father, thoughtless and angrily abusive of others. But when she lashed out like this, then she hated herself because then *she* became like her father. Eric cried through this incident, but Lars was able to reach out for him and give solace and yet to allow Velia to explore her own position of reading into Eric's behavior the full force of her internal bad father.

This recurrent projective identification was one of the factors that had been pushing Eric into a bad and powerful male identification. It was also supported by the passivity of Eric's father, Lars, which stemmed from the same internal dread of powerful males. Lars was passive, sexually and characterologically, because he shared the internal assumption that an assertive male could only be destructive. Eric then took on the shared projection of the assertive male, which both his mother and father longed for him to do, but he also began to internalize their conviction that he could not be the assertive male they longed for without also becoming the angry selfish male they feared.

We were able to establish that Velia's fear of Eric's potential badness was a projective identification, and that it was her way of evacuating the badness of her internal father, which she then felt return through Eric's behavior. This behavior of Eric's began as ordinary childhood aggression, sibling bickering, or greed. But Velia habitually read it as confirmation that her father's self-centered abusiveness was reincarnated in her son. Angry at him for this incarnation, she then felt she became her father, harming herself in Eric. The cycle haunted her, and then she had trouble tolerating Eric only because he was a persistent reminder of her struggle.

For Lars, Velia's depression and anger also represented a return of the repressed. He hoped to take care of his victim-self by refusing to be the aggressive man, only to have the aggression reappear in Velia. Further, his unconscious hope to grow a harmonious family and to do better by his son than his own father did also backfired. He, too, suffered the return of the repressed when he saw Eric and Velia in combat, and he was helpless, not knowing to whom he should offer solace.

In this session, Velia was able to express her anguish at finding her father in Eric and in herself. This allowed her to re-express her love and concern for Eric, while Lars could also find comfort in a helpful fathering activity. Relatively wordless and uninsightful, he nevertheless reached out to Eric at the same time he gave solace to Velia. He tolerated her grief, and contributed considerably to the repair of an extremely painful moment. The therapist's contribution let Lars supply the holding that he had been unable to do, and so to build toward repairing the relationship between son and mother, which, for that moment, was the leading symptom of the flaw in the family's holding. That having been done, the family experienced a sense of repair, of forgiveness and love which could overcome hate.

Shortly after the session just reported, Lars and Velia began the sex therapy described in the previous chapter. Over the next months, the family learned to work well in treatment, owning projective identifications, improving empathy, and supporting each other's growth. In addition, the sense of organization of the family had improved enormously. While sibling bickering and destruction in the play had been frequent in earlier treatment, family sessions went along smoothly with well constructed play and cooperation between the children. Now the themes that remained difficult for the family could be seen and heard inside the play, in conversations between Velia and Lars, and between them and the children.

## A SESSION FROM THE LATE PHASE OF FAMILY THERAPY

It was a year later. In sex therapy, Lars had revealed the episodes of anal intercourse with his father and brother, and Velia had first remembered that her father had been physically abusive of her and her sister. The work there, as in family therapy, had been going along well. Then I [D.E.S.] was away for a scheduled two-week vacation. The following session, fourteen months after beginning family therapy, took place upon my return. It specifies the link between the adult's sexual difficulty and the children's issues, but this time not through producing such fundamental disruption as it did at the beginning of the treatment, but through a regression contained within the treatment. At the time of this session the children are two years older than they were at initial evaluation: Jeanette is 5½, Alex is 7, and Eric is 9½.

Velia began the session, holding her head in her hands and saying, "I have a headache, and I don't feel like things are going well sexually between Lars and me. I feel helpless to change anything. And I have a terrible headache."

Jeanette, gesturing to her mother and demonstrating that she was building something to house a small paper airplane, called out, "Momma, look. I'm building his hiding place."

I could not tell for some time, but later I thought Jeanette was introducing the theme of the destructive but treasured male who had gone away (the airplane), and who must be captured and hidden. I was being seen as destructive but longed for in my absence.

I turned to Lars, and asked, "How do you feel about things, then?"

Jeanette continued talking to her mother, rather loudly, "No one knows this is his hiding place."

Lars said, in answer to me, "I'm having problems with sex, too. Probably more than Velia."

Alex was talking. I looked over, and said, "Are you worried that Jeanette will take all the blocks from your ship, Alex?"

Jeanette said, "I won't take all the blocks!"

Turning back to the parents, I asked, "Are things worse since we haven't met in two weeks?"

Velia said, "Yeah. They have been."

I noticed with dismay how depressed and disheveled Velia looked, and that Jeanette was building on her plane's hiding place. I asked Lars, "Were things worse for you in that period?"

"Yes, they have been," he said.

Velia continued, "We discussed it for 45 minutes last night, and right now I feel it would be unproductive for him and me to do anything sexual 'til we've met with you next week. There isn't any progress, and then I get resentful. For the last several days, I've had the sensation that something was snowballing out of my control. I don't know what it is." She was crying. "I feel I'm trying to put the brakes on, and I'm scared."

"Is it just in your sexual life, or are there other things?" I asked.

"Oh, other things, too," she said. "I'm cutting back my individual therapy to two times a week. I feel it's the right time, but since I did it, I've felt terrible."

A few minutes later in the session, the couple told me that they had two episodes in which the home sex therapy exercises did not go well. They referred to their sexual failures in nonexplicit language appropriate to this family therapy context.

I asked, "Do you feel worse after the two of you had those failures?"

Velia said, "I don't know if you could really call them failures. I feel worse after a period of stagnation."

Alex and Jeanette were playing with two dinosaurs who where climbing on top of each other. There was a sexual theme in the play, but it did not disrupt its thematic development. All three of the children were quietly engaged in organized play. Eric now took the space shuttle and bombed Jeanette's dinosaur.

"Oh, No!" squeaked Jeanette. The play continued with Alex asking, "What happens next, Jeanette?"

Jeanette said, "Make mine be captured by yours."

From what I heard from the corner of my ear, it sounded as though their play represented an appropriately sublimated echo of adult sexual coupling.

Velia continued, "I feel angry because I feel I work so hard to learn to do something, and then he can't do his part, so nothing happens."

I said, "So you feel left high and dry?" I turned to Lars and said, "But you feel hopeless?"

Lars nodded. "Yes!"

I continued, "And you don't want to relate the difficulty to the time away from me, even though three weeks ago things were okay?"

Lars said, "I'd say so."

I continued, "Something has fallen back."

Lars said again, "I'd say so."

I tried to lead him, "Do you want to link those?"

Lars laughed. Eric was flying his model fighter plane around in the air toward me. Then the kids began to play that one plane was chasing the other, making noises. The children's play on couple relationships was continuing, but, under Eric's influence, was getting more aggressive. Lars responded to my quest by saying, "Do you remember the problem I was having with my self-esteem? It seems cyclical, and it's coming around again."

I asked, "Does it affect just the sex, or everything?"

Lars said, "Well, that affects everything!"

A few minutes later, Jeanette and Alex were playing. Alex's helicopter flew away, and Jeanette's doll called, "Bye-bye-e-e-e." Then she explained, "She's waving at the helicopter."

"What are your two dolls doing in the bathtub?" I queried.

Jeanette set me straight. "This isn't a bathtub. It's a boat! She's waving at the helicopter and she's driving her boat."

Lars noticed that Jeanette's dress was practically up at her waist, and said, "Pull your dress down, Jeanette!" Jeanette smiled. I noticed that this attention to a sexualized issue had occurred at a moment of anxiety about separation and sexuality.

Eric was playing with the two planes, with one chasing the other in a dogfight. He intruded on Alex and Jeanette's game.

Alex whined, "Eric! We're not playing with you."

Jeanette called, "Bye-bye! We'll see you tomorrow. We'll see you when we get home!"

At this moment, I felt drawn to the play. I asked, "Eric, what's happening? I see your guy is shooting down a lot of folk!"

Eric nodded. "Yep!"

"Is he mad?" I asked.

There was no answer.

"What's happening with him?" No answer.

The plane crashed.

"I see he crashed." He now crashed the plane that had been shot at. I had the distinct impression he did not like this moment of attention on his play, probably any more than his father liked my attention to him. I felt the play was going on in parallel to the adult conversation, so I turned back to

Lars and said, "So your self-esteem is doing badly, but you don't want to link that to my absence?"

Lars said, "I don't think so. I don't feel like it is."

Eric picked up two planes again and had one chase the other, an apt metaphor for my pursuit of his father.

I said to Lars, "So you just feel empty? But I do want to link these things, Lars. It seems to me that we know that you can't make links, that's one of the troubles."

Lars said, "Yep!"

I continued the pursuit. "Since you have so much trouble making links, let's guess and see. You and Velia both feel hard hit by my not being available, and you feel it by losing your sense of self-worth and your sexual competence. I think that's linked to the sense of loss of your father." I could see that Lars was nodding now, so I continued. "You didn't get help from him, and on the contrary, you said not long ago that when you asked him for help, you got something very painful instead." I was thinking about the sodomy his father committed on him.

Lars nodded. He seemed to be staying with me. Velia was looking down at the floor in some distress.

Suddenly there was a dramatic snorting from the play table across the room. Eric was kneeling out of sight behind the table with a pink pig puppet perched on his hand.

"Snort, grunt, snort," he insisted.

"What's going on, Mister Pig?" I asked.

Jeanette joined in instantly. "We're going to do a puppet show."

"All right then," I said. "Ask the pig what it's snorting about, will you?"

Eric said, setting me straight, "He's a pig! That's why."

Jeanette and Alex went to the table, too. Eric's pig was devouring the magic markers on the table, chewing them greedily.

I said, "He's sure eating those markers up. It looks like he's a hungry pig."

Eric said, in his best deep-voiced grunt, "That's because I am!"

Velia laughed at Eric's puppet play. I continued to interview the pig. "What made you so hungry? Didn't you have anything to eat?"

"That's right," said the pig. "I didn't have nothin' to eat." Eric was fully in role as the starving pig.

"Are you mad about it?" I asked.

"Yeah!" he exclaimed.

Alex chimed in. "Here's another pig."

Velia was no longer looking depressed. She said, "Eric's stomach ought to be pretty empty by now, because he emptied it on the way up here."

I noticed Lars was smiling, too. The whole mood of the room had been transformed.

"He was car sick again. The morning traffic on the beltway doesn't agree with his stomach," she continued.

Alex and Jeanette had now fully joined in the play.

Jeanette, with the pink rabbit on her hand, said to Eric's pig, "Why are you eating my food?"

"Grrrrunt!" said the pig.

"He's eating my food!" said the rabbit. "Okay! I'll just eat his food."

Alex, with a purple large-nosed monster puppet, asked, "Is there any hamburgers anywhere? Or not?"

The pig seemed to have devoured enough magic markers. "I'm going to take a nap. I'm tired from eating."

"What have you been eating?" I asked.

Alex's monster answered, "Carrots! Where are the carrots?"

Jeanette's rabbit said, "I'll go in the house and see if I can find any carrots."

"Well, what do you think, Lars and Velia?" I asked, turning to them. "Do you feel starved for attention for two weeks, from me?"

Velia said, "I can answer 'Yes.'"

"And you can't answer, Lars?" I asked.

Alex's puppet "honked" the nose on Jeanette's rabbit. I thought it was a comment on my "picking on" Lars.

"Stop honking my nose!" said the rabbit.

Alex's monster said to Eric, "Don't eat her carrot!"

Lars answered my question by saying, "My first impression was: 'You don't even want to think about it that much.'"

Noticing a kind of slip in what he said, that his idea really seemed to refer to me rather than to himself, I said, "You mean that I don't think about it much?"

Lars pulled at his eyebrow.

Velia corrected me, "No, he means that *he* doesn't think about it."

"That's not what he said," I countered humorously. I was counting on their comfort with a teasing quality, which they used frequently themselves with each other and with me, to get this point across. It seemed to work.

Lars smiled at Velia, and said, "That's what I meant, though."

I repeated his words: "What you said was, 'You, meaning me, don't even want to think about it that much.'"

"Nyanh-nyanh, nyanh-nyanh, nyanh-nyanh!" chanted Velia. "You got caught in a Freudian slip!!"

Lars grinned widely and hit her leg in a friendly retort. "I don't think about it that much!" he insisted for the record.

"That's true, too!" I countered.

Velia added, in therapeutic support, knowing how to get through to Lars, "But you don't think *he* thinks about it either."

Lars said, "I don't know about that. But I know *I* don't."

"But," I said, "You get down emotionally, and you stop functioning."

"That's true," acknowledged Lars. "I have more difficulty functioning."

"And you feel rotten, but you don't link it to the thoughts and feelings you have."

"That's right," he said.

At this moment Eric wandered off the set, over toward one of the TV cameras.

Alex called out, "Eric, where are you going?"

Velia summoned him: "Eric, what are you doing over there!"

Eric said, "I just wanted to see what they are projecting on."

I was momentarily consumed with the pun on projective identification, but I kept silent.

Velia said sternly. "Would you get back over here!"

And Lars said with considerable insight for which I was grateful, "You just wanted to get us off the subject, huh?"

Now Jeanette joined in the diversionary activity. "Bumpty-bump-duh, a-bumpity-bump-bump," she sang to the tune of the Star Wars theme. And she took the pig Eric had previously used and marched off the carpet, and around the room, her heels clicking rhythmically on the hard studio floor.

"So you think Eric is trying to distract us?" I said to Lars.

Lars answered, "He's been trying to all morning."

Eric whined, "I just want to see what they're projecting on."

Jeanette interrupted, saying to me, "Hey! I want you to have something."

As Jeanette and Alex brought some puppets over to me, I remained focused on Eric, asking him, "How have you felt the weeks we haven't met?"

Eric rolled his big, appealing blue eyes under his blond hair, as if he had no idea.

"Stop imitating your father," said Velia. "You do too know."

As I put the purple monster puppet on my hand, I continued, "You know, Eric, I've been impressed that even though you get car sick on the awful, long ride here . . . (here Eric nods his head vigorously) . . . you keep on wanting to come."

"Uh-huh!" said Eric, nodding his head even more.

Jeanette now had the pig puppet, which suddenly giggled loudly, bidding for my attention.

"What's that pig laughing about?" I asked.

Jeanette said, "He's honking his nose." And she began to take the nose of the monster puppet on my hand in her pig's mouth and squeeze it, saying, "Honk! Honk!"

Eric got another puppet and came in to join in honking the nose of my puppet with determination.

I looked at Lars and Velia, and said, "Maybe those two aren't the only two who want to beat me up?"

Velia laughed and rubbed her eyes. Jeanette was now using puppets on both her hands to tweak the nose of my puppet. It was a kind of orgy of tweaking.

Velia said, "I can laugh, thinking what if the kids tweaked *your* nose!"

Lars said, "You love the idea!"

I said, "That's right. And they wouldn't be the only ones wanting to do it, right?"

Velia laughed, holding her head, reminding us of her headache.

Lars gently taunted Velia, "Why don't you go over there and tweak his nose? Get it off your chest."

"No!" I said, instantaneously caught off guard, feeling for a moment she might actually do it. "Why don't you talk about it." Immediately I felt foolish for acting as if she would join in the aggressive play. But it was a sign of the power of the projective identification in captivating me. Recovering, I said, "If you could, maybe you wouldn't have such a bad headache."

Velia nodded slowly and said, "It's possible."

Jeanette interrupted, "Wheee, ha, ha, ha!" And she and Eric squeezed my puppet's nose some more, as in a full-fledged torture. Then she took my puppet and marched victoriously around the room, singing, "Doopy, doopy, doopy!" as her footsteps rang again on the tile floor just off the set. Having completed her march of triumph, she came back to me and handed me a yellow dog hand puppet.

"Hi!" she said.

"What's up?" I asked, speaking for my new puppet.

She said, "I been honking someone's nose!"

"So I heard," I said. "Why would you do a thing like that?"

Jeanette answered, "Because he was mean to us, so we been mean to him!"

Meanwhile, Eric was once again asking Velia if he could do something with the TV camera. I looked over at him and said, "Eric, you're having a lot of trouble seeing what we're projecting onto right here. What do you think about what is happening here? I think today you're upset. I can tell because your "bad guys" started winning...."

At this point, Lars grabbed Jeanette by the dress, partly to keep her from interrupting, and partly to tease her.

"Hey! Let go my dress!" she insisted.

I continued, over the distraction. "And you know what else, Eric? I think the bad guys win when you're upset and when your mom and dad are upset."

"No!" said Eric. "They didn't win. The good guys won."

"I saw that in the beginning," I said. "But later your two green planes chased Alex and Jeanette's planes, and they looked like they were giving them a heck of a bad time. I think that happens when people are upset in the family. And this time the upset began when your dad said he felt he couldn't function, and your mom felt she couldn't speak." I turned to Velia, "And you felt bad about Lars, and about decreasing the frequency of therapy with your individual therapist, and about not seeing me."

Velia said, "That sounds accurate."

I continued to Velia, "And also you're clear that you would be angry, too, if you weren't so low! And so you start laughing, feeling lighthearted, when the kids tweak my puppet's nose."

"Yes, it's true," she laughed.

"And Lars," I continued, "You do, too. But you can't make a connection or think about it. We just hear that when I'm not available you happen to fall apart for no apparent reason, without your even knowing you're angry or why you're upset."

Velia said, "I didn't recognize it initially, but it's easier for me to recognize it than it is for Lars."

"Is that true, Lars?" I asked.

"Of course!" he confirmed.

"Then in the family," I said, "as the two of you withdraw the kids start to react. Today we've seen the pattern in the play, in which the angry and bad characters start to dominate. But that's what happens inside each of you. You feel taken over by the bad stuff. It used to happen with the kids getting disorganized and fighting. Things are better now, so we see it mostly in the stories in the play."

Alex was playing with a building made out of blocks with a helicopter inside. It reminded me of the fire truck and firehouse play of the first family session two years before. He now began to bomb the building with blocks as I spoke to the family. Then the helicopter emerged and flew off. Meanwhile, Eric was throwing the toy airplanes on the ground.

I said to Eric, "Boy, my planes are taking a beating. They're crashing all over the place. Eric, I do recognize those are my planes you're throwing on the ground, right!"

Eric smiled and said, "Yep!"

"Do you think they deserve it?" I asked, knowing the answer.

"Yep!"

"That's what I thought! So you're mad at me, too?"

"I don't know . . . it's just playing," he protested.

"I know you're playing, partly, But it tells us something. And that ambulance is taking a beating, too."

"No," he said, "It already was broken." Here Eric took the toy ambulance he'd been fiddling with, and rammed the block building that Alex and Jeanette were playing with together.

Alex protested, "Eric! Don't!"

"Sorry! I didn't mean it," said Eric perfunctorily.

"Eric, you did, too," said Lars.

"I did not!" said Eric.

"I wonder what it might mean," I mused, "since ambulances are associated with doctors?"

Jeanette was saying to Alex, about their dolls, "They don't have a momma or a dad."

I continued with my train of thought. "Any thoughts, Lars or Velia?"

Lars said, "I wouldn't know."

Velia said, "It's very clear, this ambulance-slash-doctor was crashing down this house that had been built up."

"You thought it was clear?" I asked.

"Yeah, when you make the connection between ambulances and doctors, it's perfectly clear," she said.

"I like the part about the 'ambulance-slash-doctor,'" I said, laughing.

Velia blushed, and laughed heartily, holding her face. "I was seeing the typographical slash," she explained as she sliced the air with her hand. "But, yeah, now that you point it out, it does have meaning: 'Slash the doctor!'" She laughed.

Eric interrupted, "Dr. Scharff! Look!" He showed me his play.

I said, "That guy is dancing with a tiger, huh?" And looking at Velia, but speaking to the whole family, I added, "Well, if you're so angry, aren't there tigerlike feelings around just like that? But if you don't know you're upset or angry, then things just disintegrate in the family. And that costs everyone a lot. This play and the session today let us see the repercussions, which ordinarily make you, Lars and Velia, feel worse because you feel like things are out of control. That's been the cycle."

They nodded. I glanced at the clock and saw it was the end of the hour, and said, "Well, we have to stop for today."

Jeanette cried out, "No! No!"

But Eric, for the first time ever, gave a gleeful, "YEA!"

"Yea?" I said.

"That's a new one!" said Velia.

"You've really had it with me, haven't you, Eric?" I said.

Eric giggled.

"I want to still play," said Jeanette, but she joined in cleaning up the toys and left cheerfully.

## DISCUSSION

We present this session to show how a chain of influence develops, from the therapist to the couple, to their children, and to the whole family. Beyond illustrating in great detail the effects of a therapist's absence and the spreading ripple of those effects, the absence set the stage for understanding the regression in the family and their recovery from it.

Because the couple's difficulties were frequently organized around the sexual issues, it was in their sexual functioning that they most acutely felt the loss of the therapist. Clearly, there was a more generalized effect, however, which they acknowledged. Velia became thoroughly depressed. This event linked her depression once again to object loss in the transference. Lars' difficulty was usually heralded by the onset of a bewildered confusion. He would suffer a loss in his capacity to think. In addition to whatever constitutional causes there were for his learning difficulties, his sexual history of sodomy and abuse by his father had left him feeling that it was dangerous to pursue knowledge and to attempt to get too much help from other people, especially men. So, the absences of the male family therapist and Velia's male individual therapist threw him into his usual state of being without the capacity to make links. He could not be potent intellectually or sexually.

Once the couple had this difficulty with loss, the children could not escape its effects. They had their own feelings about the family therapist's absence, since all three of them were dedicated to the therapy. Nevertheless, at this stage of the therapy, they did not suffer additional overt disorganization and thereby throw the family into even more distress. Before therapy, the parents' sexual distress had pervaded the family through Velia's rages at the children whenever Lars had urged sex on her. Now, that did not generally happen. But when their mother's depression and the talk of the sexual difficulty did emerge in this session, the children acted out the issues in their play, partly by regressive bickering and disruption of the play, and partly by expression of themes within the play. At the beginning of therapy a year before, it was usually Alex who was disruptive, fueled by his constitutional attention deficit. Now Eric, rather than Alex, became disruptive. But with a steady therapeutic effort in the hour, the play became well organized and expressive of the issues of greedy and desperate object hunger, which drove the parents' depression, confusion, marital stress, and sexual stumbling. Now, modified within the transference, these were the same issues that had previously regularly got into the children, where they had been amplified and passed back to the parents and all around the family.

In this case, all three children joined in pointed transferential play to lead the way to expressing and elaborating the theme the therapist was pursuing interpretively. They focused on the anger, the greed, and the neediness for him. The honking of his puppet's nose expressed many things, only some of which were put into words. At the leading edge was the anger at him for being away and becoming the monster mother–father of separation. But they were also busy hungrily feeding off him, in a way biting off bits of his puppet's nose-breast-penis for nourishment. Expressing the anger let the other feelings and neediness gain expression, too.

As the children took the lead in this play, Lars and Velia could humorously, and with relief, join in the expression of anger and need.

Velia did it quite directly, and Lars, as was usually true, did it vicariously by urging her on.

The overall pattern of the therapy hour began with the elaboration of a problem in the couple. Elements of the problem were unconsciously understood and shared by the children, but in the beginning the therapist could not understand these elaborations. As the couple explored their difficulty, the children's play and unconscious understanding became more organized. Finally the hour culminated in the children's poignant expression of the major underlying themes of neediness and of anger at privation from the transference source of parenting, holding, and provision of resources.

When this happened, the play and conversation dramatically joined in expressing and sharing the problem, as explicitly elaborated in the transference. The family felt deprived by the therapist's absence, experiencing a rekindling of abusive and neglectful themes of parenting that were embedded both in their object relations history and in their sexual disorder. Then they brought their shared themes to bear in the therapy, in their play and discussions with each other, and most especially, in a transference focus on the therapist. He, too, felt taken over by the theme, absorbing the projective identifications of the hour. He felt guilty and in need of making up to the family for his absence, confused about meaning in the course of the hour, and depressed about their regression. At one point he explicitly, although only momentarily, felt that their anger might be acted out at him— never a realistic danger with this family. And he felt an exhilaration and gratitude at the crystallization of the transference, which gave so much explanation and elaboration to the work he had been conducting with the family for so long.

The net result of the hour was a marked strengthening of the family's resilience, of their focused relationships to each other, and of their capacity to provide contextual and centered holding for each other. This hour, more dramatic than many, was nevertheless but one day of building those capacities with this family. In its pattern of regression and rebuilding, it also documents the gains of two years of work by a committed and hard-working family who were soon to enter the termination phase of their work.

The work of this session was shared between the adults' conversation, which introduced the problem of regression in their sexual life and in the contextual transference to the therapist, and the children's play, which gave a language for the issues underlying the couple's sexual difficulty, helped family and therapist to understand it, and demonstrated the way the children internalized the object relations issues.

Before treatment, the children could only absorb the issues through introjective identification, unconsciously trying to provide relief to their parent's relationship in the process. But in this session, their play demonstrates an improved family-wide holding capacity, as it is now the children who elaborate and explore the object-hunger that underlies the couple's sexual regression, invite their parents to join them in expressing it in the transference, and return the introjective identification in modified and matured form to their parents. Because of this, the session also catalyzed the couple's sex therapy, which soon went on to a successful conclusion. In doing so, the children contributed to helping their parents provide better family holding in the ensuing years.

Part IV

**Special Topics**

Chapter **12**

# THE TREATMENT OF EXTRAMARITAL AFFAIRS

Extramarital affairs commonly present as symptoms leading to or emerging during marital intervention. Often the discovery of infidelity crystallizes dissatisfaction due to marital discord that has been at a low boil for years and leads to referral. More frequently one or both partners admit to infidelity in the course of a thorough assessment.

In an assessment, it is important to ask the question whether either or both partners have had affairs, either now or in the past. Of course, when and how the question is asked often determines what kind of answer a therapist is given. For instance, we may get a different answer in asking the question with both spouses present than if we ask it when seeing each of them alone. While extramarital affairs are common, occurring perhaps in more than half of marriages, it is not usual for a spouse to admit to one for the first time while in a couple therapy assessment interview. But asking the question may lead to later revelation. If the spouse already knows about infidelity, then the couple will usually discuss it as best they can in the joint interview, but may wait for us to raise the question.

So it is worthwhile to ask the couple during the joint initial interview if either has had affairs. It is the nonverbal responses to this question that are the most valuable. It is common, for instance, for one of the spouses, let us say the husband, to answer easily, "No! I haven't and I don't think my wife has." Meanwhile, the wife has looked anxiously at the husband or is tapping her foot, before chiming in on cue, "No! I haven't either." From these statements and nonverbal cues, we do not assume that the wife has had an affair, or even that the husband has not. But we have a measure of the amount of anxiety about the subject between the couple as glimpsed in a fleeting moment. It may turn out that the wife had an affair in the past, or is having one now, or has not but feels so hurt in the situation that she has thought of it often. Or it may turn out that her foot-tapping reflects on her guardedness as she waits to see what her husband is going to say.

A major debate in couple assessment is whether or not one should see the partners separately. Primarily this is a question of the clinical management of affairs. Infidelity, however, is not the only issue about which the partners will speak differently when seen together and alone. It is worthwhile to give each member of the couple a private space in which to elaborate on difficult matters such as private fantasies that seem threatening, doubts about the marriage, or suspicions about the other's qualities as a parent. But in marital work, the secret of the extramarital affair is the most important revelation in the individual interview. If the couple is always seen together, anything either partner would only feel safe to tell the therapist when alone is blocked.

## ADVANTAGES AND DISADVANTAGES OF A JOINT INTERVIEW

The disadvantage of always and only seeing the couple together is not hearing the things that are individually known but cannot be said. Therapists in this situation do not know everything they could. The advantage, however, of this situation is that therapists are not burdened with knowing something they cannot speak about. This can be liberating. For instance, when therapists who have never met with either spouse individually detect something suspicious in the couple's interaction, they are free to say so, and even to speculate that such a feeling makes them wonder about a secret like an affair. When they have not been told, they are in a position to guess without betraying a confidence.

## ADVANTAGES AND DISADVANTAGES OF A SEPARATE INTERVIEW

The advantage of seeing each partner privately is that therapists will have more information to work with. They tend to get truthful answers to questions about secrets—not just secrets about affairs, but about secret fantasies, hidden feelings, and painful opinions. Therapists who have worked in this way will have more open knowledge about the couple, and will be in a position to work with an unfaithful spouse on the meaning of the affair and its repercussions in the marriage.

The disadvantage of knowing something that is kept secret from one of the spouses is that therapists are no longer free to conjecture, and are hampered in responding to their fantasies. Caught in a position of being silenced by the spouse with the secret, they are hobbled by the countertransference. While this can be worked with as a countertransference position—often one that gives the therapist an intimate feeling of what it is like to be the spouse from whom the secret is kept—the therapist is still not entirely free to speak. One way of working with this arrangement is to work for a while individually with the spouse with the secret toward understanding the effects both of the affair itself and of its operation as a secret in support of object relations issues withheld from the partner. When this work proceeds well, the spouse who has the secret can be prepared for sharing the fact of the affair in the interest of the therapeutic rebuilding of the marriage, thus redressing the imbalance of control in the marriage that the possession of a secret often carries. This may produce a crisis, but it is a "planned crisis" inside the therapy, one with the intent of therapeutic gain.

In the absence of this kind of cooperation—and it may be withheld for good reasons such as the conviction that the spouse will become violent or will promptly leave the marriage—therapists may want to take the position that if the imbalance of knowledge becomes constricting to their capacity to work, they will have to say so. It is entirely possible to do this without spilling the secret. If the impasse is sufficiently great, the therapist may feel it is cause to recommend individual therapy or to resign from an ongoing therapy contract. This can be done by acknowledging a lack of progress and a feeling that the work has ceased to be productive, with or without raising the dilemma of disclosing information that is not the prerogative of the therapist to disclose.

In such a case, the therapist may be able to demonstrate that the impasse is present in the couple work, or he may be able to say that the impasse derives from individual issues that the partners are not willing to share. This latter stance directly pressures the couple to disclose information each has refused to share. This stance can only be taken if it is acknowledged from the beginning that such information exists, as for instance if both partners have such information and have agreed not to share it. In the absence of this situation, therapists can still say that they do not have a sense of forthright communication between the spouses, and that this has contributed substantially to the impasse. Such a statement avoids the ethical dilemma of unauthorized disclosure, but without shirking therapist responsibility.

Conjoint couple interviews alone or combined with the individual assessment interviews are equally acceptable. In our practices, we have worked both ways. In evaluating couples for sex therapy, it is important to do such a thorough sex history evaluation that meeting with the spouses individually as well has been our standard practice. We do so because sex therapy tends to produce an additional crisis of its own, and it does not work well when a significant aspect of commitment is being kept back. Once marital or sex therapy is going on, we work only with the couple, except when the couple plans for an individual meeting for a specific reason. If one spouse has to be out of town or is sick, we do not see the remaining spouse. In summary, it is possible to be effective with either arrangement provided the advantages and disadvantages are understood and taken into the work.

## THE CAUSES AND EFFECTS OF AFFAIRS

In some marriages, affairs are sanctioned by the couple in defiance of the culture. In others, affairs are syntonic with the peer culture and may even be celebrated. As marital therapists, we do not see those marriages with affairs that claim to be successful and therefore we have little to say about affairs as a force of value for marriage.

In all cases that come to us clinically, an affair is a symptom of a flawed marriage. It arises from deficits in both the holding and centered relationships, and is most usefully understood in this way. This avoids the argument about whether affairs may be culturally normal. Couples come to see us because, by their own definition, they are in trouble. In this setting, they and we need all the help we can get in understanding them. We regard affairs as representing issues that have been split off and put outside the boundary of the couple relationship. Understanding the causes of an affair is the first step to reintegrating the couple's marriage.

It matters greatly if the relationship between the couple is one with basically a secure and loving framework in which something has gone wrong, or is one of chronic conflict and mistrust in which the affair only adds to the list of grievances. This underlying quality of the marriage is the main ingredient in the assessment of whether the affair will turn out to be, in a difference noted by Dicks (1967) a generation ago, a benign attempt to get some love into the marriage or a more malignant assault on it.

## Causes of Affairs

Categorizing affairs hardly does justice to the complexity of the human search for triangular relationships. There are as many causes of affairs as there are individuals having them. But we can generalize about different psychological sources establishing a continuum from the relational context to the individual personality (see Table 12–1).

## CONDITIONS OF THE MARITAL CONTRACT

There are some arrangements in marriage that may lead one or both partners to feel that a sexual and emotional relationship is only possible outside the marriage. This arrangement was chosen by a man whose wife had been hospitalized with severe brain damage for years. According to his principles, he could not abandon her by divorce, but there was no life between them. For him, the choice to have affairs allowed him to honor his commitment to take humane care of his wife without giving up on sexual and emotional involve-

Table 12–1. Factors Contributing to the Likelihood of Extramarital Affairs.

1. Conditions of the marital contract that sanction extramarital activity.
2. Cultural expectations of extramarital activity as integral or acceptable to the marriage contract.
3. Marital tension that undermines a couple's capacity to hold each other's intimate interests and leaves one or both vulnerable to or actively seeking openings elsewhere.
4. Reduction of individual commitment based on individual character structure and pathology in a marriage that seems acceptable.

ments. His behavior was understandable, even noble, according to his values, but he was less thoughtful of the needs of his lovers.

Other situations in which spouses choose to gratify their sexual and relational needs in extramarital activity include marriages where the spouses feel a religious obligation not to divorce, or stay together by agreement for the children, but without emotional or sexual interest in each other. When the arrangement is satisfactory, we do not see the couple clinically, although we often see the children, who do suffer the strain of living in a family with a loveless marriage. However, we do see these couples when they are attempting to hold such arrangements together despite considerable ambivalence. Then the situation devolves into one of the other two groups.

## CULTURAL OR PHILOSOPHICAL OPENNESS TO EXTRAMARITAL INVOLVEMENT

Free love for married partners is sanctioned in some subcultures although its popularity has diminished with the advent of AIDS (auto immune deficiency syndrome, a fatal illness associated with infection by the sexually transmitted HIV virus). Still, free love is fun, growth-promoting, and causes no trouble, according to its proponents. We do not meet such couples clinically. To the extent that they positively agree on having affairs, or closing their eyes to them, they have no conflict and we have no role. However, in our culture, this way of life constitutes an "at risk" situation, and we believe these marriages contain a substantial percentage of those that fail. The "open marriage," arrangement often ends when one of the partners meets someone with whom they form a more committed relationship. So, our impression, admittedly based in our experience of the failures, is that the philosophy behind these relationships may be a rationalization for difficulty in managing the continuing bond of the marriage, and a phase of "open marriage" is often a way station on the path to more open dissatisfaction with the marriage.

> Mike and Rita Minelli were in their fifties, and led a conventional life, felt committed to each other, and were more or less happy raising their children. But as their children left, they felt bored sexually. Rita took the lead in suggesting they try an open marriage. She enjoyed it and found it let her tolerate the marriage more easily. Mike felt shyly inadequate in the situation. "I'm not a very good lover," he said, "so I feel that I can't do this very well." Nevertheless it was Mike who met someone and began to fall in love. The couple came for help because Rita panicked at the threat of the dissolution of their thirty-year marriage.

It turned out that she was nonorgasmic, and had used the affairs to substitute a heightened arousal for her frustration with intercourse. But she had also been using the arrangement to deal with chronic resentment at Mike. He had initially felt hurt by her suggestion of swinging, although he had not resisted it. But when he met someone younger who made him feel better about himself, he felt enormous relief.

The causes of their chronic marital strain could, only now, be examined. Rita had longed for the affection and approval of her father, while she felt controlled by her clinging mother. Her father had many affairs, which he flaunted before her mother. One evening, her mother had sent Rita to beg the father not to go out, but he had refused and had marched out leaving the two of them. She had felt humiliated by the role her mother asked her to take, and rejected by her father. She chose Mike as reliable, a man who did not threaten to betray her, but in her identification with her father, she then felt restless. The suggestion for an open marriage was an attempt to fashion a compromise that offered the flair of the identification with her rakish father and the safety of Mike's dependency.

Mike had felt put down and ignored by his father, who preferred his older brother. He had turned to his mother to bolster his shaky self-esteem. When Rita suggested the open marriage, he had been anxious about it, partly because it was not his preference, and partly because it threatened the dependence he had transferred to her. So eventually, when he happened on a woman who was openly adoring of him, he unconsciously felt a renewed opportunity for the dependent relationship in which he felt more comfortable.

By the time they sought therapy, Mike was unsure he would choose to break off the new relationship and return to Rita. He agreed to a period of work on their relationship and on the sex, and eventually did return to the marriage. This time, both of them agreed that it would be exclusive.

## MARITAL TENSION

The third category of affairs contains most of the cases we see clinically as marital therapists. When there is relatively little contribution to marital difficulty from individual psychopathology, strain is introduced from a large variety of sources—developmental crises in the family, sexual difficulty and its frustration, chronic anger, and loss. There are endless varieties of marital strain, from developmental to economic, the strains of differing values or loyalties, of long separations or commuting marriages, too many children, too many in-laws, and so on. While some thematic categories have been described (Strean 1976, 1979; Moultrup 1990), the strains most likely to produce severe difficulties, however, are those of poor mutual fit at the unconscious, object relations level between the couple—the level of fit that determines the long-term quality of the marriage (Dicks 1967). Of the many examples of strain, one may serve to remind us of the causes.

Len and Crystal Powalski had been married twenty years and raised two children. Early in their marriage, there had been periods of breakdown from which they had recovered. They survived relocation and months-long separation required by his military career. Crystal assumed that he would need to have affairs and tolerated the inevitable. When he was at home, they got along well and she had no worries about his fidelity and commitment to their marriage. However, when she was diagnosed as having breast cancer, he fled emotionally. On the day of her emergency surgery, he was discovered to be in bed with someone he had met at a bar two days earlier.

In this case, a marriage that had been resilient in tolerating the affairs when they were geographically justified and out of sight was now under greater stress from crisis. It quickly became apparent that Len had been unable to tolerate the assault to the breast he depended on. Because of his dependent identification with Crystal, he felt mortal anxiety for himself, too, and looked for a phallic expression of his life and independence in keeping with his counterphobic defensive style, which had served him well in dangerous military assignments. Despite the betrayal Crystal felt, the couple was able to use treatment to manage a reconciliation and to achieve considerable growth by getting an understanding of the meaning of the affairs as a shared response to the difficulty of bearing the pain of separation.

Another example comes from a situation in which the adult developmental strain of the husband was the only observable cause.

Will and Sadie Bowan came to see me [D.E.S.] because Will complained that Sadie was no longer satisfying to him sexually. Will was 37, and Sadie 35, and they had been married since college. They had an apparently good marriage, loved each other, and enjoyed their family of two preteen sons. Sadie enjoyed homemaking and Will had a good career. Nothing seemed wrong except his dissatisfaction with sex, which, though routine, was certainly companionable and satisfying to her. She enjoyed their love-making, but lacked the adventurous quality he sought. He wanted to try new things, like oral sex, new positions, and enjoy a more widely ranging physical life. She felt these things were not for her. Although the problem was clear, I was left feeling dissatisfied with my understanding of the situation, with a puzzlement that often foretells that there is an unannounced affair as central to the actual difficulty.

When I saw Will alone, he did not admit to an affair. The most significant discussion involved the block in his career. He worked as a high level bureaucrat, and felt that because he had not gone to law school, he could never go further in his career. With his sons growing toward adolescence, he felt his life was almost over. The insistence on sexual variety now made some sense to me as an attempt to solve his midlife crisis of confidence.

But that was not the whole story. Sadie soon called me to say she had overheard a phone call between Will and a woman in his office. It tipped her off that they were having an affair. When she confronted him, he admitted that he had been passionately caught up with this woman, and that it was much more exciting than his marriage. It gave him a sense of being liberated from the trap of kids, a mortgage, and a dead-end job. Sadie confronted him: he had a choice between the marriage or the other woman. He elected to give up the other woman. At the same time, Sadie was able to become a bit more adventurous sexually.

Will was able to link his crisis to his own story of growing up with parents who had a quietly bitter marriage, which made him fear entrapment by family demands. In his resentment of his mother, he blamed her for hindering his father's career. Sadie felt quite happy being raised by parents in an apparently well-adjusted marriage, whose style of denial dissuaded her from looking at difficult matters growing up. She admitted being similarly determined not to know about issues between her and Will. In a brief intervention of six sessions, this affair and the midlife crisis of which it was a part resulted in considerable growth and strengthening of the couple. Such a brief treatment is typical only of our work with developmental or situational crises.

## CONTRIBUTION FROM INDIVIDUAL PATHOLOGY

The fourth category is the area of individual contribution. Some marriages are marked by affairs from the start because one of the spouses is so threatened by the idea of commitment that the primary bond has to be fragmented among many people so that no one person will have a strong claim. Character pathology affects some so that they cannot maintain sexual interest in the long-term partner. Unconsciously invoking splitting of the object, they will only feel aroused by the unavailable woman. When this situation is identified, it will usually call for individual therapy in addition to couple work. However, the fact that the condition is triggered by variations of a fear of commitment often means that the patient's capacity for commitment to therapy is equally minimal.

One special situation concerns the consequence of a male homosexual or lesbian affair. While some of these affairs precede a decision to identify openly as homosexual, many more occur as crises in marriages with such a shift of sexual identity. Many of the spouses of people who have homosexual affairs are not any more upset by the fact that the affair is homosexual than some others are by knowledge of a heterosexual affair. Male homosexual affairs now also carry the additional stress of the increased possibility of AIDS, which is upsetting because the affair now brings not just the threat of loss of the marriage but chronic illness and death of the husband and the risk of infection of the wife. Examples illustrating contrasting situations regarding the tolerance, or even internal congruence, of the spouse for the internal object relations issues involved in the homosexual liaisons will be given in Chapter 13 where we discuss the larger topic of homosexuality in heterosexual marriages.

## THE EFFECTS OF AFFAIRS

Whatever the causes, the secondary effects of affairs run the gamut from undermining the marriage by secrecy to catalyzing a renewed attempt to construct a better marriage, not uncommonly with considerable success. The affair is a symptom of the marriage, and its discovery or revelation usually constitutes a crisis, with possibilities both for danger and for opportunity. One danger follows from the splitting of good and bad, in which case the marriage is reified by keeping the sense of badness in the straying spouse and the shared goodness in the spouse who is being betrayed. Another danger stems from maintaining a secret life, which often leaves the other person befuddled, as in the following example.

Matt and Lila Mitchell had been married ten years. They had three children after an early marriage. Lila had given up college and stayed home with the children. Matt had been successful in business and then elected to go to law school. The couple came to me [J.S.S.] for therapy because they were fighting, Matt was staying out late at night to study, and Lila was depressed.

In the couple sessions, Matt railed against Lila for clinging and demanding too much of his time. He frequently belittled her for housekeeping flaws. Desperate in the face of his condemnation, Lila tried to appease him, and initiate a process of reconciliation, but he was adamant that her rages and demandingness had to stop. I found him unavailable and angry. He was almost as contemptuous of therapy as he was of Lila. Matt's unyielding and unexamined hate of Lila led me to suspect that there was someone else he thought was wonderful, which he adamantly denied.

In the face of his denial of any responsibility, I questioned the usefulness of continuing therapy. As I arrived at this point, Lila appeared in my office to say she had been told by a friend that Matt was having an affair with a classmate. She was devastated, but she also felt relief at finally having an explanation for Matt's scathing behavior towards her. The secret affair and his use of it to idealize another woman and denigrate her had had the effect of driving her crazy. The discovery of his lying let her begin the process of regaining self respect. She left the marriage and used individual therapy to begin the process of mourning and rebuilding her life.

A chronic picture of betrayal and corruption in an older couple is provided by Jacques and Yolande deGrey, in their early sixties. His impotence had come on six years after they had successfully been treated for her disinterest in sex and primary nonorgasmic status. They were a cosmopolitan, but bitterly critical couple, who told me [D.E.S.] that they had seen some of the most famous therapists in the world. Now they hoped for help with their new difficulty, which seemed to consist of a combination of an organic factor in Jacques' erectile difficulty, and a late-life depression. Jacques had had a remarkably successful career as an international architect, but several times, younger associates had turned on him. He felt as if the son he longed for had repeatedly rejected him. These episodes revived his sense of distance from his own father. Recently, the lack of a younger partner in his firm had pushed him to a decision to sell the firm. After that he had grown depressed.

When I met with him individually, he told me of a life full of many active affairs. He was deeply critical of his wife, whom he found angry and depressed, and he had made his situation tolerable by involvement in serial extramarital arrangements. One of these had been with his wife's sister. As we discussed his difficulty maintaining his sense of integrity late in his life, he decided that he might indeed feel much closer to her if he could tell her about the affairs and seek a more honest relationship. Without my urging, he did so, not telling her about the liaison with her sister, however.

The result was incredible, but not particularly helpful. When he announced the pattern of affairs to her in a therapy hour, she looked amazed. "But I knew all that! Were you worried about this?" she exclaimed. And she proceeded to give a long list of names which were, apparently, all correct. However, she took his admission as another piece of evidence that he was being self-serving, and used it as one of her reasons for ending her participation in therapy. She said she had had enough. She was going to have no part in digging up old pain, both of this sort and about her own painful development. The couple left treatment to resume their previous adjustment. Of course, this couple had not had the benefit of the revelation of the most secret affair with the sister-in-law, which might have penetrated the way Yolande distanced herself habitually from pain.

Affairs can also have the effect of draining off tension in a marriage that might be in constant conflict without them, but usually they maintain a split in object relatedness that saps the marriage. Jacques and Yolande illustrate the common malignant effect of a secret that increased the splitting of good and bad over many years.

## THE LIFE OF THE SECRET

Part of the effect of an affair comes from the unconscious meaning of secrecy itself. Gross (1951) described unconscious aspects of secrecy derived fom different levels of psychosocial development. He wrote, for instance, that when secrecy derives from the anal level it is an expression of the need for a possession to control and withhold from the object in an ambivalent urge to retain and surrender the secret to the object. In the stage of phallic narcissism, the secret is used in the service of exhibitionism, and finally at the oedipal level, it is used as a means of initiating friendships, maintaining trust, and extending intimacy. Gross thought that in the oedipal period, the infantile neurosis might take on the quality of secrecy in that "the child may identify the secret with the adult genitals and by this . . . means, internalize the secret as a substitute for his oedipal wishes, and incorporate it into his ego"(p. 44).

Gross's insights can be extended to the unconscious expression of aspects of the relationship through secrecy. Children who are negotiating issues of closeness and separation often refuse to tell something as a way of maintaining separateness, and then rush to tell any secret at all in order to promote intimacy.

The secrecy of the affair may be of more importance than the sex itself, used in the service of maintaining distance and separateness from the spouse. Secrecy may express anal control, a narcissistic self-righteousness, a defense against merger, or an oedipal triumph over the spouse. In the parlance of childhood the secret, depending on its developmental level, might be saying "you can't catch me," "you can't make me," or "you can't beat me." It may say "I'll show you," "I can win," or "I can have what you deny." All this is to make the point that just because affairs introduce a triangular constellation does not automatically establish them as oedipal level phenomena. The idea "I can have the other parent, which you would deny me if only you knew," is only one of the possible unconscious communications of the secret affair.

From an object relations point of view, secrecy about an extramarital affair or about anything else (such as money or fantasies) is a way of relating to the object, based on a technique of the relevant developmental level. The secret can be withheld as a way of distancing oneself from the object, bartered to control the object, or shared as a tender of closeness. Secrets promote object splitting in a marriage, especially in regard to affairs. A secret kept with an idealized mistress has the effect of keeping the wife at a denigrated distance, not only because she is being betrayed, but often even more because she is diminished by not being "in the know."

Because of the power of secrecy to divide or to bring together, it is important to ask the couple, where possible, to discuss the element that most constitutes the innermost secret of the affair. Sometimes that element is the identity of the third party. Demurrals based on protecting the other man or woman are rationalizations and represent a continued denigration, which runs against the stated intention to rebuild the marriage. Even a secret fantasy of an affair may carry the emotional weight of an actual affair.

## A SECRET MORE IMPORTANT THAN AN AFFAIR

Frances Simon, age 42, said she did not mind telling her husband, Dolph, about her recent affair with a man she met in art class. But she did not want to tell him about a passion she had carried throughout the marriage for an old high school teacher of hers, a man who was now in his sixties. There had never been any sex between them, but she carried the fantasy still that he was the perfect man who would have made her happier by far than her stodgy husband.

In investigating the splitting of object relations, it quickly became clear that while something about the current frustration in the marriage had been acted out in the actual affair, the more profound splitting and projective identification involved the contrast between her denigrated view of her husband and the idealized, enshrined view of the high school teacher. The secret, which carried far more impact than the affair, had been used to nurture a fantasy exciting object that was then denied to her marital relationship. In this case, as in many, the revelation of this secret offered an opportunity for taking back the projective identification and ended the export of all excitement and idealization beyond the boundary of the marriage. Only then could she begin to assess how much this marriage offered and what she could realistically expect from it.

On the other side of the secret is the spouse, kept in the dark and "not wanting to know." For some it is unconsciously safer not to know the terrible secret because of an unconscious assumption that knowledge will deal an intolerable blow. Unconscious mechanisms cause a betrayed spouse to dismiss clues about an affair for defensive reasons but do not imply that the spouse unconsciously "wanted the affair to occur." We should not be in the position of accusing the betrayed spouse of making the affair happen. It is crucial to establish the issues of unconscious collusion in affairs without assigning blame either to the betrayed spouse or to the one who sought the affair.

## OCCASIONS WHEN IT MAY NOT BE NECESSARY TO URGE REVELATION

There are times when the secrets may not any longer be close to the leading edge of the marital difficulty, where their revelation may not be crucial. Early in the investigation of the clinical management of affairs, David Scharff urged the universal tactic of pursuing revelation (D.E. Scharff 1978). Experience has dampened the claim for universality, although the principle concerning the constructive aspects of revelation remains. The following case of an older couple offers an example of a good outcome without revelation, and has constituted part of the evidence that reconstruction is possible without revelation under the right circumstances.

Rose and Gene Holt, in their sixties, came for help with their sexual life because Gene was recently having increasing impotence. However, Rose had never been orgasmic. In their forty-five-year marriage, she had seldom enjoyed sex, and she had no expectation of ever doing so. She had enjoyed physical closeness with a man in the single affair she had twenty years earlier. She was grateful to him for giving her an experience over several years that she never expected to have again. She felt he had been attentive and tender, while Gene had been perfunctory and interested in his own release.

In this case the affair seemed to have taken place a long time in the past. Even so, it was clear that the couple had projected the possibilities of tenderness and of any integration of physical and emotional tenderness outside themselves, and in Rose's case into the affair, where it now remained as a mummified relic. The therapist did not insist on revelation, but worked with Rose to revive the hopes of a more tender possibility in her marriage. In sex therapy, she was able to learn to become orgasmic and to integrate a new physical responsiveness into the relationship with Gene. He was able to learn a new openness and attentiveness to her needs that had never occurred to him before. The issues that had been expressed in the affair had long ago returned to a repressed condition inside the couple rather than being split out into current affairs. This case, therefore, did not require revelation to reinvest the marriage with the issues that needed to be addressed in couple therapy.

## THERAPY AND THE ROLE OF SPLIT-OFF OBJECTS

Our therapeutic aim is to recognize patterns of unconscious cooperation, and to establish the way an affair has dealt with splitting, projective identification, and repressed, painful issues of object relations felt to be unmanageable in the couple.

Splitting is central to the process. An affair involves not only the splitting of objects into good and bad, but splitting of the physical bond off from the primary marital bond. Then aspects of the repressed rejecting internal object are put into the spouse, and the beckoning exciting object is sought elsewhere. For instance, it may be that a husband views his wife as trustworthy and nurturing, but for him sex is so closely tied up with a dangerous but alluring exciting object, that he can only function with a denigrated woman, perhaps a prostitute. Or a wife may have picked her husband as a good and steady support at the expense of excitement, which has to be projected beyond the boundary of the couple so as not to destabilize his image as a reliable nurturing object. Then she may love and value her husband, but fear to experience excitement with him. Or she may project the rejecting and persecuting object into her own genital area, and unconsciously need to protect both him and herself from its release in excited sexual encounters.

Thus far, these dynamics are not different than those of other sexual difficulties. What marks the splitting that leads to affairs specifically is that these qualities are no longer split within the couple or the individual, but are lived out with others. This splitting goes beyond the boundary of the couple, the split-off object relations expressed in a new bodily bond. The newly formed couple of the affair is of interest for the light it throws on the married couple: Is the new liaison of longstanding and committed quality or brief with changing partners? Is it devoted to sexual excitement and little else? Or does it involve sharing of interests with little sexual activity? There are endless variations in the meaning of the split that the affair reveals.

Then there are the issues of projective identification to be understood. What was being managed in mutual projective identification by the couple before the affair began? What is it that has been split off into the new partner of the affair, and what has been put into the denigrated or betrayed spouse through the enactment of the affair? These issues are also no different than in other issues in marital therapy, but the existence of the affair often brings them quickly to crisis proportions. As these matters are understood, the nature of the repressed bad objects becomes clearer and can be taken back by the couple and reintegrated by its individuals.

## AN ILLUSTRATION OF TREATING AFFAIRS IN COUPLE THERAPY

Once the fact of the affair is known, either because it has been uncovered or revealed before therapy, or because the therapist has urged revelation in the service of promoting a planned crisis of growth, the couple that wants to rebuild virtually always has the same task: reintegrating the issues that have been split off into their ongoing relationship. The following example has been reported previously for its description of the sexual issues, the need for revelation, and the impact on the children of parental sexual difficulty (D. E. Scharff 1982, Scharff and Scharff 1987). This occasion gives an opportunity for a longer-term follow up.

Max and Ginger Wheeler, he 37 and she 27, had met during an affair. She had worked in his office and the affair was known by almost everyone except Max's wife. During the affair, Ginger had enjoyed the physical closeness and had not minded sex, but after marriage, she grew to hate intercourse. After the birth of their daughter, Ginger gave up pretending to enjoy sex, and so Max brought her for sex therapy. During the evaluation, it emerged that he had begun to have affairs again during her pregnancy, frightened by the rivalry of a child. The therapists [D.E.S and a female co-therapist] said they would not offer sex therapy unless he told her of his outside activities and unless the affairs stopped. Panicked, he stopped the male therapist [D.E.S.] on the way into the interpretive session, and said he would tell everything except that one of the affairs was with her best friend. This was the first of many times that the counter-transference echoed the couple's marriage. The therapist, feeling trapped and "manhandled," suddenly felt that he knew what the wife was living with. Feeling in a bind, and not yet experienced in working toward revelation, he simply refused to live with the knowledge. Max came clean in the following hour.

Ginger staggered under the weight of the revelation. When she recovered, she considered her options while the couple and therapists tried to make sense of the affairs and of their connection to her avoidance and dislike of sex. The first effect of the revelation was to put the two on the same footing. Ginger now understood what had been happening. She quickly said that she realized she knew without knowing. She had been avoiding going to Max's office for a long time, knowing that everyone had known about her affair with him. She realized that in a way, she had pushed him into the affairs by her sexual refusal coupled with her intense dependency on him. While she would not tolerate any more affairs, she soon offered to try to rebuild their marriage in therapy.

The therapists felt they had been let out of a collusion of corruption. While previously Ginger had regarded them with suspicion and Max had looked to them to serve his purposes, they had felt lost with no sense of alliance, in danger of being abused by the couple. From the time of the revelation, they felt on more solid footing. They were clear that the marriage was in no shape to benefit from sex therapy and they recommended that Ginger and Max begin marital therapy with one of them [D.E.S.].

In the couple therapy, it soon emerged that Ginger had been an oedipal victor in her family. She thought that her father actually had never loved her mother. He denigrated her, while being fond and admiring of Ginger. Having a daughter of her own meant that she had begun to identify herself with her mother, and she therefore unconsciously expected to be cast off by the pair of Max and her infant daughter. She had, she now thought, both expressed this fear and precipitated its likelihood by her sexual aversion.

Max had been the idealized youngest child, an only son with four sisters. His father had numerous affairs, inflaming Max's mother's continuing rage. His mother was also cruelly critical of the sisters, so that Max had a sense of exaggerated specialness, but he always felt threatened lest her rages at others turn finally on him. As an adult, he had solved this problem of internal object relations by keeping both Ginger and his previous wife at bay through splintering the object in numerous affairs. It turned out he also had premature ejaculation, a psychosomatic symptom of his unconscious determination not to let a woman or her vagina trap him.

These elements of unconscious determination could be identified soon after the revelation, but the therapy took much longer. Both Max and Ginger had phases of individual work, followed by more couple's work. Max gave up the affairs, but after Ginger did not become sexually responsive in two years of individual therapy, she discovered that he was planning to begin another affair. He said it was true, and that if she could not face sex, he was prepared either to live by having affairs or, if she preferred, to face divorce. Under this renewed impact, she did manage to become responsive and orgasmic for the first time through treatment in a nonorgasmic women's group. Max and Ginger were then able to treat his premature ejaculation in a sex therapy format introduced into their couple therapy. Ginger insisted, however, that Max renew his individual work. He did, with considerable relief.

The couple's life calmed down and proceeded over the next several years. One day, the therapist [D.E.S.] got a call from Mrs. Wheeler. When they met, she said that she was now having an affair. She knew that he would not treat the two of them when that was the case, and she was not asking that. She had decided some time ago that the marriage with Max was not the one she would have picked if she could have planned her life over again. This affair had underscored the fact that she and Max did not belong together. She was coming now to ask for advice on how to handle their two children through a separation.

In the process, Mr. Wheeler also came to see the therapist. He was sad about the failure of the marriage, but said that the therapist should not be disappointed in the work. He felt the whole family had grown enormously, and were now capable of lives of an entirely different quality. He thanked the therapist profusely, asked about issues of the management of their children through the separation, and went on his way.

In this case, the meaning of an affair had shifted fundamentally during the life of the couple. Beginning as an immature expression of individual and shared pathology, it ended as an expression of mutual decision-making and at least to some extent, of growth.

## THE AFFAIR-BASED MARRIAGE

Harvey and Anne, whom we studied at length in Chapter 8 (the apparently impossible couple) presented as a couple born of affairs, a situation that sometimes pertains in second marriages. Both had been married before, and each in their own way had felt the marriages to be quite dead. Anne's marriage to a successful builder had quickly become a matter of convenience. She could tolerate her husband's lack of interest in the family because it let her do as she pleased in running the family and raising her children. She handled her longing for emotional closeness by a series of surreptitious affairs that went on without noticeable curiosity from her husband. When she met Harvey, she found more passion and interest in the relationship than any she had ever had, but she also found that it stirred her up in disturbing new ways. His frequent erectile difficulty during the affair upset her, but did not keep her from deciding to divorce her lackluster husband in favor of Harvey.

For Harvey, his previous marriage to a depressed but undemanding wife was a matter of continuing disappointment, which he handled by an endless series of lunchtime liaisons. None of these meant a great deal to him, and were handled with as much emotional isolation as was his marriage. Meeting Anne offered welcome rejuvenation, for at 53 he was beginning to face a sense of dissipation of his powers. He had suffered occasional impotence in affairs before, but as this gripping affair took hold for him, he experienced the paradoxical difficulty of more trouble with erections. They were fairly reliable in brief and secret trysts, but when he and Anne now arranged longer periods of time together, as when he attended scientific meetings out of town with her, he began to have more sustained difficulty. This problem solidified after they were married, and was the chief reason they sought help after eighteen months of marriage.

In this case, the affairs of both previous marriages could now be seen as keeping passion and commitment at bay, split off from the safe and steady but uninvolved marriages each had. The affairs thus had an important role in maintaining those marriages as steady but unemotional and essentially nonsexual. Harvey and Anne each needed such a marriage for different reasons. Harvey was frightened of closeness to a woman, based on his fear of his needy, alcoholic mother, whose wish to impose her needs on him still plagued him. Anne had felt neglected by her parents during years of recovery from a childhood burn. Left with little visible evidence of the scars, she nevertheless felt that she was unlovable, and took her husband's lack of interest as evidence of what she should expect. The affairs allowed her a split-off relationship with the exciting object she craved, without chancing the aggressive rebuffs she had felt from her parents' neglect after the burn.

There are painful elements even in the aftermath of the affair that leads to successful marriage. The resentment of children about their broken homes often presents a reminder of the compromises involved. These children face so many recurrent hurdles around the loss of an intact home (Wallerstein and Blakeslee 1989) that the difficulties they face are a constant problem in remarriage. The remarried couple also has the stress of encumbered finances and the need for continued negotiation with ambivalently held ex-spouses.

But the more central problem comes when aspects of internal object life that had been held outside the original marriages now must be integrated into the subsequent one. For instance, guilt that was held at bay enough for the affairs to happen must now be absorbed into the marriage itself. In a general sense, the rejection of a repressed bad object that was handled by splitting and projected denigration of the spouse before, must now be handled inside the new relationship. When the remarriage offers another better chance for healing and growth, there tends to be no affair. Because of this, second marriages are less often complicated by affairs, but this is certainly not always so.

In the example of Harvey and Anne, bitter fighting alternating with passionate interest and tenderness was such a contrast to their emotionless first marriages that they could hardly identify themselves in the new situation. The search for a new other in an affair or in courtship is also a search for a new self. Hoping to find a completely different other person in the new liaison and, later, in the marriage, Harvey and Anne each also found a completely different self. Now the contempt each had exercised toward the previous spouse came back with such force that projective identification occurred in projectile form. The selves that Anne and Harvey each found were both intriguing and terrifying—that is, they represented enlarged, unstable images of parts of themselves tied to vastly magnified images of the exciting and rejecting objects. Anne, in particular, felt so betrayed by the image of herself in this new relationship that she contended over and over that she could never trust Harvey. The disorienting effect of their present marriage made sense of their choice to spend their younger adulthoods with stable, even if disappointing, marriages to which they could tie stable selves, splitting off the exciting and craving parts of themselves to objects that did not threaten them.

## AFFAIRS SEEN IN INDIVIDUAL THERAPY

The perspective with which a therapist sees affairs in individual therapy is a different one, without the primary emphasis on the meaning to the marriage. While this may still be relevant, the therapist's responsibility is to the single patient, without responsibility to the marriage and the spouse. Certainly, if the patient professes an interest in working on the marriage, then the factors we have been considering will be relevant and may be introduced, worked with, and interpreted. The patient may want to work with them in individual therapy, may accept referral for couple therapy, or may decide that the work on the marriage is not of interest.

Often, however, an individual patient is ambivalent. In the following case, a woman expressed strong interest in her marriage but acted to continue and even increase the splitting of the exciting object.

> Raquel Gaddis spent many days in psychoanalysis in agony over the relationship with her distant and unemotional, but stable and reliable husband, Nigel. She longed for a closer, more emotional relationship. He was more interested in his work, in music, and in politics. She began to have a series of affairs, with the idea that if he found out, it might mobilize him. The men were always more interesting and passionate, but less reliable than Nigel. The analyst felt that her desperation stemmed from her difficulty confronting Nigel with her dissatisfactions, but he understood that when she did, she felt she got little response.
>
> When Nigel continued to be moved neither by her increasing travel schedule, which barely disguised her liaisons, nor by her confrontations, Raquel finally told him of her affairs, and urged him to try one, too, in order to see if he wanted to learn how to be more sexual and passionate. She had the idea that an affair might possibly return Nigel to the marriage more energized, but she said she understood it might also end the marriage. She was willing to take that risk. She was therefore disappointed when he returned to her to seek advice about the first woman he met through his music, with whom he did not at first begin a sexual relationship. Raquel felt he had treated her more like a mother than a wife. Later he did launch a sexual relationship. At that point, the analyst referred them to a colleague. Nigel and Raquel began couple therapy, but to little avail. The distance between them remained, and the projections of unemotionality onto Nigel and of unreasonable demandingness onto Raquel could not be altered. Eventually, Raquel decided that Nigel would never change enough to satisfy her, and she moved out.
>
> Here, the affairs on both sides were initiated by the wife. The therapist's suggestion that the affairs were an alternative to facing Raquel's growing desperation that the marriage was already one she could not tolerate was ignored, and life for the couple grew much more tumultuous before the marriage died. Raquel's use of the affairs enabled her to post-

pone her loss over considerable time, but she was not, in the end, convinced that her delay had been useful.

Another patient, Felicia Marti, entered psychotherapy after the failure of her marriage. Even in high school, she had had the equivalent of affairs, running around with a friend of her boyfriend whenever he was out of town. She had married her husband soon after college, desperate at the prospect of having to be on her own otherwise. He was much older, a reminder of her rude but beguiling father. Father and husband were like two peas in a pod and got along famously.

Mrs. Marti's marriage was rocky and sometimes threatened violence. She found her husband more like her irascible father than she had realized in the six-week whirlwind courtship. She took a job in a nearby city, with her husband's blessing, and began a series of affairs there, always with older, usually married men who were more sophisticated than her husband. Her marriage finally broke up when her husband threatened her with a gun one night while he was drunk. Even after the collapse of the marriage, she was unable to connect with men who were closer to her age or were more available. After six years of this self-defeating pattern, she finally sought psychotherapy for her increasing loneliness.

Once beginning intensive psychotherapy, Mrs. Marti tried to seduce her male therapist, noting, "No one I've ever taken a fancy to has ever turned me down." When that failed she began another series of affairs, both with married men and with men who might be more available but who were a great deal older. She also shoplifted minor items like wine glasses, ostensibly to give to her boyfriend. In therapy, dreams led her to understand that these stolen items signified both her mother's vagina and her father's penis, and that it was her feelings of abandonment due to an absence of the therapist that had triggered the shoplifting. As she realized how much the affairs during the marriage, and the liaisons and shoplifting now, were all in unconscious reaction to her early privation and envy of her parents, she became more appropriately depressed. She stopped all delinquency and all sexual activity for almost two years, before resuming dating in a markedly more appropriate and centered way. After three years of trial relationships, she was, at 36, able to meet and marry a man who was only three years older than she was, and with whom she had developed a stable relationship.

This woman expressed a pattern of affairs that began in her adolescence and continued after her first marriage. Finally it was reenacted in the transference, where it could be understood. It was only then that she was able to give it up, and begin a slow path toward forming a solid relationship. This happened because the pattern of affairs moved into the transference early in therapy. It was not until a focused transference to the therapist as the depriving father and mother figures developed that this therapy took hold and helped her to understand, and ultimately to surrender, a lifelong pattern.

## PRINCIPLES OF THERAPEUTIC MANAGEMENT

When an affair is a significant part of a couple's trouble, we proceed through a series of tasks in assessment and therapy, as summarized in Table 12–2.

### Assessment of Commitment

Early on, the couple's degree of commitment needs to be assessed. This is the best indicator of therapeutic potential. Despite the strain of an affair, partners in therapy do best if they are committed to each other, or at least if they wish to be, provided things improve. Once one of them has a sense that commitment is beyond repair, they are not likely to do well.

### Examination of Splitting and Projective Identification

The therapy of affairs begins with an exploration of the meanings of events and secrets as they have stemmed from and affected the couple's object relations.

### Revelation

When possible, full revelation of the secrets and affairs clears the ground for repair of the foundation on which the relationship is built. It is an axiom that "A house built on a poor foundation will not stand." Getting out all the hurt can be painful, but if it is done not in order to be hurtful, but to build a foundation for therapeutic repair, it almost always helps.

Table 12–2.  Dealing with Affairs

1. Assess degree of commitment.
2. Examine the meaning of splitting and projective identification contained in the affair.
3. Explore revelation of marital secrets in the service of building a new foundation.
4. Suggest that the affair cease.
5. Interpret to facilitate reintegration of split-off and projected meanings contained in the affair.
6. Use transference and countertransference to understand the meaning of the affair as reenacted in therapy.

If however, a couple comes to us with a substantial expectation of marital separation or divorce, we do not urge revelation. If the couple is going to separate, then secrets can remain private. The revelation will not contribute to the marriage and may compromise the individual in the legal divorce process. It is still true, however, that the children of such a marriage may benefit from knowing what actually happened in the predivorce family. This, however, is a separate matter.

When conducted in the interests of therapeutic change, revelation can put the couple, often for the first time, on equal footing. The wife who was disadvantaged, because in the dark, now has equal knowledge and power. She *could* choose to leave, giving her also the option to stay willingly, no longer as hostage to her unconscious need to "not know." And the revealing husband has willingly surrendered the power he held through the unrevealed secret. Now they may well be in a position to share vulnerability equally, relinquish self-serving protection, and establish a firm foundation for rebuilding.

## No Ongoing Affair

We insist that there be no ongoing affair. That activity is too demeaning to the stay-at-home spouse and to the therapist. A continuing affair can certainly be worked on in individual therapy, but after an initial period of assessment and evaluation, it is not consistent with good-faith efforts at rebuilding in couple therapy. We believe it is better to withdraw from couple's work than to collude in tolerating such an imbalance. Then the couple can be offered the opportunity for one or both of the partners to work individually.

## Interpretation and Reintegration

The bulk of the therapeutic work will, as always, center on helping the couple reintegrate the split-off aspects of the relationship—exciting, feared, denied aspects—that have been projected into the affair. In this task, specific therapy for the couple's sexuality may be important.

## Transference and Countertransference

As in all object relations marital therapy, the role of transference and countertransference is important. The treatment will itself contain the quality of an affair with a third party, namely the therapist, and of the marriage whose difficulties led to therapy. The therapist will feel the emotions of guilty excitement about the affair, pity for the victim of its secrecy, or anxiety about the illicit and risky quality. Most of all, the therapist will experience their projections in him as a third party to the dyad. Attacks on the therapist's holding and direct appeals through individual transference are likely ways that the couple will express their deficits in shared holding that have led one or both of them to breach the couple boundary.

When therapists are willing to absorb these projective identifications in the contextual transference, they begin the process of reversing the splitting and pathologically polarized projective identifications, and of reuniting physical and emotional aspects of the couple's bond. By tolerating the anxiety of the projections, but ultimately refusing to go along with them, therapists offer the possibility of renewed holding to marriages that could not contain a fragmenting affair.

The management of extramarital affairs is a common issue in marital therapy, so common that a full discussion of it would involve almost everything that can be said about marital therapy itself. Nevertheless, it has been written about relatively infrequently, and is especially overlooked in the literature of the psychodynamic therapies. This chapter is intended to help well-rounded marital therapists include knowledge about the issues arising in affairs as part of their standard therapeutic armamentarium.

Chapter 13
# HOMOSEXUALITY AND PERVERSION
# IN MARITAL THERAPY

When there is co-existing homosexuality or perversion (now termed paraphilia) in one member of the couple the therapist faces a particularly perplexing problem. For a heterosexual couple, the question of the impact of a shift of sexual identity or the intrusion of an alternate identity raises the fundamental question of the survival of the couple as a unit. Indeed, some couples do come to a therapist for help to negotiate this shift, to adjust to the break-up of the marriage, and to plan for the children. In the more frequent situation that is brought to a marital therapist, the couple comes because one of them has ambivalence about homosexuality and is at least willing to see if the pull of the marriage will keep the heterosexual orientation dominant.

Equally challenging are the paraphilias (or perversions) when one marital partner has a pull toward transvestism, or a fetish, or has been exhibiting or committing a sexual act with children. These matters cannot be tolerated by society because they are harmful to the children and so the paraphilias are assumed to be evidence of severe psychopathology. However, in the couples we see, it often turns out that paraphilic tendencies are there in a latent form, and only become manifest under stress of some kind. It is our task to see if the overt manifestation of homosexual or paraphilic issues is related to stress in the couple or in either of the spouses, and, therefore, if it is subject to treatment either for the couple or the individual. Too often, we assume that it is a sign of such serious psychopathology that it is untreatable in couple therapy or incompatible with heterosexual marriage. With treatment, the issue may be returned to its point of departure from the marriage. Then with continued therapy the couple can resume course on a more even keel.

There is also the situation, well known to many sex therapists, where a paraphilic spouse lives in a relationship in which the couple decides to live with the paraphilia intact and to adjust around it. The most common example is provided by the heterosexual couple that accommodates a male transvestite. There are, in many cities, formally organized groups of these couples, with social gatherings in which the men wear feminine attire and the wives are included in the event, some with enthusiasm, and some more reluctantly. Similar accommodations are made in a substantial number of couples that include a homosexual partner who has enough bisexual identification to wish to stay married, and even sexually active, and who also engages in homosexual activity. Of course this particular adjustment is markedly more problematic now in the era of AIDS.

While therapists who are unaccustomed to this kind of adjustment are uncomfortable with it, and may have difficulty supporting it, they may feel helped by two pieces of information. First, there is a significant number of couples who seek such an adjustment, and for whom it is comfortable. Any efforts we make to talk them out of it because of our own discomfort will simply drive them away from us. In such cases, if the therapist is uncomfortable with even tolerating such an adjustment, it is better to say so and make a referral.

Second, the existence of such couples underlines a subtle but more important point. For couples to seek help in reaching any of these accommodations, even that the partner with the ambivalence about sexual identity be helped to resolve it, requires a great deal of tolerance by the other partner for the inner conflict about sexual identity. Marital therapists who might not personally tolerate a homosexuality or a paraphilia conflict in a partner could be blind to acknowledging that there are spouses who can include such individual conflict without intolerable couple conflict. There is, as in any other marriage, a considerable congruence of inner object relations issues, and in these cases, most especially for the grey areas of sexual identity. These considerations apply to all levels of paraphilia and homosexuality—from fantasy to overt acting out. Until we have given a trial of treatment, there is no reason, per se, to assume the situation is doomed by relentless confusion of sexual identity undermining the couple's possibility of a satisfactory fit.

Before considering further the implications of some of these situations for marital therapy, it might be well to comment briefly on the origin of homosexuality and the paraphilias from a psychoanalytic and object relations point of view.

In the beginning of analytic thought, Freud (1905b) postulated that homosexuality was considered to be simply the most common among the many perversions. Only later have the complex factors of the object relations of the individual been seen as central to the development of homosexual object choice and to the splintering of the object, which is expressed in the paraphilias.

There has been controversy about the role of hormonal balance in the predisposition to homosexuality. Meyer (1985a) concluded:

> In terms of present knowledge, there appears to be no definitive action of hormonal or other biological factors on sexual identity or object choice. Rather, there appears to be a complex interaction between biological, environmental, and mental factors that affect the expression of sexually dimorphic behaviors. The concept of a 'nature vs. nurture' controversy seems anachronistic. [p. 1058]

Controversy also exists about whether ego-syntonic homosexuality is a pathological process. This discussion is well beyond the scope of our consideration here, but we can comment on questions that puzzle us in the clinical situation. How do we explain the coexistence of an intact gender identity accompanied by homosexual object choice? Many authors have linked difficult relations with parents to homosexual development, with a predominant pattern that includes a domineering mother and an absent or ineffective father. Roiphe and Galenson (1981) documented the importance of experiences beginning in the second year of life, while Meyer (1985a), reviewed the evidence for events during oedipal development. There are often crucial additional turning points as late as adolescence (D. E. Scharff 1982), so that it can now be understood that events and issues from all points in development through adolescence play a role in the development of homosexual object choice.

In homosexuality, as in the paraphilias, the expression of a feature of childhood sexuality is a required component of adult sexuality.

Sachs (1923) was the first psychoanalyst to describe the way a person uses a surviving remnant of infantile sexuality to allow displaced expression for other, more feared pregenital components of sexuality, which are only then susceptible to repression. This has been known as the Sachs Mechanism. While Sachs' description now seems inexact, his early contribution ranks as important. More recently, writing from an object relations point of view, Kernberg (1975) and Socarides (1978) have noted that homosexuality may express a range of internalized object relationships based on increasing levels of ego maturation. Thus they postulate that a homosexual operating at the oedipal level submits an infantile self to a domineering parent of the same sex. In high level pre-oedipal homosexuality, the sexual object stands partly for the self and partly is a representative of the pre-oedipal mother. In the less mature, narcissistic brand of pre-oedipal homosexuality, the object is purely a representative of the homosexual's grandiose self. Relationships are brief and there is scant concern for the object as another person. In schizo-homosexuality, homosexuality coexists with schizophrenia. There is a lack of separation of self from object (Socarides 1978).

The family constellation that contributes to both male and female homosexuality is critical to the formation of the underlying object relationships. Bieber and colleagues (1962) found that in men with severe homosexuality there had been a family pattern of a detached hostile father and an overly close, seductive mother who dominated the husband. Homosexual object choice fundamentally involves major difficulties in early development. Female homosexuals also show a mixture of pre-oedipal and oedipal issues, with failures in their relationships to both mother and father. Saghir and Robins (1973) noted that a variety of etiologic patterns exist for lesbians, ranging from domineering, hostile mothers and unassertive, detached fathers to intensely seductive fathers and narcissistic, detached mothers. The common underlying factor, they concluded, is the presence of a vigorous anti-heterosexual pattern in the home. McDougall (1970) has described her analytic understanding of a lesbian who sacrificed her relationship with her father to her mother in order to maintain the mother as an ideal image of the self.

Often the relationship with mother has been close but ambivalent. The boy who later becomes homosexual fails to let go of an early identification with his mother to form an adequate identification with his father. The girl who later becomes lesbian cannot risk her mother's displeasure in solidifying father as an object choice, or else she faces palpable danger when he is too exciting and rejecting, perhaps intrusive or even molesting. Thus the potential for homosexuality in a child is one possible locus for parental disturbance expressed in seriously distorted family interaction.

From our observations, we can add our impression that there are essential contributions to homosexuality by both parents, but also by the child's experience of their relationship to each other. This is influenced first by the relationship to each parent. Second, as Ogden (1989) has noted, each parent presents an unconscious image of the other as an internal object. That means that the first image of father (or the only one in single parent families) may be the mother's internal object of a father, presented to the child unconsciously, Similarly, the father presents his internal object set of women and mothers to the child. Lastly, what the growing child internalizes of the actual parental couple relationship matters greatly—quite apart from the child's internalized relations with each parent individually. This will become important for us in examining adult couples when the heterosexual or paraphilic spouse in a heterosexual marriage re-creates a couple based on the internal couple formed in identification with the heterosexual parents' relationship, which includes an alternative couple in the intrapsychic sense and one that may compete with the marriage in fantasy or in actuality when affairs occur.

In sum, overt homosexuality develops when supported and encouraged by the parents' shared conscious or unconscious processes (Kolb and Johnson 1955), when parental needs override the child's needs for autonomy in the phases of separation–individuation (Socarides 1978), and when family-wide conscious interaction and unconscious projective identification support the development of the splitting and sorting of internal objects such that the exciting, safer internal object is identified with the same sex and the threatening object is opposite-sexed (D. E. Scharff 1982). These same general issues determine perverse solutions: relationships in the family that make direct sexual expression dangerous, but which turn general problems of relating into sexualized matters fraught with danger and excitement, contribute to the development of paraphilias.

## THE MARRIAGE WITH A HOMOSEXUAL SPOUSE

Let us now turn to the situation of the couple with one partner who exhibits homosexual elements of sexual identity and object choice. In some cases, both members of the couple may have had previous homosexual experience. More often, the tolerance of one for the penchant of the other expresses the overlap in object relations issues.

Homosexual issues may be expressed within the couple along a continuum from a fantasy without enactment to a brief, single affair to prolonged or repeated homosexual affairs and finally to the individual's becoming primarily homosexual. Our work as marital therapists is confined to those cases where there is partial expression of homosexuality through fantasy or periodic enactment without one partner's insistence on making that the major orientation.

## Homosexual Fantasy

It is common for one or both partners to have homosexual fantasies. Often the fantasies have been kept secret from the partner out of shame, and when this is so, these fantasies usually grow in influence and autonomy, as happens with the suppression of fantasies or secret thoughts (D. E. Scharff 1978, 1982, Wegner et al. 1990). Usually it is helpful to have the fantasies shared between the couple, and it often then happens that their force and obligatory quality dissipate. This happens partly because of the frequent, although unexpected tolerance of the partner, which is usually greater than the partner with the secret imagines it will be. In any case, it is almost impossible to work in any depth with the couple as long as the secret is maintained, so that the sharing of the secret is important in giving the therapy a chance, even if the results are not uniformly positive. If these fantasies are distasteful to the one who has them, and if they do not dissipate, they may be regarded as an indication for individual therapy as well as couple therapy.

## Homosexual Affairs

The more difficult question concerns the meaning and consequence of a husband's or wife's homosexual affair. While some of these affairs presage the decision to identify as homosexual, many more occur as crises in marriages without a permanent shift of sexual identity. It is important to know that many of the spouses of people who have homosexual affairs are not any more upset by the fact that the affair is homosexual than some others are by knowledge of a heterosexual affair. Of course, the issue of AIDS has made male homosexual encounters particularly dangerous now, and that is a matter that must always be taken up in couples where life is thus threatened.

Conrad and Jennifer Bailey, he a successful Navy captain of 47 and she a housewife of 44, came because of his lack of sexual interest in her. It turned out that he had had numerous brief liaisons while on cruises, not much caring whether the liaisons were homosexual or heterosexual. Jennifer was outraged at the affairs, but the homosexual ones did not offend her more than the heterosexual ones. She did insist that all the affairs stop if the marriage was to continue.

Conrad's childhood was marked by a high level of parental neglect. A series of maids substituted for his largely absent, working parents. One of the maids had invited him to her room for intercourse in the years when be was between 11 and 14 years old. There had also been a faulty institutional parental substitute in boarding school where parenting was done by male teachers, one of whom seduced him on several occasions. These relationships in which older men and women stimulated his sexual needs in lieu of satisfying his needs for basic care had been carried along in his adult pattern of bisexual affairs, where he split the object into a steady wifely one who provided support, and exciting others, male or female, to whom he could relate sexually. This served to keep his primary relationship to Jennifer safe but unexciting. Diffused sexual object choice modeled on his childhood care situation was continued in adult liaisons.

Jennifer's previous tolerance of his affairs and now of his ambiguous sexual identity was harder to understand. She, too, seemed to have had a childhood of enough neglect that left her willing to tolerate a great deal of ambiguity in exchange for caring she thought was reliable. She was concerned not about the exact nature of the extramarital sex, but about the fact that there was any of it at all. She was most concerned about Conrad's lack of sexual interest in her. In all likelihood, her internal organization, which had tolerated affairs and homosexuality, shared many of the object relations issues with her husband, expressed through projective identification. In these couples, the female's silent paraphilia or homosexuality is often overtly expressed by the male (Meyer 1985b).

The unconscious fit in tolerance for an undifferentiated, diffuse sexual identity and choice of objects apparently allowed this couple room for the reworking which they were able to do. Conrad agreed to have individual therapy, and to renounce the affairs. With a few months of insight-oriented psychotherapy, he developed a tolerance, for the first time in his adult life, for enough depression to allow a beginning understanding of the losses of his childhood. In the midst of his tolerating the depression within the therapy, his interest in sex with Jennifer returned, and the pressure toward outside affairs seemed to dissipate. While this was by no means a thorough treatment, follow-up indicated that Conrad had apparently gotten enough help to strengthen his tie to Jennifer to give up the affairs. Over the next years, the relationship settled into a new equilibrium.

A second example, from quite a different point of view, is provided by Mrs. Phoebe O'Malley. Mrs. O'Malley regarded marriage as a context for getting on with her life, a marriage to be carried on without passion. She had many heterosexual affairs, but she also had a long and stormy affair with a young woman she had hired to take care of her daughters. This one caused no more stir in a marriage of convenience than did the heterosexual ones. It went on under her husband's nose, and without his wanting to know about it. What the affair did produce was a close liaison between the other woman and the older of the two daughters, a connection in which this other woman continued to act seductively with the daughter long after Mrs. O'Malley's divorce. That relationship with the daughter brought the issues Mrs. O'Malley had tried to keep splintered out of her marriage back to her, and to her daughter, in a continually alarming way over many years.

I [J.S.S.] saw Mrs. O'Malley during her second marriage, some years after the affair with the woman, when the complications with the continued pull by the other woman on her daughter were still active. However, the issues of bisexual object choice that had been involved in the lesbian affair were no longer prominent in the second marriage. Mrs. O'Malley's second husband was an artist with a considerable tolerance for her bisexuality born out of similar issues in himself. He had never acted on his homosexual issues, but he had open sympathy for hers. Both of them were, however, united in agreeing that in this marriage they were interested in maintaining an exclusive relationship, so that questions of sexual identity and object choice were ones of unconscious fit, not action.

## THE PARAPHILIAS

The paraphilias—exhibitionism, voyeurism, or fetishism—are repetitive, involuntary situations of sexual arousal or masturbation characterized by unusual or bizarre imagery or acts involving the use of nonhuman objects for arousal. They may alternatively include those situations of sexual arousal that are accompanied by the imposition of humiliation or suffering—that is, the sadomasochistic perversions, or by sexual acts involving nonconsenting partners or children too young to give their consent—rape and pedophilia. Arousal and orgasm are dependent on the eliciting of a special fantasy that has conscious and unconscious components but its influence and elaborations extend beyond the sexual sphere to pervade the individual's life (Meyer 1985b). Stoller (1975, 1979) has helped us to understand the way in which sex and aggression are always fused in these symptoms, so that the paraphilic expresses anger toward the sexual object along with sexual arousal.

The group of paraphilias includes fetishism, transvestism, sexual sadism and masochism, exhibitionism and voyeurism, pedophilia, zoophilia, a group associated with excretory functions such as coprophilia and urolagnia, and a longer list of less common and more bizarre syndromes. The paraphilias are far more common in men than women, which Meyer (1985b) attributes to reaction to the threat of castration more obviously posed to the boy's genitals due to the externality of male genital anatomy.

"Male perversions are external, often flamboyant structures with concrete props that tell the story of triumph over a castration threat. Female perversions are largely unobtrusive, being revealed by a particular willingness to accommodate to the perversion of sexual partners . . . a clandestine insurgence against a sense of genital inferiority" (Meyer 1985b, p. 1069).

The formation of a perverse symptom as an expression of internal object relations is different in each person, but similar in its economy: one compromise formation allows expression of individual and family conflict. A function that ordinarily has an important but minor role in sexual expression, and which is usually a passing expression in childhood of early sexuality, comes to the forefront. In these pictures, anxiety and aggression are inextricably bound with sexual desire and arousal.

In classical psychoanalytic theory, it was suggested that the motivating force behind perversion was the boy's concern with castration (Freud 1905b). To calm castration anxiety, he used unconscious fantasy to establish repetitively the existence of the imagined maternal phallus. In convincing himself that his mother had a penis, he could counter his own anxiety about the threatened loss of his own penis (Bak 1968).

From their study of an infantile fetish, Roiphe and Galenson (1981) postulated that phases that are usually transient in children can be extended to variable lengths, and that at the outer limit of such a continuum rests the adult persistence of paraphilias. It has been thought that the unconscious fantasies that underlie these syndromes could be uncovered only when in-depth exploration was available, as in psychoanalysis or detailed observation of child development. However the fantasies also emerge in couple therapy, when we explore the underpinnings of the interpersonal behavior of the paraphilic spouse and the coercible mate.

The paraphilias, then, have been classically described as representing ordinary transient pieces of early development that have become fixed, stereotyped components of arousal through the confluence of many unconscious factors during development. The study of the paraphilias has been enriched by such recent contributors as Khan, McDougall, and Coen.

Khan (1979) sees perversion as "auto-erotism *à deux*," as an "engineered re-enactment of masturbatory practices between two persons as a compensation for that insufficiency of maternal care which is the prerequisite of infantile auto-erotism and narcissism" (p. 24). This fits with McDougall's (1970, 1985, 1986) idea of the perversions as a stage for internal sexualized dramas in which the drama reflects a rigid and impoverished fantasy elaboration and a need to enact internal object relations rather than to handle them through symbolic thought. This brings to perversion Segal's (1981) idea that the lack of a capacity for symbol formation leaves a person using instead a "symbolic equation," that is, a concrete act or equivalence that is substituted for a fantasy or metaphor.

McDougall (1985) writes, "Disavowed or repudiated from the psyche rather than repressed," the destructive desires toward the controlling image of the mother "are directed against the parental objects or their part object representatives, all of which have been fragmented and damaged in the internal world of psychic representations." They are then played out in what she calls "the neosexual scenario" in ways that conceal their meaning. Then

> the sexual partner is required not only to embody the idealized image that the subject desires but also to incarnate all the reprehensible elements that the subject does not wish to acknowledge. In every neosexual production, valued as well as dangerous parts of the self are in this way recovered, mastered, or rendered innocuous. Thus we come to understand that in order to reverse an intrapsychic conflict the subject seeks an attempted solution in the external world. The partner, by participating in and enjoying the act, furnishes proof that the intrapsychic stress has no need to exist, that castration is harmless, that the genital difference between the sexes is not the source of sexual desire, and that the true primal scene is the one presented in the neosexualities.... The role of the other... is to facilitate the disavowal and dispersal not only of phallic oedipal guilt and castration anxiety but also of more primitive anxieties, the fantasies of having attacked and destroyed the internal objects. The fantasy need to castrate the other—or to complete oneself at the other's expense... demands an illusory reparation of the original objects and an expression of archaic sexuality in which body parts and substances are exchanged as reparative items. [pp. 255–256]

Coen (1985) has summarized an object relations overview of the paraphilias: general early problems between the self and parental objects become focused on a sexualized solution. He cites a number of writers who describe the mother's role in seductively sexualizing the relationship with the child. What has not been as well described in the analytic or developmental literature, but is clearly crucial, is the family support and encouragement, through projective identification, of the paraphilic solution to family-wide problems in relating.

## PARAPHILIAS EXPRESSING FAMILY EXPERIENCE

I saw a transvestite 10-year-old boy who was internalizing and expressing his parents' shared fear of the dominating, so-called phallic woman and of the threat of castration, as well as his own developmental fears. His mother openly said that men were no good, and had chased off the boy's father while pressing herself upon the boy in a seductive way. The family came to treatment when a new stepfather entered the scene, shifting the family's balance toward intolerance of the boy's cross-dressing.

In another example, a woman who begged that her husband tie her and whip her genitals during sexual encounters had grown up with an abusive father who nevertheless was her only source of emotional support, while her mother, a depressed and passive woman, seemed to be completely ignored by the father except when he was drunk. She was also masochistic in most of her personal relationships. This woman could be seen to have incorporated the suffering of both father and mother, both in the general makeup of her character and in explicit sexual terms that expressed the internalization of both her own and her parents' disappointed longing.

An example of a couple in therapy will illustrate some of these points further.

## TREATMENT OF A COUPLE WITH A PARAPHILIA

Ralph and Audrey S., married twelve years, parents of two children, sought consultation because Audrey could no longer tolerate Ralph's insistence that she dress in a tank top and shorts and consent to "wrestle" before intercourse. Ralph complained that he could not achieve arousal without these circumstances. A joint interview revealed that this obligatory aspect of their sexual life had not been present in the beginning of their marriage, but had first become pressing after the birth of their son, eight years earlier. Ralph had experienced this child as a potential rival, reactivating his fear of exclusion from his own parents. His father had been largely absent from the family. The only memory of his father was the few occasions when they had roughhoused when Ralph was very young. Ralph's mother had been attentive but harsh, preferring his two sisters. A second contribution to Ralph's wrestling paraphilia came from Ralph's having spent many boyhood afternoons watching wrestling on television with his beloved grandfather. As he was telling me his story, an adolescent contribution emerged from the times he had engaged in an arousing form of "horsing around" with male peers during puberty soon after his father's death, at a time he felt most lonely in his loss and excluded from his family.

In turn, Audrey had felt lost in her large family. Her father was also largely absent. It seemed to her that whenever he was there her parents argued vociferously. Audrey was the oldest of four, and felt excluded by her mother's preference for the younger children. When her mother became ill, she had to care for them.

In the consultation interview, we were able to establish that for Ralph, the wrestling had come to symbolize the required conditions of being loved while being able to discharge the rage he felt over being excluded. The resurgence of sexuality and aggression during puberty, supported by the many occasions of "horsing around" with his friends, contributed also to his compulsive choice of the wrestling as an act required for his sexual arousal.

For Audrey, submission to wrestling was also a form of paraphilia, the kind of submissive perversion described by Meyer (1985b). Early in the marriage, Ralph's demand constituted a form of suffering that she felt unconsciously she should bear as the price of her husband's interest. With time and maturation, however, her need for a perverse solution decreased, and not surprisingly, it was she who grew beyond her tolerance for the perversion and demanded therapy. By then, Ralph's dependence on her, and his own hope for a more developed object relationship, allowed him to ask for help. The couple were able to give up stereotyped sex within a few sessions of therapy, but stayed in treatment to explore the issues and anxieties about rejection that had led to their original object relations compromises.

This vignette illustrates, first, that in couples there generally is a mutuality to the perversion that satisfies the object relations needs of both partners. Both of them contribute to it, and while this is so, the shared perversion is maintained with stability. Secondly, deviant sexuality expresses and symbolizes the object relations and fantasies of the person. The developmental histories of Ralph and Audrey and of their relationship made sense of their symptoms, and of the shift that now brought them for treatment.

Finally, like all symptoms, including all sexual symptoms, the severity of paraphilias varies along a continuum from the situations in which they are normal variants to those of severe pathology. The mildest cases may be comfortable variations on sexual expression. Next on the continuum are those paraphilias that are more distressing to the patient and/or the partner, such as the man driven into occasional transvestism when the marriage is under extraordinary stress. Many of these will be rather easily treated. The severe cases, on the other hand, will be more difficult to treat. The importance of thinking of the paraphilias as existing on a continuum is that we can then hope to uncover the milder cases that will respond readily to treatment by the marital therapist.

## UNTREATABLE TRANSSEXUALISM IN A MARRIAGE

An example at the more severe end of the spectrum illustrates the usual stereotype held by many therapists who see paraphilia as a hopelessly untreatable condition.

Oliver Winchester came for help to assist him to obtain a sex change operation. He had first begun to think he was really meant to have been a woman not long after the death of his first wife ten years ago. Nevertheless, he had maintained his macho job as a navy frogman, and had married again. His second wife, Sally, came along for the second consultation. She desperately wanted to stay married. Failing to talk Oliver out of the sex change operation altogether, she wanted him to try wearing women's clothes. She offered to help him learn feminine skills, do his hair, and stay with him to help with his preadolescent children. For a while Oliver felt drawn to this solution, but then pressed for more and more radical aspects of the process toward sex change. The therapist never encouraged or even supported the progress toward Oliver's living like a woman or his obtaining the sex change surgery but aimed his psychotherapeutic approach at maintaining Oliver's stability and keeping him from the more impulsive aspects of this way of life. Oliver separated from Sally, and moved rockily toward the surgery, which he ultimately obtained, changing his name to Olive. He refused further individual therapy. He was able to get a job in a field allied to his previous work and always maintained a steady commitment to the children, who were, however, never able to discuss their issues with the change in any depth.

Obviously, this kind of case does not profit from marital work aimed at marital reconstruction. Our efforts then are limited to the support of the individuals in their adjustment to the many losses. One of the important jobs to be done, although only minimally successful here, is the support of any children who must adjust to these radical changes in their parents.

## TREATABLE TRANSVESTITE ISSUES ARISING IN A MARRIAGE

Raoul and Mabel Gonzales were sent to me [D.E.S.] for evaluation as a couple by Mabel's individual therapist because a troublesome sexual symptom had developed. They had had intercourse infrequently until now that Mabel was wanting to get pregnant. Under pressure from her to increase the frequency, Raoul had begun to make demands that articles of women's underwear become an obligatory part of their sexual life. Increasingly, he was unable to approach Mabel without this. He told her that he now realized that this wish had been there for a long time and that he had suppressed it until the past year. Then he had begun to suggest that it would mean a lot to him if they could go shopping for women's underwear together, or if he could put it on before they went out together, so it would be their secret. He was also interested in getting her to wear special items of women's underwear, like black bikini underpants, which he liked to smell and then wear himself. He recalled a special thrill once early in their relationship when she had draped a pair of her underpants over his head so that he could smell them.

Their marriage of eight years had been stormy. In their frequent fights, Mabel screamed and sometimes lashed out at Raoul physically. Raoul, who, according to Mabel, also had a temper that could burst out of control, presented Mabel's rages as one of the main problems about their marriage, while Mabel downplayed them. When I mentioned these disparate views in the final couple session, they looked at each other and smiled. Raoul said, "Yeah, it's really beautiful!" And then after a minute, he added, "It's awful. We don't want that to continue." The fights were highly invested moments of tension release, probably more orgastic than overt sex.

Raoul's fetish had been largely dormant during most of their relationship. Recently, under pressure to impregnate Mabel, he found that he would feel more like having intercourse if he could wear women's underwear, especially twisted into a tight "cock ring" encircling his penis, or if Mabel would talk as though she were a prostitute. He wanted her to say things to him such as, "Hurry up, I haven't got all day. You only have five minutes more." He wanted her to be aggressive, surly, and dominant. He told her that this set of wishes and fantasies of a dominant, cruel woman had been there since he was 5. Yes, it was in the background over the years but he had known it all along. As far as I could tell, it had been prominent in his thinking only for the last two or three years.

Mabel tried to go along with the demands, only to find that they escalated. While she had not minded the first, rather timid requests, she found that she was deeply resentful of the idea that Raoul could be aroused only with the aid of women's underwear or sadism. After a few months, with the support of her individual therapist, she refused to go along with him and asked that they seek couple therapy.

Both Raoul and Mabel had difficult backgrounds and had internalized a sense of deprivation. Mabel said that she hated her mother, who had resented her deeply, because, as she was frequently told, she was her father's favorite, though he never had time for her. She felt in the end that she had no one. She had left home at 17 after a fight about her mother's disapproval of her boyfriend, who was abusive of her. She then supported herself through college.

Raoul felt he had grown up tormented by his mother and sisters. He was the youngest by twelve years of three children, and his sisters taunted him mercilessly. They taunted him about being little, but they were also endlessly seductive. They found him in bed in their underwear once when he was 3, and the next Halloween they dressed him as a girl. They frequently said it was too bad he was not a girl, because he would be so cute. More than once, the girls sent him to the store to buy feminine napkins for them, and then refused to give him the dime they had promised. Once, when he was 10, his 22-year-old sister and he were changing clothes in the same room. He remembered the scene in which she was in a transparent bra and panties while she tried to seduce him. He was too terrified to respond. As an adolescent, he masturbated to fantasies about his two sisters in their underwear.

Raoul was resentful of his mother both for sanctioning the girls' torture of him and for imposing herself on him. He had been born when she was 43, and she felt he was special. That meant she was also critical of him, expecting him to perform perfectly and live up to high ideals. None of his girlfriends was ever good enough. In previous therapy, Raoul had recovered a sense of having been special to his father for the first two years of his life, only to have had his father abruptly become resentful of his little boy's assertiveness. His father withdrew, leaving Raoul to his controlling mother and sisters for the rest of his childhood. The recovered memory of the loss of his father's love explained something to Raoul about his lifelong resentment of women.

Raoul had many relationships with women before he met Mabel. He thought there was a recurrent pattern: after a period of good feeling and enjoyable sex, he would begin to feel they were "bitches" like his mother and sisters. Then he would retreat from them sexually and emotionally. He had no doubt that this pattern was his own individual problem, and that sooner or later he would have to work it out himself, regardless of what happened with Mabel.

The transference that emerged during Raoul's evaluation is of interest. He reported never having had any homosexual experiences or fantasies except for the one that he had after the first individual interview with me. After that hour, while masturbating he had an exciting fantasy of a man performing fellatio. The fantasy suggested that he had found the explicit sexual questions of the hour arousing, and experienced me as seductive in much the same way his sisters had been. The intimacy of the interview with me had reawakened a sexualized longing for his rejecting father. His fantasy also alerted me to the possibility that his personality had more of a polymorphous component than he had presented.

The problem we formulated was whether there was any possibility for improvement in the couple's sexual life. They were at an impasse because Mabel, who had progressed in individual therapy, had balked at going along with Raoul's fetish, which he presented as increasingly obligatory. So the two seemed to be headed on a confrontational course, which would have the logical outcome of separation.

The question I asked myself during the process of evaluation was whether the fetish and the transvestite direction it implied were a fixed matter, only now being declared but rooted in Raoul's history, or whether they represented a regression under the current strain. As we worked, I heard from Mabel of her therapeutic progress, which had let her take an increasingly strong stand against suffering in the marriage and develop her own self esteem to a point where she was no longer a victim of her own masochistic version of a paraphilia in the grip of Raoul's demands. But it was initially unclear if Raoul would be able to back away from the obligatory fetish of women's underwear and its escalating area of influence.

Both members of this couple were in intensive analytic psychotherapy. This case illustrates the not uncommon logical consequence of a collision between the spouses that stems from the emergence of progressive trends in their individual work. Their collision came at a time when the work each was doing was taking them in opposite directions. What I mean by this paradox is that Mabel's therapy was in a phase of leading her to consolidation, an assertion of her "right" to self-respect, and a narrowing of her areas of masochism and abuse, which had been explored for a considerable time.

Raoul had explored aspects of his marginal adjustment for several years, and had achieved considerable growth. However, he had recently begun work with a new therapist after the death of one he had seen for some time. In the wake of that loss, he stayed out of therapy for two years, and then sought help as the question of the fate of his marriage resurfaced. The issues that brought the fetish to the fore now included those of added strain—pressure to consolidate his marriage and have children, and the death of the previous therapist, who had been a good father figure to him. But on the progressive side was an added capacity to tolerate exploration of the issues expressed through the fetish.

Because of these factors, I came to the conclusion that the fetish was not an insuperable obstacle to effective couples work, and not such an enormous issue in itself that it had to divide them. It was a complex product of a breakdown in the relationship in time of crisis. Although Raoul felt it had been there for a long time, he had also given evidence that it had been in the background until the crisis of permanent commitment to marriage and children had emerged. This crisis was in other respects almost identical to ones he had experienced in previous relationships. In several earlier relationships, he had been able to function comfortably sexually without the aid of women's underwear, but as each relationship grew toward commitment, he began to think of the woman as a bitch, and would then break it off. It was his angry resentment about Mabel that he now was trying to counter with the underwear.

The crucial area for the couple was, indeed, their commitment to each other as embodied in the decision about children. Toward the end of the evaluation, they told me something that caught me short—and that

Raoul's individual therapist had not known—that, in fact, although they presented themselves as married, they were not actually married! They had divorced several years ago for tax reasons and had never remarried. I recalled out loud that Raoul had told me that he had serious questions about the viability of the marriage, and about Mabel's capacity as a mother. He had, after much reluctance, finally arrived at the point of wanting a family and children, but he was unsure Mabel was the right mother for his children. Mabel had said she wanted clarity about the fate of the marriage, although she also did want this marriage and—even though they were not married—to work for its improvement.

The couple agreed with me that their divorce for tax reasons also expressed the profound shared underlying issues of difficulty in commitment. They recalled that after their divorce, they had openly discussed the idea that being unmarried had perhaps strengthened their relationship. They joined their ambivalences and escaped a semblance of control by each other in maintaining their relationship as an unmarried marriage.

The perversion was a shared one in this couple. Raoul expressed the outward form of the perversion, the search for the mother whose cruelty will not become castrating because he appeases and controls her. In another way, he identified with the exciting mother in donning her apparel. Mabel expressed the common complementary feminine side of the picture. She submitted to the contempt and control, becoming the denigrated object, and felt an unconscious comfort and familiarity in the sense of being controlled, possessed, and denigrated, until she achieved a new view of herself in individual therapy.

## Transference and Countertransference in Evaluation

In this case, the transference and countertransference could be seen to echo the shared perversion and to bring it into the evaluation process. The couple came with focused projective identifications to each other. Raoul unconsciously put the feared, persecuting, and denigrated object into Mabel, while she put the abusing, but sought-after, exciting object into him. Before the evaluation, these focused transferences to each other, which were designed to shore up fears about their capacity to love each other, had taken over their shared holding. In therapeutic consultation, they joined together to project these elements into me in an attempt to get them outside their shared holding boundary and to shore that up by cooperatively denigrating me. During this process, they enhanced their sense of commitment to each other, which they had not been able to do before. They did so by focusing on me as a rejecting object and a sorry provider of help and solace. During the interviews they barely managed to work with me. If they felt I had misunderstood something, even if it were because they had indeed said what I was merely quoting, they took it as evidence for my fallibility. Raoul doubted that they needed couple work at all and was dubious of me on that count, although he did listen to my conclusion that individual therapy, as important as it was to each of them, would not get them to understand how their mutual fears interfered with their relationship. Mabel, on the other hand, felt that she knew that they needed help before they came. That being so, she demanded to know why I was making such a big deal of what she had already known. In the process of confronting me, she blotted out the worries she had shared with me that the fetish was unacceptable to her, that she had doubted she could stay with Raoul.

This process was supported in part by the way the two of them expressed different attitudes in each setting with me. There was a sense of crisis in the initial couple's interview. Then Mabel seemed desperate and angry at Raoul in my individual interviews with her, doubting if the marriage would survive. When I saw Raoul individually, he was also reserved and doubtful about the marriage, but he then turned quickly to a rejection of my services and of their need for couple therapy. And then in the couple setting again, they agreed on their need for couple therapy, as though neither of them had expressed doubts about the viability of the marriage. They also agreed upon the uselessness of my understanding and the irrelevance of my conclusions.

Yet, surprisingly, when I began the referral process to find them a more acceptable therapist, they pressed for me to see them—and they felt entitled to be seen on their terms: a reduced fee and evening hours. I could not meet their needs in terms of fee reduction and therapy hours taken out of my family time. In its paradoxical way, their offer to see me on terms they could tolerate was a tender of love and trust, which I was seen as rejecting. As Raoul's insistence on conditions Mabel could not accept questioned the viability of the marriage, so their challenge to me exceeded the frame I was willing to consider.

The whole process of transference denigration and disapproval of me could now be seen in the light of their attempt to possess and control me through their contemptuous ridicule, so that their shared envy of me for possessing something they wanted would not leave them feeling so belittled themselves. That is to say, Raoul's fetish could now be seen to clothe the maternal transference object in order to completely control it and guard him from danger—perhaps to emasculate a feared phallic mother. In the transference, they joined in handling their fear of being controlled by an object by attempting to contemptuously control me, disguising the longing and envy, which were even more painful. In the countertransference, I felt in danger of being rendered impotent therapeutically.

In short, the threat I posed transferentially to Mabel and Raoul, namely the threat of disruption of their mutual pattern, closed their ranks. Their shared contextual transference was riddled with the shared perversion. Their joint effort to belittle and then contemptuously control me as a captured object was an attempt to maintain their own holding capacity.

Work with the couples we have been discussing shows that marital therapy does not take place only within the relatively tame boundaries of straightforward love and aggression. Internal object relationships can be too complex for that. It is not only for work with the couples with openly perverse or homosexual organizations that we need to know about this. It helps us to understand the many couples for whom more subtle forms of similar issues are present.

Couples whose situation includes homosexuality or paraphilia present disturbing constellations for therapists not accustomed to these issues. We hope we have made the point clearly in this chapter that the existence of these issues does not, in itself, mean that marital therapy is either impossible or necessarily unusually difficult. These pictures exist on a continuum; from variations on normality, mild stress-induced reactions to situational or developmental crises, moderate emergence of underlying pathology, to severe deviations where no marital resolution is likely. During evaluation, it is our job to estimate which cases are treatable. Then, both in evaluation and treatment, the transference-countertransference constellation can be expected to reflect and express the object relations of homosexuality or paraphilia, requiring flexibility, knowledge, and comfort in the therapist who undertakes their treatment.

# Part V
# Endings

Chapter **14**

# TERMINATION AND FOLLOW-UP

## THE CRITERIA FOR TERMINATION

Couple therapy may end smoothly, the result of work well and completely done, or it may end for reasons short of success. Sometimes patients and therapist agree on the quality of the outcome and sometimes not.

For instance, a couple may come with one spouse hoping against hope that the marriage can be restored. In the therapist's view it may be beyond repair, either because the other partner has already decided that it is over, or because, for a variety of other reasons, the conditions for reworking the marriage will never be met. If the therapist is right about this, couple therapy may end because of its failure to restore the marriage, or it may continue past the separation to the point of divorce. Difficulties in ending the couple therapy may reflect the couple's inability to terminate an unsatisfactory marriage. Sometimes the therapist's confrontation of the hopelessness of the marriage challenges the couple to renewed commitment that leads to an unexpectedly good outcome in the ensuing therapy.

The one common theme in a termination, whether it be after one disappointing session or after several years of fruitful work in therapy, is loss. This ranges over loss of the marriage, loss of the ideal of being married, loss of the treatment opportunity, loss of the treatment setting as a home for the couple's relationship, and loss of the relationship to the therapist.

Loss is addressed not only in termination. In an important sense, the ending of each session is preparation for eventual termination. Sometimes this issue is openly in focus, for instance on those occasions when there is a separation for the couple, or when the therapist is away. More often it is a matter of sensing the couple's response to loss of support toward the end of the hour, when the sudden occurrence of something subtle or disquieting is best explained by the impending separation.

In this chapter, we portray the nature and quality of termination of therapy in a variety of situations, focusing on the tasks to be accomplished and the limits of the work.

## TERMINATION BEFORE THERAPY BEGINS

Often the work ends soon after the referral, and often abruptly, because one or both of the partners either has already decided or soon decides that they no longer want to stay in the marriage. Sometimes they have come to a first session only out of a sense of duty. In these cases, the work may end promptly, or one of the partners may stay to do individual work, which itself may be either brief or as thorough as psychoanalysis.

> Don L. called me [J.S.S.], desperate for an appointment. After a twenty-year marriage, his wife, Lenore, had said she wanted a separation, and he wanted to do anything he could to avoid it. He told me on the phone that it was a complete shock to him. As far as he knew, they had been happy. Could I see them quickly?
>
> When I met with them two days later, Lenore said that her view was completely different. She had been telling Don for years that things were not going well. She felt that several years ago she had begun the process of detaching herself, and now she thought her preteen children could manage a divorce. One of her grievances was Don's inattentiveness to their son, who had a learning disorder and was a less satisfactory child. She resented his leaving the boy to her.

Don protested that she should give him another chance. Besides he was in a time of crisis at work, between jobs, while Lenore had plenty of money. She was not being fair. Lenore was steady, saying that Don's inability to understand what she was talking about had not changed over the years. She had, for many years, agreed to nurse him through one such crisis after another. Really, she had come hoping I would take Don into therapy, because she knew this separation was going to be hard on him.

Don still hoped desperately to find a way to save the situation, and Lenore did not definitively say no to him for some weeks. I said to them that if she really meant that it was over, it was probably better, less anxiety-provoking, to make that clear. In an individual interview, she told me that she was, for the first time, involved with someone else, but that she thought Don would be extremely vindictive if he found out. She was definite that she was ending the marriage, but she had enough compassion for Don to want him to get the help he needed.

When I saw Don alone, he was desperate, anxious, and panicky. He obsessively reviewed the unfairness of the situation with no insight into the level of dysfunction in the marriage that his spouse had complained of for years. As Lenore prepared to leave the house, he became increasingly anxious, severely depressed, and suicidal. He responded moderately well to antidepressive medication prescribed by a colleague, but he continued to display an uninsightful insistence on his right to fair treatment, which only served to justify his wife's judgment of him.

In the end he could do no mourning. Instead, he fought her at every step of the way through the divorce and property settlement proceedings. He substituted an angry battle for mourning the marriage and family, and only settled down two years later when he began a new relationship. Lenore, on the other had, attempted to avoid mourning by jumping into a newly idealized relationship. This minimized her need for absorbing psychological loss, although in a different way than Don. It was only when the second relationship turned sour that she began to compare the two, and found that she had picked two dependent and demanding men who initially presented themselves as charming and cooperative. She could then begin to use therapy to understand elements of her experience with her delightful but disappointing father, which she had previously tried to manage through the two men she had chosen.

This marital therapy hardly began. Some work was done, in helping each of the partners manage the losses they had already incurred and those they were about to undergo, but even that was not particularly successful, so that a stuttering, incomplete therapy echoed the sense of the marriage between one apparently reasonable spouse who maintained a bland and "optimistic" denial, and one obsessional and paranoid spouse who cried "foul" and "take care of me." Don made virtually no progress, while Lenore did get some support and advice on the management of the children. But even she did not actually do any significant therapeutic work until the failure of a second relationship.

## TERMINATION WHEN THE THERAPIST FAILS

In this demanding work, there will be therapies that end because the therapy fails. Either the fit between the couple and the therapist is not good enough, or the therapist makes mistakes that make it difficult for the couple to continue with that therapist, or at worst, to continue at all. Often, it is difficult to tell if the failure is one purely of technique or even of countertransference, or if it is intermixed with difficulty the couple has that is so significant that the therapy could not have proceeded under any circumstances.

> Mr. and Mrs. Field were referred when I [J.S.S.] had no clinical time to see them. But the referral agent was a close colleague who said they were a deserving and interesting couple whom he would especially like me to treat. He thought I would enjoy seeing them and so I made time for them. But when I saw them they seemed stuck and unmotivated. The husband, Mr. Field, complained of Mrs. Field's lability, and she complained of his passivity and unavailability. In fact, she said, she did not think she could stand it any more. She was thinking of divorce.
>
> I quickly picked up on her seeming to be at the end of her rope, and wondered about her thoughts about separation. But in the next hour, she accused me of pushing them toward separation when she had no such intention. I felt in the middle of a lion's den. She let me know that she felt misunderstood, and that she was not sure she cared to come back under the circumstances.
>
> She did stay away the next session although Mr. Field came. He then canceled a session on short notice. It is my policy to bill couples for cancellations in any event, but in reviewing this situation, I knew without thinking it through that if I sent them the bill without discussing the situation with Mr. Field, he, too, would feel hit. Indeed, he did not pay for the canceled session, nor did he call to schedule any further ones.

In reviewing this case, it seemed to me that it was my feeling of seduction by my referring colleague that made this couple difficult for me. Thinking I had been promised a treat, I felt unprepared for being subjected to the ordinary bruises of the couple's transference. Without realizing my sense of letdown, I passed the letdown on to the couple, who certainly provided enough opportunities that it was easy to do so. Nevertheless, I assume this couple may not have been substantially less treatable than many other couples, and that in this case, the failure was mine.

## TERMINATION FOLLOWED BY TRANSFER
## FOR BETTER FIT

A case that occupies the grey area was reported in our earlier book (Scharff and Scharff 1987). Mr. and Mrs. Kyley, he 55, she 41, were referred by her individual therapist. A couple who had been fighting throughout their marriage, they filled the therapy session with their battles, so that the therapist [D.E.S.] felt abused, walked out on, and left with their unruly burdens. Mrs. Kyley was demanding—nothing was enough. Mr. Kyley would passively absorb stinging attacks from her for extended periods of time, and then finally erupt, sometimes banging the office furniture so hard that it might break. When he did do as she asked, she gave him little credit. However, he blithely did as he pleased much of the time, with the idea that she would come down on him sooner or later anyway. After a few hours in which they showed improvement, they would regularly come in with one of their fights, which seemed to spoil all progress. Interpretations about their shared spoiling were to no avail. In these times, Mrs. Kyley would regularly talk divorce and express contempt for her husband.

After these cycles repeated perhaps a dozen times, I [D.E.S.] confronted the couple with their inability to move beyond this repetitive pattern, and wondered if the therapy was of any use. I said that it certainly did not feel so to me. Mrs. Kyley said that she was going to move to a separation in any event. It was not my fault. Her husband was impossible. Mr. Kyley shrugged his shoulders passively. He said he did not want the marriage to end, but he agreed there was no sense of progress or change. We agreed in two closing sessions to review this decision, but they were instead marked by the same tempestuous arguing that had been the hallmark of the couple. In the end they left, she sullen, and he looking beaten. I felt beaten as well.

Two years later Mrs. Kyley's individual therapist gave me a follow-up. They had not separated, but had asked for another referral. In the subsequent couple therapy, they had apparently had a much calmer course. Perhaps the improved quality of the work, and of their subsequent relationship, reflected Mrs. Kyley's continued progress in her intensive individual psychotherapy. Perhaps it was the confrontation with failure in the ending of therapy with me. Or perhaps it was a better fit with another therapist, perhaps one less impatient for progress and more tolerant of their sadomasochistic way of relating. Hearing the follow-up certainly gave me pause. A couple I had seen leave treatment with a sense of failure, but at least with the feeling I had done all I could, had gone on to survive and do better. Perhaps I had a role in their improvement, and on the other hand, perhaps I could have done better by them.

This ambiguity is, at bottom, one we deal with all the time. We try to learn our craft, we follow our experience and intuition, and then we must admit how much we do not know. Many patients treat us well, perhaps better than we deserve. Other couples put us to the test—and we do not necessarily pass. Here we want to document that there are many such cases, where the ending is not perfect, the outcome not necessarily good, and sometimes the fault lies with the therapist. It is all we can do to face this possibility honestly, to keep trying to hone our skills, and to understand that such is the nature of human endeavor. When therapy does not go well, it is indeed a loss for our patients. It is also a loss for us!

## TERMINATION AFTER BRIEF INTERVENTION

Useful work can occur in brief encounters with couples. Some couples are in crises that have presented them with challenges to a marriage that has many strengths. If we can help such couples to resolve the crises, they are quickly on their way. In such cases, the termination is folded into the brief work we do for them. It is helpful if they can leave with an open door to return, but many of them never feel the need. Others will use the boost of the brief intervention, and later return, often for individual work for one of the partners.

If the couple is going to be able to work well in the brief mode, they usually come with a positive contextual transference, which supports them through the therapeutic encounter, and which enables them to leave with their own shared holding substantially repaired.

Linda T., age 25, came to see me [J.S.S.] for an individual consultation. She complained that her husband, Nick, a 28-year-old lawyer who was meeting extraordinary success, had been ignoring her so thoroughly for the last year that she could no longer stand it. She enjoyed her job in broadcasting, but they had planned to have children about now. He seemed oblivious to her entreaties that he invest more in marriage and family. She responded positively to my recommendation for a couple assessment and her husband agreed to attend.

In the first conjoint session, Nick was resistant to anything she or I said. Then she compared their marriage to his parents', a couple who had stayed together over years of substantial resentment. Suddenly Nick began to cry. "You're right," he said. "I just had the idea that you were trying to keep me from working so hard in a kind of envy, but as you were talking, I suddenly saw that having children made me scared that our marriage would be like theirs. And that's what I have been most afraid of all my life." His reluctance to talk melted, and he seemed transformed.

They scheduled two more appointments, but there was almost nothing to say. He had stopped straining at the bit and taking her for granted, and with an air of relief, he was investing heavily in the marriage. The termination work went on in the third and last of these interviews. The couple considered the question of whether they could make it on their own. We reviewed their strengths and difficulties, and they agreed that neither of them would block the other from asking for therapeutic help if strain grew between them again. I felt a sense of tentativeness about the capacity of their recovery to endure, but there was not enough remaining sense of difficulty to justify continuing. So at the parting, I carried some sense of worry.

Six months later, Nick dropped me a note to thank me for the help. Linda was two months pregnant, and they felt they had refound the marriage they wanted. I ran into them three years later at a fast-food restaurant. Linda came across the restaurant to tell me that things were going well. They had a second infant, and she was staying home to care for both children. She said that Nick was still the man she had hoped he would be, and had turned into a terrific father. The encounter left me wishing that more of my interventions had worked so easily and so well.

We have found that all couples for whom brief therapy suffices have come for crises in taking developmental steps, but with marriages built on basically sound foundations. While other couples may themselves be satisfied after a few visits, if we have felt that their marriages carry longer term risk, we part from them with substantial concern.

## TERMINATION LEADING TO INDIVIDUAL OR FAMILY THERAPY

Either successful or unsuccessful marital therapy may result in a shift to individual therapy. Sander (1989) has described the use of this shift as a strategy. He often plans to use couple therapy as preparation for individual work with one or both spouses. In our experience, it is equally likely that individual work leads to a phase of couple work. That is to say, one phase and focus of therapy may lead to any other focus that seems to form the next logical intervention.

For instance, let us say that the couple therapy has been successful in allowing a couple to take back the projective identifications, support each other, and work together in their wider family. This may still leave areas in either of them to be worked with in individual psychotherapy or psychoanalysis. Or it may leave issues in their wider family, either with their children or between the couple and their own parents and siblings, that warrant attention. When this is the case, such shifts should have a progressive feel to them. The termination may cover the full force of the loss, as the couple surrenders a setting that has been supportive and enriching to them, or it may be

muted if both are continuing in family or parallel individual therapies. Nevertheless, there is a real loss to be grieved. As much as possible of this work should be done before the dissolution of the couple's work, in order to facilitate the work in the next setting.


## SUCCESSFUL COUPLE THERAPY LEADING TO INDIVIDUAL PSYCHOTHERAPY

Bea and Dick Neill came to marital therapy without much hope. This
was the second marriage that had gone bad for him, and he felt that there
was little he could do to reverse the decline. He had moved to Washington
to be with Bea, and had been unable to find work in his specialty area of
computer design. Bea was in training in foreign affairs. She was beginning
to change her mind about not wanting children, but she now felt that Dick
had been passive in pursuing his career, and that this would continue
when she accepted an overseas assignment, so she wondered if he would
make a good father if she did decide to have children.

Nevertheless, the couple did well in therapy. Bea found the insights
about her willingness to make a compromised marriage helpful. She
learned that her fear of having a marriage like her parents' battling one
had led her to pick Dick for his passivity, but now she wanted him to be
more active. Dick was not especially articulate in therapy, but he listened
and he tried. He understood the shift in Bea's wishes, and talked about the
pressure it put on him. Mostly he talked about his job and the difficulties
of being in an area with little opportunity for advancement.

And then, almost imperceptibly, he showed more initiative in looking
for a job, and landed a spectacular new position. He began to brighten up.
There was a new liveliness between them, and they seemed to get better
and better. The couple therapy had done its job, but Bea now asked for
referral for individual therapy for the issues of her self-esteem that had led
her to a marriage that had begun with significant compromise. She felt it
had worked out better than she had a right to expect, and she wanted to
investigate the causes of her prior attempt to sabotage her own growth.

The couple said goodbye with a sense of encouragement, but also of
sadness. Their work over the period of fifteen months had turned their
shared life around, and they were a bit anxious as to whether they could
keep it up. They contacted me a year later to say that Bea had completed a
year of individual therapy and had been given her first overseas assignment, which she felt eager to accept. Dick had done so well at work that
his company had set up a special project he could carry out from their new
location overseas.

## FAILED COUPLE THERAPY LEADING TO
## SUCCESSFUL PSYCHOANALYSIS

In another case, let us say the marital therapy runs aground or at least reaches an impasse, the marriage breaks up, or one of the partners withdraws. These cases may lead to individual therapy by default. Often, any work on the ending of the couple's therapy is only done by the partner who remains in individual therapy. Nevertheless, the ensuing individual therapy may be carried out to great advantage to the one who undertakes it.

Belinda Levitz, age 40, called to ask for therapy for her marriage, which she thought was in severe difficulty. She had been given my name [J.S.S.] by her husband's therapist when she called him. When they came for a first consultation her husband, Joel, was on his good behavior. He expressed surprise at Belinda's dissatisfaction with the marriage, and offered to do anything he could. Nevertheless, it quickly became clear that he was both alcoholic and abusive. While usually managing to front a benign exterior, he stayed up late nights at home drinking, and then terrorized Belinda, yelled at the children, and had once broken her rib while coercing her into sex, something he referred to as giving her a "friendly bear hug." Although charming in public, he terrorized his household. This quality soon came to dominate the couple's sessions as well.

Belinda had not been able to give up an anxious masochistic dependency on him. In the couple therapy she saw that she had been hostage to her fear of being alone and to her low self-esteem. She now moved to confront him in the therapy: either he stopped drinking or she would have to initiate a separation. Under this pressure, Joel's difficult behavior increased, and he began an affair with his secretary, coming home late drunk.

The situation was rapidly deteriorating in the face of therapy, even though Joel was still also in individual therapy. Belinda asked for individual appointments, but I could not agree to these requests until the marital issues were resolved. I did so feeling that seeing Belinda alone would alienate Joel and prematurely end any hope of marital therapy. Joel confirmed that this was so. He agreed to consultation between me and his individual therapist, but it did nothing to halt the decline. Finally, Belinda decided that she had had enough. She set a deadline for improved behavior. It came and went without change. She took the children and moved out of the house, and in the next couple's session, announced that she was only interested in further sessions to focus on the care of the children. Joel was furious, and began a series of abusive phone calls, took money from their joint account, and refused to cooperate. Although he was not apparently drinking before our next session, his demeanor was changed as though he had been. He turned on the therapist, accusing me of unethical behavior in siding with Belinda, and then ended therapy by storming out.

Mrs. Levitz was now faced with mourning both the couple's therapy and her marriage. She had moved reluctantly to the recognition of the physical and verbal abuse that had been her secret lot for many years. Now she had to mourn the marriage she had never wanted to give up. She questioned whether couple's therapy could have saved the marriage. Could anything have been different? But she did not think so, and trusting me despite the sense of enormous loss that had been precipitated by the confrontation in the therapy, she asked for intensive individual treatment. Mrs. Levitz wanted to consider the reasons she had tolerated the abuse for so long. She wanted to work on her issues of depression and low self-esteem that she now understood to have provided the context for her hopelessness and victimized position. A full psychoanalysis eventually allowed a thorough exploration of these matters, including the previously unknown childhood and young adult losses that had led to the compromised marriage in the first place. This allowed Mrs. Levitz to make fundamental intrapsychic changes reflected in her capacity to work at a much higher level and ultimately to be in a caring relationship with a strong and kind man.

## TERMINATION WITH COMPROMISED OUTCOME

Some outcomes are compromises, the best that can be hoped for in imperfect situations. In these cases, the giving up of the therapy has all the markings of mourning an imperfection.

Andy and Maxine W. had a turbulent marriage for which they sought couple therapy with one of our students. Maxine felt that Andy gave too much attention to his son from his previous marriage but neglected their three children, which she resented. She was jealous and hot-tempered, while he was cool and kept a defended distance. The sessions were full of rage and envy. After six months of work, the therapist reported that the couple had made a major life decision, to relocate geographically. Andy left the son of his first marriage behind with ambivalence, but hoped he would be able to see his son, who was now in college, enough to maintain their relationship. Maxine felt this would give them the best chance for a new start.

As the end of the work approached, Andy and Maxine still had a turbulent marriage, but one with a modicum of agreement and marginally more expression of mutual support. Maxine had a sense of optimism, which from the therapist's perspective was maintained by manic denial. Andy came alone for the last session. He reported that Maxine had said that she did not need to come, because everything had worked out. He expressed his thanks to the therapist for her tolerance, and said that a great deal was in the balance. He had bet his livelihood and his capital on the survival of the marriage, and it was not clear it was a good bet. Nevertheless, he had done it. He was sorry to leave the therapist, but he was unsure they could have done more with additional opportunity. At the end, we shared the therapist's sense of risk about the marriage.

A different picture can be presented by those couples in sex therapy who may get a partial result, or for whom the sexual part of the work is successful, only to find that issues in their relationship cannot be solved as easily. We had seen one case of sex therapy in which the couple found a great deal of help for their relationship, but could not master their sexual dysfunction, since the husband's impotence turned out to be organically based. This couple had refused to resort to papaverine injections or prosthetic implants. They left therapy with a mixture of gratitude and relief by the wife who did not like being pried into, and sadness that the husband's erectile difficulty had persisted throughout his whole life, and now had an additional organic basis. A year after leaving therapy, the husband did return to request referral to a urologist. The couple then learned to use penile papaverine injections successfully. The husband was grateful for that and they now enjoyed sex as never before.

## WHEN TERMINATION IS PREMATURE

We employ the framework of termination to contain the regression that is commonly expected during its course. It is important for the therapist to have a working confidence in the therapeutic format within which these regressions can be understood and lived through without changing the frame.

But while this is usually the best course, it is not always so. New material may emerge during the termination that persuades the therapist that more can and should be done. The following case makes this point and lets us follow through from a premature first termination to a later one, which nonetheless was still somewhat incomplete. Only in the last few minutes did the work come together and the therapist was left hopeful but unsure of the outcome.

> As soon as their children were away at college, Lydia and Alex Gordon, a couple in their early fifties, had noticed a poisonous interaction that substituted for intimacy in their relationship. Lydia, a compact, vivacious redhead, had boundless energy for her full-time career as a journalist and her horseback riding avocation, while her much less athletic, overweight husband liked to relax after his day's work at the drawing board by listening to music and cooking gourmet meals. Alex felt constantly hounded and criticized, while Lydia felt cast as the witch. Alex's individual therapist referred them for assessment for marital therapy to see if divorce could be avoided.

In subsequent therapy with me [J.S.S.], they had come a long way from being on the point of separation to falling in love again. They owned their projective identifications and developed a more cooperative relationship with direct communication. After working on their guilt-provoking masturbation fantasies, they were amazed to discover between them a vital sexuality that brought comfort, intimacy, and excitement to their relationship. When they were almost ready to terminate, their newfound sexuality further surprised them with an unplanned pregnancy. After feeling initial joy at their creation, they began to question the feasibility of having another child at their stage of life. As Catholics and right-to-life advocates, they were in agony over their need to make a choice. Alex decided he definitely did not want to father a young child again and Lydia, who had always wanted one more child, sadly decided to have an abortion as Alex wished in order to preserve their newfound freedom and intimacy. Together they worked to understand their shared ambivalence, to reach a shared decision and to help each other through the ordeal of the abortion and the psychological aftermath. They had supported each other with love and concern through the crisis; they took a short but refreshing vacation during which Alex decided to go on a low-fat diet for weight reduction and cholesterol control; they were actively mourning the loss of their baby; their relationship was stronger than ever, and they felt ready to finish therapy. The date was set to allow for a month in which to terminate.

During termination, the couple regressed. Alex became lethargic and had no sexual energy. Lydia attributed this to his reduced food intake at first but her sympathy turned to disappointment that he was no longer able to create excitement for them. He slipped back to his habit of withdrawal, passivity, and depression while she, desperately trying to get him out of it, became controlling, critical, and nagging as before.

Some regression during termination is not unusual and indeed is to be expected. The loss of therapy anticipated during termination reactivates conflicts and allows for a final working-through. In this case termination of their relationship with me rekindled the losses of terminating their pregnancy. Gains and losses were in an uneasy balance. I was puzzled as to why our work was not enabling recovery from the regression. I became unsure of my formulation and began to search for other possible explanations. I remembered that I had earlier asked them about their current choice of contraceptive. Their response had been disquieting. They planned to use the same contraceptive as had been in use when conception occurred. I had explored safer alternatives with them and they decided to supplement their method with condoms. But Lydia refused to have her tubes tied because she still wanted the possibility of having another child and she opposed Alex's choice of a vasectomy because of her knowledge of dreadful complications. She made it clear that she would never again use abortion as a second line of defense against an unwanted pregnancy. Alex's investment in her fantasy of their procreativity meant that he could not assert his choice to have a vasectomy.

Now in the penultimate session, I remembered that I had previously pointed out that a long-held wish for a child was still active and creating a deadlock. I reminded them of this and said that I realized that they had slipped back since the day I said that. They disagreed: that wish was not the reason for their coming apart, and the proof was that Alex had bought condoms and both felt secure in that choice. The problem was he hadn't felt like needing them. At first they were sure that by having more time together they could resolve this problem themselves but by the end of this penultimate session, they were asking for a follow-up session with me after termination. They also discussed Lydia's need for individual therapy to focus on relationships in her family of origin, her feelings of loss now that her children were grown, and her work inhibition. Alex planned to continue with his individual therapist to work on his tendency to depression. I remained unsure whether this was a problem of the termination phase that would resolve in the final session or with ongoing individual therapy, a reasonable outcome, or whether this termination had been premature and represented a manic triumph over the loss of the pregnancy termination. With this uncertainty in mind, I approached the final session.

Lydia opened the session: "I'm just thinking that maybe we're not ready to terminate." Alex disagreed. Lydia continued, "There's been no sex for weeks; we're just not reaching out. Alex is depressed and he's not saying anything."

Alex, who looked grey and drawn, said, "I've talked about it. I know we've lost our closeness. I've had sleeping problems. I'm worried about money. The big design project is finished and there's plenty of work for now but I don't know where the next big project's coming from. Mainly it's just that there's no excitement at work. We haven't any trips to go on. I'm in a lull. I've no sexual energy. I don't think it's to do with fear of another pregnancy. I think Lydia's not over the abortion. Lydia, maybe you should get going with individual therapy now. You've been talking about it for years and not . . . ."

Lydia interrupted, "Well, Alex, what are you doing to create excitement at work?"

Alex shriveled up. Lydia pointed at him and said sharply, "Look how you are reacting! You're all depressed."

Alex rose to the challenge, retorting, "Lydia, you're doing more of this. You're always on me to do something, like you're telling me why don't I go exercise. I am working out and I haven't gone off the diet. I'm just in a lull and I'll be fine. I still think we should terminate."

I said, "You're aware of problems stemming from the loss of the pregnancy and how you each suffered that. Perhaps you're also reacting to the loss of the therapy."

Alex replied, quickly, "Yes, I'll miss this. But most of all I miss what it did for us. I wish we still felt as we did before the abortion."

Lydia followed, "I miss the baby. I think it was just a horrible decision.

I'm so angry with myself about it. And that baby was so strong. It really held on. The gynecologist had to use the vacuum twice. It was awful for me and I kept feeling that the baby really tried to live. It was really a good, strong baby. I'm so mad at myself. And I'm mad at you, too."

"I'm sorry," said Alex. "I still think it was the right decision." Then he asked tentatively, "Do you still want a baby?"

"Yes," said Lydia flatly.

"Oh," sighed Alex, "That's a big problem. The only way we can ever have sex is if I have a vasectomy."

Lydia, alarmed, said, "Oh, no!"

Alex looked hopeless, caught in a trap. "There's nothing more we can do in couple therapy to work this through. Lydia, you'll have to deal with this individually."

"That was my last chance to have a baby," cried Lydia. "I'd be crazy to try to have one now. I should have had that one. It might have been our girl."

"Well, I still think you should work on this in individual therapy," Alex concluded.

*I was beginning to agree with Alex. Lydia had spoken from the outset of her intention to have individual therapy to work on her work inhibition, and on issues arising from her family of origin, in particular her overexcited relation to her father. I was thinking of her wish to have a baby as a fantasy of having an oedipal baby from her father. Work of such psychological depth might require intensive individual therapy.*

But Lydia brushed aside Alex's suggestion, saying defiantly through her tears, "I'm angry with you for deciding we should have done this; I'm angry with you for saying I have to go to therapy; I'm angry with you because I knew what I wanted but I did what you wanted and it's your fault. And I don't wanna say all this someplace where you can't hear me say it. I want you to hurt."

Gently, Alex told her, "I'm not gonna hurt about it as much as you are. It was your body and you felt it more."

Lydia, even angrier now, replied, "This happened between us. It's not for me to work on by myself. You're over it but just because I'm not, I'm not gonna grieve over it by myself."

*I could feel how Lydia, being the woman, had had the physical experience that let her feel more pain. I knew that her fantasy of a baby left her vulnerable to loss when its enactment ended. Her clarity about her pain had tended to support a projective identification in which Alex projected all the hurt into Lydia, who could speak about her feelings so clearly, leaving Alex impoverished and inarticulate, not able to talk about his experience. His lackluster approach to life was bringing out in Lydia even more anger, which drove him further into retreat.*

I said, "It's difficult to see how Alex is hurting because he is unaware of it and doesn't speak about it. You, Lydia, are clear that you hurt because you have lost the joy of creating and mothering another child, but Alex, I think, is suffering in his own way. Alex, you are not hurting because you can't be a father again. You are settled with that." Alex nodded. "You are hurting because you have lost excitement, which is one of the qualities a father brings to the baby. Perhaps that is Alex's way of mourning the baby."

This comment gave Alex an opening. He began to talk at length about how deeply joyous he had felt and how excited and thrilled he was at the news of the pregnancy. When he realized he just couldn't go through all the years of devotion it takes to raise a child, he felt quite depressed. He had enjoyed fathering their babies, toddlers, and schoolchildren. He had loved being his boys' soccer coach and he could not stand the idea of handing over those functions to a caretaker or to other fathers, but he just could not do physically all he had done as a younger man. "Yeah," he said, "I still feel depressed about it. And Lydia doesn't really reach out to me. But I'm not angry at Lydia about it. I just wish she wouldn't keep nudging me out of it."

Lydia said, "I'm just trying to get you to be active again so we can have what we lost. I gave up that baby to preserve what we had found between us. And now it's not there. I'm disappointed and I'm mad: I don't have the baby and I don't have our wonderful, close, sexual relationship either. We've had a double loss: the loss of our pregnancy and the loss of vitality in our relationship."

I said, "You found your sexuality and it was expressed in the form of that good, strong baby. But when you couldn't have the baby, you found your sexuality was gone too. You can't get back your sexuality until you get over the loss of that baby. But until you get back your sexuality, you can't give up the baby that represents it. Right now, your feelings for the baby give it too much weight, both as the proof of your vital relationship and also as the destroyer of it. It's a circular problem. How do we break the cycle?"

Lydia responded, "I don't know. I worry we'll never get the liveliness back and that's why I try to get Alex to be active. Because I don't feel confident about inviting him to be with me, I don't."

"I know you don't," said Alex, kindly, "But I wish you would." He leaned toward her and his thick, straight, silvery forelock fell forward on his brow.

Lydia brushed the hair out of Alex's eye.

"What are you doing that for?" he said warily like a boy whose mother should not have embarrassed him with his friends.

"That hair! In your eyes again," Lydia almost tutted.

*I could see the surface of their physical interaction as a rejecting plane, conceal-*
*ing a deeper level of physical caring. I thought Lydia needed an excuse for her*

*impulse to touch Alex's worried brow. And I noticed that Alex's skin turned from a wan, grey color to a healthy glow.*

So I said, "The unruly thatch of hair may have been one reason, but Lydia, I thought that you were trying to reach out to Alex past your own difficulty in believing he would accept your invitation."

Alex asked, "Is that what you were doing?" and inched toward her.

I continued, "And I noticed that the moment you touched him, Alex brightened right up."

"Oh, yes," Alex acknowledged, smiling. "I like lots of that." He moved close to Lydia and put his arm on her knee. She snuggled up and put her arm around his neck.

*They looked so pleased with each other. I felt as a child might feel—definitely excluded from their physical space, yet basking in their happiness. I thought that they might now be able to terminate after all.*

But Lydia said, "This proves what we can do when we work on it together. I know we need more sessions but you feel it's time to get over this and tough it out."

"No," said Alex, "I agree with you now. We're not ready quite yet." Turning to me, he asked, "I know we can't have our old time back but can you see us weekly for a while longer?"

*Because of the work they were doing on this together, I felt able to give up my investment in this being the termination date. We think of a termination date as a guide or as an intention, not as set in stone. Admittedly, we might sometimes interpret some requests to continue as a regressive wish to avoid the pain of separation from the therapist, when we think that is so. But in this case I felt convinced that the termination phase had enabled them to express more grief than before and to acknowledge their need for more time to resolve it.*

So I offered them a new regular time and Lydia commented, "I'm glad of some more time to deal with the sadness of losing Dr. Scharff and this time together every week."

"So am I," added Alex.

*I felt some release of tension as they arrived at this compromise, and I imagined that I was sharing their feeling of relief.*

And then, as if I needed proof of the ubiquity of resistance to progress, Lydia left the room, saying to Alex, "I can't believe how you just flipped. Sometimes the way you change really bothers me." He shook his head in disbelief. How difficult it was for them to accept their progress in moving beyond an impasse!

For this couple, the threat of termination clarified the dynamics of their difficulty. The conception, representing their sexual vitality, also carried the seeds of its destruction, whether the fetus lived or died. The sense of destruction did not stem from the abortion itself. The paralyzing grief was not over the conscious aggression involved in the abortion decision, but was due to unconscious aggression against the internalized loving, sexual couple. The forces of unresolved hatred against their parental couples were unleashed against their own couple relationship because they could not bear to have happiness that they had felt excluded from before. Feeling excluded from the therapy brought these unresolved issues to the fore.

*Working on my countertransference to them as an intimate couple was crucial in enabling me to understand and help them beyond their determination to stop therapy according to our previous agreement. I was able to metabolize my feelings of exclusion without retaliation, and so to hold in my mind their coupling and, like a child, to feel warmed by it. This work was not spoken but exemplifies the nonverbal expression of the healing aspects of the holding capacity, even in termination.*

Two months later Lydia and Alex set a date to terminate. Alex had by now agreed that he was ready to make a stronger commitment to his individual therapy. During this termination phase, they had further discussion about the pregnancy. Lydia experienced enormous shame and guilt over it. These feelings were associated to her continued longing to have a baby, an intense wish she could remember from childhood. With help from Alex's associations she discovered that this longing also related to her persistent masturbation fantasy of thinking of her father. She thought she was now looking forward to doing further work on this in individual therapy some day. "It's all so oedipal!" she concluded.

This realization led to a confirming dream, which Lydia reported.

"I was going upstairs, my mother behind me. The stairs started shaking, but I got to the top. As soon as I got there the stairs turned into a slide and my mother fell down and got ground up. It was horrible."

Lydia, who was familiar from previous therapy with the dream use of stairs to represent sexuality and parental intercourse, went on: "So my having sex with Alex is gonna kill my mother! Oh! Wait! My fantasy of having sex with my father is gonna kill my mother! I must've really wanted to."

Alex helped her to continue, asking: "Want to what? Kill your mother or have sex with your father?"

"Probably both," sighed Lydia. "To feel turned on by your father, that's normal. But to the point of obsessing over a fantasy of sex with him, that's sick. And I didn't make that happen. He must've been stimulating it. I know he was. He was crazy."

"The way he cut you off as a teenager must have made you want him even more," said Alex sympathetically, caressing her shoulder.

Lydia turned on Alex, "When you cut me off, I feel that way again and I feel dirty about it. Then I can't touch you, I don't feel good enough." Lydia was responding to the rejecting object she projected into Alex to repress the exciting object evoked by his touch. But this time he did not get taken over by it.

"But," he remonstrated, "though I withhold from you, I still express love for you. I don't do what he did."

Lydia softened and replied kindly, "I know. And I'm glad you don't But it still feels the same and then I can't bear to approach you physically. And I want to. I want to get back to the lovemaking that we had."

*I was taken over by Lydia's sophistication in working on her dream. And I could see the way her projective identification was modified by Alex's containment of it. I felt they hardly needed me. Perhaps that is why I failed to see the transference implications of Lydia's dream. Having a satisfying intimate and sexual relationship with Alex would mean the death of me as they left treatment. Oedipal aggression had been transferred to my holding of them. Because I was partly in its grip, my capacity to see this was thrown off, just as the mother was thrown off the stairs. The termination phase as a stairway to completion and health remained a slippery one.*

Over the next weeks the couple progressed like this in their capacity to work on their exciting and rejecting objects at times, regressing to enacting the rejecting object in their former less cooperative relationship in which Lydia badgered Alex to stop cheating on his low-fat diet in case he clogged up his arteries while he silently resisted. His head hung even lower when she begged him to stop acting depressed, because she couldn't stand the pain of his not being there for her. This pattern of accelerated progression alternating with regression is characteristic of termination. In a progressive moment of outstanding self-confrontation, Lydia was able to admit the extent of her need to control Alex to keep him alive for her and the skill she exercised in manipulating him into taking decisions that she agreed with but not openly so that it appeared as if she were being overruled: for instance, she had really wanted Alex to decide as he did on the abortion, and she might be doing the same about the contraception decision.

Alex's response was to take control. He promptly and boldly went off his diet, much to Lydia's distress. In trying not to control him, she had nothing to say. He reassured her he would go back to it, but only when he was ready to do it for himself. Still she had said nothing. Then Alex thought she was withdrawing in anger, giving him a dose of his own medicine. So it went, up and down, progression and regression until the new termination date.

In keeping with his new assertiveness, Alex was the one to begin the final session.

"Well," said Alex dramatically, "this is it!" After an expectant pause that Lydia did not fill this time, he went on to say he had learned that he should not let the ups and downs of the therapy and the relationship throw him so much. For years he had tried to make the marriage perfect, wanting to make it up to her for her miserable, chaotic family. When he had failed, he felt depressed, which was worse for her. Suddenly he had the revelation that it was not his responsibility to make Lydia happy and that the failure was not totally his fault. "Things don't have to be made perfect, and I don't have to get depressed about failing," he declared. "Ups and downs! That's life!" This all came to him after a dreadful fight that led momentarily to their considering living separately. The fight was about Alex's doing what he wanted without considering Lydia over the weekend when company was there. Still Lydia said nothing.

Alex continued: "It was the way she pounced on me. That got me mad! Why does she have to get so angry? She scowls at me shouting, accusingly, 'Why didn't you make time for us? You said you would!' Like I've failed in a promise." Turning to Lydia, he said, "Lydia, you could have just said, 'Do you want to have some time together, like we agreed?' But no, you have to harass me and accuse me." Turning back to me, he said, "So I thought I'm not going to be controlled by her anger any more, and I walked out in the middle of the conversation. Later, she told me she wasn't angry, she was hurt." Then again to Lydia he suggested kindly, "If you could say 'I'm hurt,' I could say, 'But I want to be with you!'"

I said that of course she could and that equally he could remind himself that she was hurt and reassure her as he had proposed. "Yes, I could," he agreed.

Still Lydia said nothing, even when I commented on Alex's talking for both of them. Alex said that he thought his progress in being more separate and his renewed commitment to individual therapy was hard for Lydia. Now Lydia spoke, "Yes, it's hard," she admitted. "I have nothing to say. Well, I'm afraid to say something. It might spoil your efforts at being your own person. I would have to say that I'm angry. You said you'd be with me but you forgot all about me when you were with your parents." (So this is what they meant by company!) "They are wonderful to him and they're nice to me too, but they dote on him. He forgets he's the only family I have. It hurts," she sobbed. Then getting over her tears she continued, "But I will say this. I love you, Alex. I know you're changing and I'm trying to give you room. I'm trying to stay separate and let you define yourself. It's hard for me but I'm trying." Alex was moved.

"Now you are depressed and angry!" she claimed.

"No, I'm not," he countered. "You have just said some wonderful things and I appreciate it."

Here he did not accept her projection.

Now Lydia looked upset again. Tears filled her eyes and her face lost its vivacity. Alex talked to her as if he were trying to put words on a child's distress to make it go away. "I know how angry you are at your parents for what they did to you, what I saw them do to you. I know you are angry at my parents for loving me too much, when yours were so rotten. I have a lot of anger at your parents, too, for what I saw them do to you. But my parents love you, too."

"Excuse me," I interrupted. "I notice that you, Alex, have just moved away from hurt to anger, something you wish Lydia could stop doing." As he was nodding, I continued. "Something is making it hard to look at her sad face. Does anything come to mind?"

Alex held Lydia's arm. "I can't stand it," he answered. "I feel her upset, just like I always felt my mother's. If she stubbed her toe, I felt it in the pit of my stomach." He brushed his eyes and sat up straight, as if recovering from a blow to the abdomen.

"He's had a much better family than I had," said Lydia. "I just want him to hear me say it without thinking I'm mad at him."

*We were within ten minutes of the end of the session, and they were working away as if termination was not at hand. I felt like Alex that I had failed and could not do enough, and like Lydia I had to let go. I was also feeling excluded from their ongoing therapy, where work done here would come to fruition. I thought that I was feeling the loss for them because the hurt of losing me was difficult for them.*

So I said, "I think you're talking about good and bad parents instead of about me, and changing hurt into anger, because of the difficulty in feeling the loss of me. "How do you feel about ending in midconversation?"

Lydia said, "It's a loss."

Alex said, "It's true, but the rest of my own conversation can go on in my individual therapy at any rate."

Lydia agreed, "I feel he needs that now, and I'm going to do something for myself. After that I imagine we might come back here."

"Perhaps that softens the loss," I said. (I was aware that it did so for me.) "But I still have a sense of loss to be finishing at this point."

Anxious to make me happy, as he had tried to do for Lydia and for his mother, Alex said, "Well, I'm free next Tuesday if Lydia—"

"No," I said. "I don't mean to get rid of the loss. I'm trying to talk about my feeling of loss that the work is incomplete. You were talking of having to separate because being close seemed so impossible. You are finishing before you have refound the sexual intimacy that you discovered with such pleasure during therapy. And although we've worked on the loss of the pregnancy, I haven't heard of a resolution to the contraception dilemma."

Lydia replied to the last part first. "That I'm doing in four weeks. I've decided that I need a tubal ligation."

"I know it was difficult for you as a couple to take such a final decision because of your longing to give each other a baby to love," I acknowledged.

Lydia responded to the earlier part of what I had said: "But we don't want to separate. We want to be close. I want that closeness that we had. I want his attention twenty-four hours a day."

"Oh, I see!" I said with a sensation of quickening. "Attention twenty-four hours a day is what a baby gets." In finishing earlier, they had been defending against experiencing in the transference the wish to be my baby. I continued, "I remember you made the painful decision to have the abortion, so as to make time for your relationship with its newfound sexuality. That meant getting back the possibility of giving to and getting from each other the twenty-four-hour love and devotion you would have given to a baby. That helps me to see that what's still not fully worked on is how the fantasy of having a baby represents your longing to be a baby."

"That's it, I'd like to be loved like a baby," Lydia said.

"I'd like that, too," Alex agreed.

Then with resignation they each said almost in unison, "Yes, we want to be each other's baby, but that's not reality."

*I had said all this before, but at this moment it seemed to come to fruition through the transference at the moment of separation. And after I delivered myself of this comment, I felt some postpartum letdown.*

As they left, they were talking of how to make use of shorter times to enjoy each other. I saw out the office door that they took the opportunity as they walked to the bus stop to give each other a long embrace.

## COMMENTARY

In Lydia's dream and their combined associations at the end of this extended termination, two elements in the transference stand out: (1) an individual focused transference regarding Lydia's rivalry with her female therapist also expressed (2) the couple's shared aggression in the contextual transference. The therapist's failure to interpret this negative transference was mitigated by her capacity to survive the attack without retaliation and without provoking the reaction formation that could have contributed to the need for another extension.

Then, in the final moments of the termination, a new aspect of the transference that had been implicit in the couple's earlier work became explicit: their longing to be the therapist's baby. At the last minute the therapist thought the shared fantasy of unmet need could be named and interpreted and maybe resolved. But without certainty of that, even though the therapist agreed the couple was ready to terminate, therapist and couple still had a sense of incompleteness, an experience of leaving a conversation in mid-sentence.

This is, of course, in the nature of living endings. The idea of a "completed termination" is an illusion. There is finality only in death;

for while life goes on, there is always another thought, the possibility of another formulation, another chapter—but not always another baby. What matters at the end of our work is the possibility for the next thought, the capacity for renewal of intimacy, and the continuing ability to accept the end of a development phase and move forward.

## TERMINATION AFTER SUCCESSFUL MARITAL AND SEX THERAPIES

Successful therapy comes in many stripes. There is no single criterion for termination, except perhaps that the couple is satisfied at least that they got what they came for. Often the partners get more than they bargained for, and sometimes they leave with a sense that they got a great deal, even if it was not everything. Termination is emphasized in the format of sex therapy, in our experience, because the couple sees it coming from quite a distance. As sex improves, it occurs to them many weeks before they finish that if the improvement continues, they will be doing well enough to carry on without the therapist. Anticipation of termination and its eventuality takes on an acute significance. For most this is unsettling, although it is a relief for others who long for return to treasured privacy. In marital therapy, termination may have a considerable impact, or it may occur as a calm winding down without drama.

Rebecca and Quentin (Chapter 1) provided the first example in this book. In their late thirties, they came to sex therapy for her vaginismus and aversion and for his frequent inability to ejaculate intra-vaginally. There was an anxious naïvete about Rebecca, and a narcissistic self-preoccupation in Quentin. In the course of treatment, Rebecca's anxiety about her capacity to be a mother emerged.

Therapy was successful for the sexual dysfunctions, and then went on in a marital therapy format that dealt with their relationship more generally and with Rebecca's anxiety about having children, an issue Rebecca took up in concurrent individual therapy. Even as they did so, she began to say that she was afraid to resolve this issue, because then they would have to stop therapy. They were afraid that a decision that they could have children would mean that they could no longer enjoy being children.

Nevertheless, they pushed on. As Quentin admitted his own fears about his capacities to support a family emotionally, Rebecca grew less anxious and in Quentin's words they became "a well functioning sexual team." Although still frightened, they eventually felt they were ready to have a family, and even more frightening, they felt able to leave therapy. They spent several weeks discussing the anxieties they would have to bind in order to carry on without their therapist, a loss that poignantly echoed the loss of support each had felt in their families growing up. And finally, after what felt to the therapist to be one of the longest terminations in history, they went on their way—less anxious and, in their own way, confident.

## A CASE LEADING TO SUCCESSFUL TERMINATION

Here at the end of the book, we want to give a case that integrates the kind of work we try to do, a case that offers an example of work in the transference and countertransference, the principles of which can be encapsulated in a brief report. The denouement in this case came from dream work.

In this couple, both partners lacked sexual desire. Many years of low desire had been complicated by an increasing problem with the husband's impotence. I [D.E.S.] was initially suspicious that individual therapy or psychoanalysis might be indicated because the inhibited desire might be part of a profound neurotic problem with identity and with fear of a dominating exciting object. Nevertheless, sex therapy alone proved sufficient for its correction.

Dr. and Mrs. T. were both 35 when they were referred by an adoption agency a month after they had adopted an infant girl, Tammy. Never sexually assertive at best, Dr. T. had experienced impotence occasionally during the infertility evaluation and attempts to conceive. After that time two years ago, he had withdrawn and had shown little interest in sex. Mrs. T. had hardly noticed at first, being busy with her own career as a sports executive, but gradually she realized she felt neglected. It had taken the perspicacity of the adoption social worker for the couple to admit that their sexual difficulty was a source of concern in a relationship they otherwise both viewed as one of continuing joy and mutual love.

During the evaluation, Dr. T. admitted freely that he had become distracted from sex by his interest in professional and community matters. He was consciously aware that he withdrew from sexual encounters because of his fear of impotence, but he underscored his feeling that he had not been motivated about sex since his marriage. The only time this was not true was during vacations, when the couple relaxed and enjoyed sex easily. The problem was one partly of impotence and performance anxiety, and partly of inhibited sexual desire. Dr. T.'s history supported both pictures. His interest in sex had always been rather low, and during his years in boarding school, he had several homosexual encounters, which spoke to his difficulty establishing an adolescent sexual identity. He said that his relationship to his parents had been good, as was the parents' relationship itself until his mother began to look her age while his father's energy continued unabated. Then when Dr. T. was in college, his father ran off with another woman. Dr. T. had felt sympathetic to his mother although he still got on well with his father.

Mrs. T. told me she came from a loving family. She was the baby sister, with an athletic older brother. Pushed to be as athletic and competitive as her brother, she never had much confidence as a woman. The difficulty with her sense of feminine sexuality left her on shaky ground in now asking Dr. T. to be more interested in her sexually.

When I saw the couple for the interpretive session, they brought their recently adopted infant, and I was therefore able to see an enactment of their physical awkwardness. Mrs. T. held Tammy straight out from her body, balanced on the edge of her lap with Tammy's feet crowded in her genitals. She supported Tammy's head with one hand and offered the bottle like a syringe with the other. The whole scene seemed awkward and stilted—not a cozy, cuddling experience. While she was tender and obviously loving, Mrs. T. handled the child at an unusual distance from her body. I felt I could imagine a similar awkwardness with her own body and her husband's. When Dr. T. took the baby, he seemed lost and overwhelmed, yet he was clearly overjoyed to hold her. The whole situation was not the slightest bit unloving or pathological—just physically restrained and awkward.

I told the couple they shared in the avoidance of sexuality because of a shared shakiness about themselves as sexual people. I had already encouraged Dr. T. to tell his wife of his anxiety about impotence and the shame he had been feeling about it. He had done so, to their shared relief. I said now that underneath the performance anxiety that led to the impotence seemed to be a difficulty with desire that they shared, but which Dr. T. expressed for both of them. I suggested we begin with sex therapy, with the option of turning to marital or individual work. I wondered silently if Dr. T. would eventually need intensive psychotherapy or psychoanalysis. But as the couple was open, friendly, articulate, and trusting, I felt optimistic. I felt that my optimistic countertransference should bode well for their treatment outcome. They readily agreed to my suggestions for treatment.

The first crucial intervention involved the question of whether Dr. T. would stay in town to begin therapy. He was scheduled to spend several weeks in a postgraduate training program during the summer. My own schedule dictated that I begin treatment then or else refer them to a colleague. When I told them this, Dr. T. became obviously anxious. The choice this required of him hit close to the defensive way he put his marriage second to professional interests. Mrs. T. colluded with his avoidance. At first she encouraged him to go on his trip. With my help, she was able to say that she could hardly bear to ask him to stay in town and put their relationship first. She related this to her guilt about asking for anything for herself, just as her mother would never have offended her father by asking for consideration.

Their struggle to decide on treatment was a blow to my optimism about them, but at least I was now warned about the depth of their resistance. Thinking that it might be difficult to hold them in treatment, I felt on my guard. After considerable distress, Dr. T. finally decided to stay for therapy. Within hours of doing so, he felt he had passed a crisis of commitment. He said he felt like a renewed man, almost as if he had made a decision not to leave his wife. He said the decision made him different from his father.

The early exercises went well. The couple relaxed with the protection from anxiety, and felt the loving feelings they had been missing. But when genital stimulation was assigned, Dr. T. reported in several sessions that he could feel no arousal. When I asked in a session if he had any dreams, he obliged promptly by reporting one from two nights before.

> "I dreamt that a teacher I hardly knew at medical school came over and sat down to talk to me. He never would have then, all the more so because he was arrogant about students. That was the dream. I had read the day before that he had killed himself because he was depressed. That reminded me of my wife's brother, who had been depressed but he did not kill himself. He got through it. We used to worry that her brother had an organic condition, just as I worry that my impotence is organic."

I said that since we knew from the evaluation he had no organic basis for his sexual difficulty, we could look to the dream for help with causes. Mrs. T. joined in, "I worry that he is uninterested because I'm just not sexually attractive." And she continued to elaborate on the feeling that she had a boyish figure. She had not had a menstrual period until the age of 21, presumably because of physiological inhibition from the strenuous exercise of college athletics. "I never feel I can be sexy like a real woman. I never got there: I got stuck at 14."

I said to them, "You both have a sense of having deficient bodies. This contributes to your sexual fear and disinterest, Dr. T., and to your feeling, Mrs. T., that you cannot expect any better." They were then able to reassure each other about their mutual attraction to each other's bodies and other attributes.

I thought that they both seemed to be stuck in midadolescence, in a period whose focus is the shaky sense of self as attractive and sexual. I said that we should not underestimate Dr. T.'s fear about the depth of the problems—the life-and-death quality expressed in the dream. In addition, I pointed out to them the anxiety in their relationship to me, "the medical school teacher" of the dream. They shared a fear that I might be disdainful of them, and also that their condition would kill me off—making me unavailable to them.

The next two sessions produced the same reports of mutual enjoyment. Mrs. T. became easily aroused but Dr. T. enjoyed the massage without arousal or erection. Even during the individual sessions of self-pleasuring that I assigned each of them, he did not feel arousal.

*In the countertransference I now began to worry—to feel the anxiety that they shared. The thought seized me that perhaps they would not get far, and that they were less easily treatable than I thought. This is to say that in the countertransference, I began to absorb their doubts about whether I could help them—that they would "kill off" my efforts to help them. So now, in the countertransference, I was experiencing them as disappointing exciting objects. I had the fantasy that they might leave treatment without improvement, and that, if they did, I would be relieved. To use the language of their symptoms, I felt "sick of treating them" and, in a way, lost my "desire" to do so. They had now recruited me, through their shared projective identification, to join in their shared unconscious view that sexual desire would bring them to a hopeless and potentially lethal impasse. So in this transference-countertransference replay of their internal problem, I now felt seduced by them, as exciting objects, into hopefulness, and let down by the failure that they also feared.*

Then Dr. T. brought in a second dream. He began by assuring me that it was completely unrelated to the therapy.

"I was standing with ten or fifteen people in a large room with our backs to the wall. It occurred to me that we were going to be executed one by one. Whoever had organized it was huddling at the head of the room. My first reaction was to be defeatist. I took off my jacket and rolled up my sleeves, just as I did a few minutes ago in here, and I thought, 'If they are going to do it, I hope they'll hurry. Waiting is agony.' Then I realized they hadn't started, and it was a long time. I thought, 'I don't want to die, so why not fight?' They were demonstrating how people died by carbon monoxide poisoning, the same way as that teacher of mine in medical school died recently. They showed that you went to a bed covered with garbage baggies and you have a gas mask with oxygen until it is changed to carbon monoxide. I thought it was awful, so I asked to use the telephone. They let me, and I called my mother. But there was no answer. My fight juices were finally going by now, so I just walked out the front door of the office. I took off my shirt because somehow it was a telltale sign, and I started to run. It felt terribly slow. After two or three minutes, I realized a motorcycle policeman was following me. I still ran for my life. I was running through a territory like the strip places on a highway, gas stations which were closed because it was 2 A.M. The policeman caught up with me. I thought he was going to catch me, but just at that moment, a bad guy came out of a trailer and took a shot at the cop, who took off after him, so I got away."

Dr. T.'s association left all three of us in no doubt that the execution he feared was the sexual exposure of the exercises. Mrs. T. was the one to notice that the odd method of execution, on a bed that felt threateningly smothering, recalled the assigned sexual exercises. In the dream, he had called his mother as he had done in his youth when he felt helpless. He said, "Hers is the one number which hasn't changed all these years. I was counting on her. She should have been home in the middle of the night, but she wasn't there. So I ran for my life." When I said that I was the cop he feared, he replied, "No doubt about that!" But Mrs. T. joined in to add that she had identified with the cop, since he often treated her as being after him to do things. He talked about fearing being controlled by the demand for sex implied by me in giving exercises, by his wife in being attractive to him, and even by himself since he cared for her.

I asked him about the building in which the dream occurred. It reminded him of the junior high school at home, the one he had left to attend boarding school at a time he felt he had to escape from his mother. But when he left home, he missed her terribly.

I said I thought he might have felt he had to leave home as a young teenager out of his fearful recognition of his parents' sexual life.

He replied, "Well, they did have a last child just after I left. In fact we named Tammy after that sister."

The fear of the persecuting object was now out in the open—in the dream, in his acknowledged fear of sex, in his acknowledged fear of me, and in the person of their infant named for a child born of the parents' intercourse. The couple could see the way their transference fear echoed the feelings they were trying to keep at bay between themselves.

I summed up my speculations about this dream in dialogue with the couple. Here I will condense our conversation to my formulation. Dr. T. had felt threatened with annihilation by me as the representative of parental sexuality. He also felt afraid of being annihilated by sex itself and by the smothering engulfment of his wife, who now stood for the seductive and threatening part of his mother, but who stood at other times for the cop. But he was also expressing (through projective identification) a fear of sex for both of them, for she was identified with the threat of sex that he felt in a more obvious way. He had been on the run, but early in their marriage, they both had. I ended by saying, "You can't get aroused when you're on the run, Dr. T., just as you, Mrs. T., can't get pregnant when you run so much that you have no menses!"

Although I was the cop and executioner in the treatment, it was his wife who had been in that role up to now. She had accepted it because she felt no one would willingly have her.

In the exercise following this session, Dr. T. was easily aroused, and the treatment followed a rapid course to successful completion. Dr. T. found that he was able to relax through any periods of anxiety he felt, and progressively his anxiety and fear receded. Mrs. T. also found it progressively easier to avoid backing off lest she be seen as the cop. The couple continued on to a new level of integration of their sexual and emotional intimacy.

Termination was a pleasure with this couple who had got what they came for. Nevertheless, there were moments of anxiety about whether they could maintain their progress, because of the loss of giving up their former adjustment. The distancing from each other sexually, which they had maintained over the first years of their marriage, had allowed them to enjoy each other's company like a fond and sexually unthreatened brother and sister. Now they worried about whether they could manage a new intimacy.

Nevertheless, they said they were willing to take their chances, knowing they could come back. They brought their daughter, Tammy, with them to the last meeting. She made the perch at the end of her mother's knee a throne from which to command parental attention and joy—a giggling 3-month-old with her loving and physically more confident parents. There were traces of the awkwardness from two months before, but the exchange between Tammy and her parents had a new and lively rhythm.

This couple demonstrated throughout their work a positive shared contextual transference. Their loving relationship and their motivation allowed them to work through their shared problem and their individual parts of it quickly but thoroughly, taking back projective identifications to and through the improvement of their psychosomatic partnership.

## LIFE AFTER THERAPY

There was more to learn from this couple. I did not see them again clinically, but I did hear from them on two occasions. In the first, I got an announcement of a natural birth from them eighteen months after termination. There, pictured with his doting parents and 23-month-old sister, was a baby boy. The note from Mrs. T. said, "We never expected this could happen. Thanks for your help!"

Then, three years later Mrs. T. came up to me at a film. She asked to speak to me for a moment, and said that she just wanted me to know that she thought of me often. They had been able to conceive yet another child, and their marriage had remained solid and loving. Treatment had turned their life around.

Like most analytically trained therapists, we do not send letters to keep in touch or approach former patients to find out how they are. This practice arises not from any lack of interest but from the therapist's responsibility to preserve the boundary of the treatment. We do acknowledge letters former patients may write to us and we respond appropriately in social situations. When a couple initiates a conversation that reports the outcome of treatment we are especially interested. Nothing is more rewarding to a therapist than knowing that therapy has turned a life around.

Chapter **15**
# EPILOGUE

We do not seek follow-up from the couples we treat, because doing so has seemed intrusive and self-gratifying. We have tried to let go of our patients, to welcome their autonomy, and to tolerate not knowing what happens in the future. Could this be the rationalization of the clinician who has not wanted to do research? Of course, there is nothing wrong with conducting a follow-up study, even an informal one, to determine the longer term efficacy of therapy, but we have never done so. Consequently, the follow-up we get comes randomly. There is the informal follow-up from the couple that stays in touch, calling for a periodic appointment for the couple, one of the partners, or perhaps one of their children. Over time, we have the pleasure of becoming psychotherapeutic family practitioners, getting to know the development of a small number of people through several years of their life course.

Quentin and Rebecca, the first case reported in this book (see Chapters 1, 9, and 14), made contact from another state two years after treatment ended. Quentin's ejaculatory problem had returned while they were in the middle of an infertility work-up in which he had been under enormous pressure to perform. They had found out that his sperm count was too low to allow for natural impregnation, and they were proceeding with one or another form of in vitro fertilization. Their sexual adjustment had crumbled and they were calling for advice. As a first-aid measure, it was suggested that Quentin and Rebecca should not demand ejaculation intravaginally at this time. Both of them enjoyed the long duration of intercourse, and both of them achieved orgasm easily at the end with manual stimulation. This gave them back their capacity to use sex for holding their anxiety during their infertility crisis. They were also referred to a marital therapist who could help them work on mourning the loss of fertility and bearing their anxiety about conceiving artificially. Rebecca wrote a few weeks later to say they had relaxed and things were back to an enjoyable—although not perfect—state.

An older couple, Gene and Rose Holt, described in Chapter 12, did well in therapy for a paired sexual dysfunction, but had further trouble with aging. As they left their sixties, they periodically saw their therapist for occasional lapses in sexual functioning and strain in their marriage from the management of their grown children. They came back in their seventies because Gene's occasionally recurrent erectile failure was now permanent, due to organic factors in aging. Since their original treatment, penile papaverine injections had been developed. When Gene accepted referral for prescription, he and Rose were able to regain the sexual adjustment fashioned in the original therapy. Now in their late seventies, years after first seeking therapy, intercourse was more reliable than ever.

As they faced another termination, Gene and Rose experienced renewed anxiety about working things out on their own. In this echo of their old termination, Gene withdrew crustily and Rose became confused. After the therapist pointed out the use of this pattern to express neediness for him as though they were children who could not be left, they were able to face the loss, refind their own holding capacity, and terminate. Through the next few years, Rose asked, on several occasions, for further psychotherapy of a few sessions. In these brief encounters, she reworked old resentments at Gene, recovered childhood contributions of her anger at her mother for cutting her off from her father, and reworked the transference loss of the therapist as a longed-for parent who could never give quite enough—

but who was there for her to tell about it. And that, she characteristi-
cally agreed, was *almost* enough!

Another couple, Max and Ginger (Chapter 12), had gotten a great
deal out of marital, sex, and individual therapies, but these gains did
not, in the long run, secure their marriage. Both reported that eventual divorce was a reasonable outcome of their marriage and did not
gainsay the help they had received. Their children did well, and each
of them managed a subsequent marriage with a better fit.

After a couple's evaluation another such couple elected to have
parallel individual therapies. One of us saw the man in psychoanalysis for his lack of emotional involvement and sexual interest, while a
colleague saw the wife in intensive psychotherapy for her neurotic
oedipal configuration in which she denigrated her mother—and
therefore herself—and idealized her father. Both did well in treatment
and eventually were able, to their enormous pleasure, to have children and an extremely happy marriage. They returned briefly when
their son at 9 months old had sleep difficulty, which related to the
mother's anxiety and to his constitutional difficulty in self-quieting,
and again when the boy at 5 years launched an oedipal attack on his
father that stirred up some of the old issues. The couple has had a few
visits periodically since then for a variety of midlife, developmental
issues.

Such informal follow-ups from the couples we have treated give us
a sense of the thread of life and of the enduring effects—and of the
limitations—of their work with us. They give us the chance to review
their progress and our therapeutic efforts. Having known a cohort of
couples over ten or twenty years, we find that the sense of sharing
the human condition, of traveling a trajectory through life in shared
times, becomes more significant that the differences in perspective of
therapist and patient.

# References

Althof, S. E., Turner, L. A., Risen, C. B., et al. (1988). Why do men drop out from intracavernosal treatment for impotence? Presented March 1988 at the Society for Sex Therapy and Research meeting, New York.

Bak, R. (1968). The phallic woman: the ubiquitous fantasy in perversion. *Psychoanalytic Study of the Child* 23:15–36. New York: International Universities Press.

Bannister, K., and Pincus, L. (1965). *Shared Phantasy in Marital Problems: Therapy in a Four Person Relationship*. London: Tavistock Institute of Human Relations.

Barbach, L. G. (1974). Group treatment of preorgasmic women. *Journal of Sex and Marital Therapy* 1:139–145.

—— (1975). *For Yourself: The Fulfillment of Female Sexuality*. New York: Doubleday.

—— (1980). *Women Discover Orgasm: A Therapist's Guide to a New Treatment Approach*. New York: Free Press.

Bieber, P., Dain, H., Dince, O., et al. (1962). *Homosexuality: A Psychoanalytic Study*. New York: Basic Books.

Bion, W. R. (1961). *Experiences in Groups*. New York: Basic Books.

—— (1962). *Learning from Experience*. London: Tavistock.

—— (1967). *Second Thoughts*. London: Heinemann.

—— (1970). *Attention and Interpretation: A Scientific Approach to Insight in Psycho-Analysis and Groups*. London: Tavistock.

Bollas, C. (1987). *The Shadow of the Object*. New York: Columbia University Press.

Box, S., Copley, B., Magagna, J., et al. (1981). *Psychotherapy with Families: An Analytic Approach*. London: Routledge and Kegan Paul.

Brazelton, T. B. (1982). Joint regulation of neonate-parent behavior. In *Social Interchange in Infancy*, ed. E. Tronick, pp. 7–22. Baltimore: University Park Press.

Brazelton, T. B., and Als, H. (1979). Four early stages in the development of mother–infant interaction. *Psychoanalytic Study of the Child* 34:349–369. New Haven, CT: Yale University Press.

Brazelton, T. B., Koslowski, B., and Main, M. (1974). The origins of reciprocity: the early mother–infant interaction. In *The Effects of the Infant on Its Caregiver*, ed. M. Lewis and L. A. Rosenblum, pp. 49–76. New York: Wiley.

Brazelton, T. B., Yogman, M., Als, H., and Tronick, E. (1979). The infant as a focus for family reciprocity. In *The Child and Its Family*, ed. M. Lewis and L. A. Rosenblum, pp. 29–43. New York: Plenum.

Breuer, J., and Freud, S. (1895). Studies on hysteria. *Standard Edition* 2.

Coen, S. (1985). Perversion as a solution to intrapsychic conflict. *Journal of the American Psychoanalytic Association* 33 (supp.):17–59.

Comfort, A. (1972). *The Joy of Sex: A Cordon Bleu Guide to Love Making*. New York: Simon & Schuster.

Dickes, R., and Strauss, D. (1979). Countertransference as a factor in premature termination of apparently successful cases. *Journal of Sex and Marital Therapy* 5:22–27.

Dicks, H. V. (1967). *Marital Tensions: Clinical Studies towards a Psychoanalytic Theory of Interaction*. London: Routledge and Kegan Paul.

Dunn, M. E., and Dickes, R. (1977). Erotic issues in co-therapy. *Journal of Sex and Marital Therapy* 3:205–211.

Ezriel, H. (1952). Notes on psychoanalytic group therapy II: interpretation and research. *Psychiatry* 15:119–126.

Fairbairn, W. R. D. (1944). Endopsychic structure considered in terms of object relationships. In *Psychoanalytic Studies of the Personality*, pp. 82–135. London: Routledge and Kegan Paul, 1952.

—— (1952). *Psychoanalytic Studies of the Personality*. London: Routledge and Kegan Paul. Also published as *An Object Relations Theory of the Personality*. New York: Basic Books.

—— (1954). Observations on the nature of hysterical states. *British Journal of Medical Psychology* 27:105–125.

—— (1958). The nature and aims of psycho-analytical treatment. *International Journal of Psycho-Analysis* 39:374–385.

—— (1963). Synopsis of an object-relations theory of the personality. *International Journal of Psycho-Analysis* 44:224–225.

Fisher, S. (1972). *The Female Orgasm*. New York: Basic Books.

Flugel, J. C. (1921) *Psychoanalytic Study of the Family*. In *International Psycho-Analytical Library*, no. 3, ed. E. Jones. London: International Psycho-Analytical Press.

Freud, S. (1894). Unpublished draft G. *Standard Edition* 1:206–212.

—— (1895). The psychotherapy of hysteria. *Standard Edition* 2:255–305.

—— (1905a). Fragment of an analysis of a case of hysteria. *Standard Edition* 7:7–122.

—— (1905b). Three essays on the theory of sexuality. *Standard Edition* 7:135–243.

—— (1912a). The dynamics of transference. *Standard Edition* 12:97–108.

—— (1912b). Recommendations to physicians practicing psychoanalysis. *Standard Edition* 12:111–120.

—— (1914). Remembering, repeating, and working through. *Standard Edition* 12:147–156.

Gill, M., and Muslin, H. (1976). Early interpretation of transference. *Journal of American Psychoanalytic Association* 24:779–794.

Graller, J. (1981). Adjunctive marital therapy: a possible solution to the split-transference problem. *The Annual of Psychoanalysis* 9:175–187. New York: International Universities Press.

Greenson, R. (1965). The problem of working through. In *Drives, Affects and Behavior*, vol. 2, ed. M. Schur, pp. 217–314. New York: International Universities Press.

Greenspan, S. I. (1981). *Clinical Infant Reports No. 1: Psychopathology and Adaptation in Infancy and Early Childhood*. New York: International Universities Press.

Gross, A. (1951). The secret. *Bulletin of the Menninger Clinic* 15:37–44.

Grotstein, J. (1982). *Splitting and Projective Identification*. New York: Jason Aronson.

Guntrip, H. (1969). *Schizoid Phenomena, Object Relations and the Self*. New York: International Universities Press.

Heiman, J. R., and LoPiccolo, J. (1988). *Becoming Orgasmic: A Personal and Sexual Growth Program for Women*. Second Edition. Englewood Cliffs, NJ: Prentice Hall.

Heimann, P. (1950). On counter-transference. *International Journal of Psycho-Analysis* 31:81–84.

Hite, S. (1976). *The Hite Report: A Nationwide Study of Female Sexuality*. New York: Macmillan.

Jaffe, D. S. (1968). The mechanism of projection: its dual role in object relations. *International Journal of Psycho-Analysis* 49:662–677.

Kaplan, H. S. (1974). *The New Sex Therapy: Active Treatment of Sexual Dysfunctions*. New York: Brunner/Mazel.

—— (1977). Hypoactive sexual desire. *Journal of Sex and Marital Therapy* 3:3–9.

—— (1979). *Disorders of Sexual Desire and Other New Concepts and Techniques in Sex Therapy*. New York: Brunner/Mazel.

—— (1983). *The Evaluation of Sexual Disorders: Psychological and Medical Aspects*. New York: Brunner/Mazel.

—— (1987a). *The Illustrated Manual of Sex Therapy*. Second Edition. New York: Brunner/Mazel.

—— (1987b). *Sexual Aversion, Sexual Phobias, and Panic Disorder*. New York: Brunner/Mazel.

Kernberg, O. (1975). *Borderline Conditions and Pathological Narcissism*. New York: Jason Aronson.

—— (1987). Projection and projective identification: developmental and clinical aspects. In *Projection, Identification, Projective Identification*, ed. J. Sandler, pp. 93–115. Madison, CT: International Universities Press.

Khan, M. M. R. (1979). *Alienation in Perversions*. New York: International Universities Press.

Klein, M. (1946). Notes on some schizoid mechanisms. *International Journal of Psycho-Analysis* 27:99–100. And in *Envy and Gratitude & Other Works, 1946–1963*, pp. 1–24. London: Hogarth Press and the Institute of Psycho-Analysis, 1975.

Kolb, L., and Johnson, A. (1955). Etiology and therapy of overt homosexuality. *Psychoanalytic Quarterly* 24:506–515.

Langs, R. (1976). *The Therapeutic Interaction. Vol. II: A Critical Overview and Synthesis*. New York: Jason Aronson.

Levay, A. N., and Kagle, A. (1978). Recent advances in sex therapy:

integration with the dynamic therapies. *Psychiatric Quarterly* 50:5–16.

Levay, A. N., Kagle, A., and Weissberg, J. (1979). Issues of transference in sex therapy. *Journal of Sex and Marital Therapy* 5:15–21.

Levine, S. B. (1988). *Sex Is Not Simple*. Columbus, OH: Ohio Psychology.

Levine, S. B., and Agle, D. (1978). The effectiveness of sex therapy for chronic secondary psychological impotence. *Journal of Sex and Marital Therapy* 4:235–258.

Lieblum, S. R., and Pervin, L. A. (1980). *Principles and Practice of Sex Therapy*. New York: Guilford Press.

Lieblum, S. R., and Rosen, R. C., eds. (1988). *Sexual Desire Disorder*. New York: Guilford Press.

Lief, H. F. (1977). What's new in sex research? Inhibited sexual desire. *Medical Aspects of Human Sexuality* 11:94–95.

—— (1989). Integrating sex therapy with marital therapy. Paper presented at The 47th Annual Conference of the American Association of Marriage and Family Therapists. San Francisco, California, October 27, 1989.

Loewald, H. (1960). On the therapeutic action of psychoanalysis. *International Journal of Psycho-Analysis* 41:16–33.

LoPiccolo, J., and Lobitz, W. C. (1972). The role of masturbation in the treatment of orgasmic dysfunction. *Archives of Sexual Behavior.* 2:163–171. Also in *Handbook of Sex Therapy*, ed. J. LoPiccolo and L. LoPiccolo, pp. 187–194. New York: Plenum, 1978.

LoPiccolo, J., and LoPiccolo, L. (1978). *Handbook of Sex Therapy*. New York: Plenum.

LoPiccolo, J., and Steger, J. (1974) The sexual interaction inventory: a new instrument for assessment of sexual dysfunction. *Archives of Sexual Behavior* 3:585–595.

Mahler, M., Pine, F., and Bergman, A. (1975). *The Psychological Birth of the Human Infant: Symbiosis and Individuation*. New York: Basic Books.

Malin, A., and Grotstein, J. (1966). Projective identification in the therapeutic process. *International Journal of Psycho-Analysis* 47:26–31.

Masters, W. H., and Johnson, V. E. (1966). *Human Sexual Response*. Boston: Little, Brown.

—— (1970). *Human Sexual Inadequacy*. Boston: Little, Brown.

McDougall, J. (1970). Homosexuality in women. In *Female Sexuality: New Psychoanalytic Views*, ed. J. Chasseguet-Smirgel, pp. 94–134. Ann Arbor: University of Michigan Press.

—— (1985) *Theaters of the Mind: Illusion and Truth on the Psychoanalytic Stage*. New York: Basic Books.

—— (1986). Identification, neoneeds, and neosexualities. *International Journal of Psycho-Analysis* 67:19–33.

Meyer, J. K. (1985a). Ego-dystonic homosexuality. In *Comprehensive Textbook of Psychiatry IV*, ed. H. I. Kaplan and B. Saddock, pp. 1056–1065. Baltimore: Williams & Wilkins.

—— (1985b). Paraphilias. In *Comprehensive Textbook of Psychiatry IV*, ed. H. I. Kaplan and B. Saddock, pp. 1065–1076. Baltimore: Williams & Wilkins.

Meissner, W. W. (1980). A note on projective identification. *Journal of The American Psychoanalytic Association* 28:43–67.

—— (1987). Projection and projective identification. In *Projection, Identification, Projective Identification*, ed. J. Sandler, pp. 27–49. Madison, CT: International Universities Press.

Mitchell, S. A. (1988). *Relational Concepts in Psychoanalysis: An Integration*. Cambridge, MA: Harvard University Press.

Money-Kyrle, R. (1956). Normal countertransference and some of its deviations. *International Journal of Psycho-Analysis* 37:360–366.

Moultrup, D. J. (1990). *Husbands, Wives and Lovers: The Emotional System of the Extra-Marital Affair*. New York: Guilford Press.

Murray, J. M. (1955). *Keats*. New York: Noonday Press.

Ogden, T. H. (1982). *Projective Identification and Psychotherapeutic Technique*. New York: Jason Aronson.

—— (1986). *The Matrix of the Mind*. Northvale, NJ: Jason Aronson.

—— (1989). *The Primitive Edge of Experience*. Northvale, NJ: Jason Aronson.

Paolino, T. J., Jr., and McCready, B. S., eds. (1978). *Marriage and Marital Therapy: Psychoanalytic, Behavioral and Systems Theory Perspectives*. New York: Brunner/Mazel.

Pincus, L., ed. (1960). *Marriage: Studies in Emotional Conflict and Growth*. London: Methuen.

Racker, H. (1968). *Transference and Countertransference*. New York: International Universities Press.

Raley, P. E. (1976). *Making Love: How to Be Your Own Sex Therapist*. New York: Dial.

Roiphe, H., and Galenson E. (1981). *Infantile Origins of Sexual Identity*. New York: International Universities Press.

Sachs, H. (1923). On the genesis of sexual perversion. *Internationale Zeitschrift fur Psychoanalyse* 9:172–182. Trans. H. F. Bernays, 1964, New York Psychoanalytic Institute Library; quoted in C. W. Socarides, *Homosexuality*, 1978.

Saghir, M. T., and Robins, E. (1973). *Male and Female Homosexuality.* Baltimore: Williams & Wilkins.

Sander, F. (1989). Marital conflict and psychoanalytic therapy in the middle years. In *The Middle Years: New Psychoanalytic Perspectives,* ed. J. Oldyam and R. Liebert, pp. 160–176. New Haven, CT: Yale University Press.

Sandler, J., ed. (1987). *Projection, Identification and Projective Identification.* Madison, CT: International Universities Press.

Scharff, D. (1978). Truth and consequences in sex and marital therapy: the revelation of secrets in the therapeutic setting. *Journal of Sex and Marital Therapy* 4:35–49.

—— (1982). *The Sexual Relationship: An Object Relations View of Sex and the Family.* Boston, London: Routledge and Kegan Paul.

Scharff, D., and Scharff, J. S. (1987). *Object Relations Family Therapy.* Northvale, NJ: Jason Aronson.

Scharff, J. S., ed. (1989). *Foundations of Object Relations Family Therapy.* Northvale, NJ: Jason Aronson.

—— (in progress). *Projective Identification.* Northvale, NJ: Jason Aronson.

Schmidt, C. W., and Lucas, M. J. (1976). The short-term, intermittent, conjoint treatment of sexual disorders. In *Clinical Management of Sexual Disorders,* ed. J. K. Meyer, pp. 130–147. Baltimore: Williams & Wilkins.

Segal, H. (1964). *Introduction to the Work of Melanie Klein.* London: Heinemann; Hogarth Press and the Institute of Psycho-Analysis.

—— (1981). *The Work of Hanna Segal.* New York: Jason Aronson.

Semans, J. H. (1956). Premature ejaculation: a new approach. *Southern Medical Journal* 49:353–357.

Shapiro, R. L. (1979). Family dynamics and object relations theory: an analytic, group-interpretive approach to family therapy. In *Foundations of Object Relations Family Therapy,* ed. J. S. Scharff, pp. 225–258 Northvale, NJ: Jason Aronson.

Skynner, A. C. R. (1976). *Systems of Family and Marital Psychotherapy.* New York: Brunner/Mazel.

Slipp, S. (1984). *Object Relations: A Dynamic Bridge between Individual and Family Treatment.* New York: Jason Aronson.

Socarides, C. W. (1978). *Homosexuality.* New York: Jason Aronson.

Spitz, R. A. (1945). Hospitalism: an inquiry into the genesis of psychiatric conditions in early childhood. *Psychoanalytic Study of the Child* 1:53–74. New York: International Universities Press.

Spitz, R. A. (1965). *The First Year of Life.* New York: International Universities Press.

Stierlin, H. (1977). *Psychoanalysis and Family Therapy*. New York: Jason Aronson.

Stern, D. N. (1985). *The Interpersonal World of the Infant: A View from Psychoanalysis and Developmental Psychology*. New York: Basic Books.

Stoller, R. J. (1975). *Perversion: The Erotic Form of Hatred*. New York: Pantheon.

—— (1979). *Sexual Excitement: Dynamics of Erotic Life*. New York: Pantheon.

Strean, H. S. (1976) The extra-marital affair: a psychoanalytic view. *The Psychoanalytic Review* 63:101–113.

—— (1979). *The Extramarital Affair*. New York: Free Press.

Sutherland, J. D. (1963). Object relations theory and the conceptual model of psychoanalysis. *British Journal of Medical Psychology* 36:109–124.

Wallerstein, J. S., and Blakeslee, S. (1989). *Second Chances*. New York: Ticknor & Fields.

Wegner, D. M., Shortt, J. W., Blake, A. W., Page, M. S., et al. (1990). The suppression of exciting thoughts. *Journal of Personality and Social Psychology* 58:409–418.

Winer, R. (1989). The role of transitional experience in development in healthy and incestuous families. In *Foundations of Object Relations Family Therapy*. ed. J. S. Scharff, pp. 357–384. Northvale, NJ: Jason Aronson.

Winnicott, D. W. (1947). Hate in the countertransference. In *Collected Papers: Through Paediatrics to Psychoanalysis*, pp. 194–203. London: Tavistock, 1958, and The Hogarth Press, 1975.

—— (1951). Transitional objects and transitional phenomena. In *Collected Papers: Through Paediatrics to Psychoanalysis*, pp. 229–242. London: Tavistock, 1958, and The Hogarth Press, 1975.

—— (1956). Primary maternal preoccupation. In *Collected Papers: Through Paediatrics to Psychoanalysis*, pp. 300–305. London: Tavistock, 1958, and The Hogarth Press, 1975.

—— (1958). *Collected Papers: Through Paediatrics to Psychoanalysis*. London: Tavistock, 1958, and The Hogarth Press, 1975.

—— (1960a). The theory of the parent–infant relationship. *International Journal of Psycho-Analysis* 41:585–595, and in *The Maturational Processes and the Facilitating Environment*, pp. 37–55. London: The Hogarth Press, 1965.

—— (1960b). Ego distortion in terms of true and false self. In *The Maturational Processes and the Facilitating Environment: Studies on the Theory of Emotional Development*, pp.140–152. London: The Hogarth Press, 1965.

—— (1963) Communicating and not communicating leading to a study of certain opposites. In *The Maturational Processes and the Facilitating Environment: Studies on the Theory of Emotional Development*, pp. 179–192. London: The Hogarth Press, 1965.

—— (1968). The use of an object and relating through cross-identification. In *Playing and Reality*, pp. 86–94. New York: Basic Books.

—— (1971). *Playing and Reality*. New York: Basic Books.

Williams, A. H. (1981). The micro environment. In *Psychotherapy with Families: An Analytic Approach*, ed. S. Box et al., pp. 105–119. London: Routledge and Kegan Paul.

Zetzel, E. (1958). Therapeutic alliance in the analysis of hysteria. In *The Capacity for Emotional Growth*, pp. 182–196. New York: International Universities Press, 1970.

Zilbergeld, B., and Evans, M. (1980). The inadequacy of Masters and Johnson. *Psychology Today* 14:29–43.

Zinner, J. (1976). The implications of projective identification for marital interaction. In *Contemporary Marriage: Structure, Dynamics, and Therapy*, ed. H. Grunebaum and J. Christ, pp. 293–308. Boston: Little, Brown. Also in *Foundations of Object Relations Family Therapy*, ed. J. S. Scharff, pp. 155–173. Northvale, NJ: Jason Aronson, 1989.

—— (1989). The use of concurrent therapies: therapeutic strategy or reenactment. In *Foundations of Object Relations Family Therapy*, ed. J. S. Scharff, pp. 321–333. Northvale, NJ: Jason Aronson.

Zinner, J., and Shapiro, R. (1972). Projective identification as a mode of perception and behavior in families of adolescents. *International Journal of Psycho-Analysis* 53:523–530, and in *Foundations of Object Relations Family Therapy*, ed. J. S. Scharff, pp. 109–126. Northvale, NJ: Jason Aronson.

—— (1974). The family group as a single psychic entity: implications for acting out in adolescence. *International Review of Psychoanalysis* 1 1:179–186, and in *Foundations of Object Relations Family Therapy*, ed. J. S. Scharff, pp. 187–202. Northvale, NJ: Jason Aronson.

# Index

# About the Authors

David E. Scharff, M.D., is Co-Director of the International Institute of Object Relations Therapy and Clinical Professor of Psychiatry at Georgetown University and the Uniformed Services University of the Health Sciences. Dr. Scharff earned his M.D. from Harvard and is board certified in adult and child psychiatry and certified by the American Psychoanalytic Association in psychoanalysis. He is a former President of the American Association of Sex Educators, Counselors, and Therapists.

Jill Savege Scharff, M.D., is Co-Director of the International Institute of Object Relations Therapy and Clinical Professor of Psychiatry at Georgetown University. Educated in Scotland, she moved to England for further training at the Tavistock Clinic and received membership in the Royal College of Psychiatrists. Dr. Scharff is board certified in adult and child psychiatry and certified by the American Psychoanalytic Association in adult and child psychoanalysis.

The Scharffs have a national and international reputation as authors, editors, teachers, and therapists. Among their books are *Object Relations Individual Therapy*, *Object Relations Family Therapy*, and *Scharff Notes: A Primer of Object Relations Therapy*. Both maintain private practices in individual, couple, and family object relations therapy and individual psychoanalysis with adults and children.